DATE DUE

TEJANO LEADERSHIP IN MEXICAN AND REVOLUTIONARY TEXAS

NUMBER THIRTY-FOUR

*Elma Dill Russell Spencer Series
in the West and Southwest*

Andrés Tijerina, *General Editor*

SERIES BOARD

Alwyn Barr, James E. Crisp

Rebecca Sharpless

Eric Van Young

TEJANO LEADERSHIP IN MEXICAN AND REVOLUTIONARY TEXAS

Jesús F. de la Teja

Editor

Foreword by David J. Weber

WITH CONTRIBUTIONS BY
RAÚL A. RAMOS, DAVID R. MCDONALD
ANDRÉS TIJERINA, STEPHEN L. HARDIN
ROBERT E. WRIGHT, O.M.I.
CAROLINA CASTILLO CRIMM
ANDRÉS RESÉNDEZ, JAMES E. CRISP
TIMOTHY MATOVINA
ALONZO SALAZAR
AND
JESÚS F. DE LA TEJA

Texas A&M
UNIVERSITY
PRESS

This paper meets the requirements of
ANSI/NISO Z39.48-1992
(Permanence of Paper).
Binding materials have been chosen for durability.
♾ ♻

Library of Congress Cataloging-in-Publication Data
Tejano leadership in Mexican and Revolutionary Texas / Jesús F. de la Teja, editor ;
foreword by David J. Weber ; with contributions by Raúl A. Ramos . . . [et al.].—1st ed.
    p. cm.—(Elma Dill Russell Spencer series in the West and Southwest ; no. 34)
Includes index.
ISBN-13: 978-1-60344-152-0 (cloth, unjacketed : alk. paper)
ISBN-10: 1-60344-152-2 (cloth, unjacketed : alk. paper)
ISBN-13: 978-1-60344-166-7 (pbk. : alk. paper)
ISBN-10: 1-60344-166-2 (pbk. : alk. paper) 1. Mexican American leadership—
Texas—History—19th century. 2. Mexican Americans—Texas—History—19th
century. 3. Texas—History—To 1846. 4. Texas—Politics and government—To 1846.
I. Teja, Jesús F. de la, 1956– II. Ramos, Raúl A. III. Series: Elma Dill Russell Spencer
series in the West and Southwest ; no. 34.
    F395.M5T453   2010
    976.4′0046872—dc22

                                                                2009023275

This book is dedicated
to David J. Weber,
whose work inspired
so many of us to explore our
Tejano heritage.

CONTENTS

FOREWORD

OVER THIRTY YEARS AGO, in the pages of the *Western Historical Quarterly*, I lamented the fact that historians had failed to explore the lives of Mexicans in the Southwest, even when those historians wrote about the era when the Southwest belonged to Mexico. Historians had written numerous biographies of Anglo-Americans who entered northern Mexico, from California to Texas, in the years before 1846. These writers paid scant attention, however, to the Mexicans who received those Anglo-American visitors. Thus, one could find article- or book-length biographies of any number of Anglo-American settlers, trappers, or traders who operated in northern Mexico but would look hard and long for a study of a single Mexican governor, military commander, rancher, or businessman.

I had pointed to the dearth of biographies of Mexicans to make the larger point that Anglo-American historiography on the Southwest's Mexican era was imbalanced and ethnocentric ("Mexico's Far Northern Frontier, 1821–1854: Historiography Askew," *Western Historical Quarterly*, July 1976). How times have changed. When I advanced that argument, the Chicano movement had peaked and a new generation of historians had begun to come on the scene. Trained with Ph.D.s and sensitized to think about history from the bottom up, they wrote about minorities as well as majorities, and they sought to explain how peoples accommodated to or resisted their would-be oppressors. Out of that intellectual milieu came new studies that began to redress the region's unbalanced historiography.

Of the four border states, Texas had the least balanced historiography in the mid-1970s. In the popular imagination, in particular, Texas history began with its "father," Stephen Austin, shepherding his Anglo-American children into the "howling wilderness" of Texas. The area's long history under Spain and Mexico was little more than a stage set for Anglo-American actors to win Texas independence and set Texas history into motion.

This collection of biographical vignettes, *Tejano Leadership in Mexican and Revolutionary Texas*, shows how far we have come. It contains eleven biographies of people whose lives historians have recovered from historical oblivion and fleshed out with fresh, interesting details, much of it drawn from archival sources. Each Tejano life explored in this book is male. Only men served as public figures in those days, and so their activities remain in public records. Tejanas—the women—surely provided leadership from the vantage point of hearth and home, but skimpier records make their stories more difficult to reconstruct.

All of the Tejanos in this book had to navigate rapidly changing political seas as Texas underwent the turbulence of a revolutionary decade that ended with Mexico's independence from Spain. Then, as citizens of a newly independent Mexico, each had to negotiate a relationship with a government in Mexico City that seemed endlessly under construction. Closer to home these men had to come to terms with a state government in Coahuila, to which Texas became an appendage. Still closer to home, all had to confront the surge of Anglo-Americans who spilled over the border from the United States and began to alter the local Mexican economy, society, and government.

These years of rapid change, as the essays in this book make clear, affected Tejanos from all walks of life, whether rancheros, military officers, bureaucrats, priests, or politicians. If the subjects of these biographies lived until the Texas Revolution of 1836, they had to choose between siding with Anglo-American rebels, remaining loyal to Mexico, or trying to remain neutral—and neutrality was a nearly impossible option, as Plácido Benavides discovered. If they stayed in Texas after the revolution, they had to cope with the rising tide of Anglo-Americans that washed over them. Either they learned to stay afloat in a sea of racist English-speakers who despised them, as did José Antonio Navarro, or they found themselves submerged and reduced to the status of foreigners in their native land, as happened to Juan Seguín.

Writing about the Tejano experience in the 1850s, toward the end of his long, active life, José Antonio Navarro became the first Tejano historian. Now, in this volume, many historians interested in Tejanos have added their voices to Navarro's pioneering work, going beyond it to look at Tejanos as leaders at a time when historians imagined them as followers.

This book on Tejano leadership did not happen by happenstance. Leadership came from Jesús F. de la Teja, who teaches history at Texas State University in San Marcos. Professor De la Teja sought out historians working on Tejano history, enlisted them to examine individual lives, brought those historians together in a conference on his campus, and then edited their work for publication. *Tejano Leader-*

ship also builds on De la Teja's pioneering work as a biographer of the once-forgotten Juan Seguín, whose story he retells in this volume. We owe much to Professor De la Teja and the other contributors to this volume for moving us toward a less ethnocentric and more fully realized picture of the Texas past, giving us multidimensional portraits of Tejano participants during the tumultuous years before, during, and after the Texas Revolution.

David J. Weber, *Director*
Clements Center for Southwest
Studies and Robert and Nancy
Dedman Professor of History
Southern Methodist University
Dallas, Texas
March 2010

PREFACE

IN HIS ESSAY "Native Latin American Contribution to the Colonization and Independence of Texas," which appeared in the April 1943 issue of *Southwestern Historical Quarterly* and was first read at the 1935 meeting of the League of United Latin American Citizens in Harlingen, Texas, the Stephen F. Austin biographer and prominent Texas historian Eugene C. Barker attempted to explain the problem of incorporating Tejanos (Texans of Mexican heritage) into the fabric of the Texas Revolution story:

> I should have liked to talk more about individuals: about Bastrop and Martinez and Antonio Saucedo, the first political chief, who preceded Múzquiz. About Múzquiz, himself, who belonged to an ancient family in northern Coahuila, where a town is named for the family. About Miguel Arciniega, a reserved old gentleman whom Múzquiz thought perhaps too loath to believe evil of his fellow man. About the Verramendis, interwoven with the Navarros, and into whose family Bowie married. About the Seguins, father and son, and the Ruízes. And about Antonio Padilla, who, as Secretary of State in Saltillo, rendered Austin and the first colonists invaluable service, and who later became a resident of San Antonio. But here again it is hard to be concrete; one sees them weaving in and out of the picture; one feels a very definite friendliness. Specific facts are not wanting, but they are too fragmentary to lend themselves to orderly narrative.
>
> For a good many years I have sought to interest my graduate students in these early Mexican residents of San Antonio. I wish that we might compile an authentic biographical record, showing their services in the formative period of Texas history. I hope that someone may be interested in carrying on such a study.

For whatever reason, Barker's graduate students remained uninterested. Although the individuals cited by him have articles in the *New Handbook of Texas*, to date only Juan Seguín and José Antonio Navarro have been subjects of published biographical works. Also, in addition to the men mentioned above, the De León family has been the subject of Carolina Castillo Crimm's research efforts, and José María de Jesús Carvajal, whose career principally took place along the Rio Grande border region as a Mexican caudillo, has been the topic of a major biography by Joseph Chance. Much remains to be done.

Despite his apparent friendliness toward the subject matter, Barker himself betrayed the biases of generations of Texans brought up to believe that Mexican heritage and being Texan were not entirely compatible. Even in applauding their efforts, Barker could not fail to frame the men he spoke of as "early Mexican residents of San Antonio." Well, the ancestors of some of these men may have been early residents of San Antonio, but by the 1820s San Antonio was past its "early" history. And, although those he mentioned may have resided in San Antonio, they were no mere residents. Moreover, although adhering to a certain logic, lumping Padilla, the Coahuila secretary of state who supported Anglo immigration, with the others brings out a second subtle bias—that as "Mexicans," San Antonio residents and Saltillo residents were pretty much the same thing.

And what about those Tejanos who lived in other parts of Texas? The De León clan from Victoria, Rafael Manchola and Carlos de la Garza from La Bahía/Goliad, and Vicente Cordova from Nacogdoches all were major participants in the events of the Mexican and revolutionary period. Well over 1,500 Tejanos lived in the East Texas woodlands and the South Texas prairies. These communities, along with San Antonio, were a century old when Anglo-Americans began to arrive in the 1820s. Their residents included the descendants of men who fought Apaches, Comanches, Wichitas, and Frenchmen, drove cattle to markets south into Mexico and east into Louisiana, and built the first churches and public buildings in Texas.

For Barker and most Texas historians who followed, Tejanos remained minor characters in the drama of the Texas Revolution, and they remained Mexicans. Accepting and perpetuating the ethnocentrism of an Anglo-American population that quickly gained demographic superiority and socioeconomic hegemony over Texas in the 1830s, the concept of Texan was tied to race and ethnicity. White European and Euro-American Anglophone immigrants easily became Texans. Dark skinned, Indo-American, Spanish-speaking natives were Mexican. To counteract this bias, which had social, economic, and political repercussions for Tejanos despite constitutional protections, local Tejano elites emphasized their Canary Island, Iberian, or

European origins, even when these were not true. Hence, José Antonio Navarro was the son of a Corsican, Juan Martín Veramendi the son of a Spaniard. The organizations that the growing Tejano middle class began founding in the early twentieth century reflected this bias: Barker spoke to the League of United *Latin* American citizens. For Tejano elites the term *Mexican* applied to recent immigrants and those of racially mixed heritage.

Nonetheless, there was some consciousness of the damage that the ethnoracial terminology that had developed in the course of the nineteenth and early twentieth centuries was doing to social relations in the state. In 1936, Rubén Rendón Lozano, a San Antonio resident, published a slim volume on the occasion of the Texas Centennial titled *Viva Tejas: The Story of the Mexican-born Patriots of the Republic of Texas.* In its preface Lozano declares that "the average writer of Texas history, I believe, has to some extent done an injustice to the heroes of Texas by almost completely ignoring the Latin, or Spanish-speaking element." He goes on to assert that "the Saxon [revolutionary] leaders of that era, who are justly praised, would not approve of the manner in which the deeds of their Latin brothers have been ignored and neglected." After establishing that Tejanos, a word he never himself employs, participated fully in the revolution, Lozano advises, "The apparent tendency of the modern historian to create a gap between the two races should by all means be discouraged. Such works should be abolished in school rooms, libraries and all public institutions of learning, and instead, we should face the cold, blunt facts, and give credit where credit is due." Finally, he declares his purposes in writing the book to be fostering greater understanding between "Anglo-Americans, Mexican-Americans and our sister republic, Mexico" and concludes, "Above all, it is my earnest hope to create again the realization of the founders of the Lone Star Republic that the word 'Texans' should mean Anglo-Texans and Latin or Mexican-Texans alike."

In the past thirty years substantial efforts have been made to address Lozano's concerns. Along with the studies mentioned above, the works of Arnoldo De León, David Montejano, Félix Almaráz, Armando Alonzo, Andrés Tijerina, and a few others have begun redressing the shortcomings identified by Lozano. Two books that appeared in the 1990s directly attempted to incorporate Tejanos into the mainstream of revolutionary era events—Stephen L. Hardin's *Texian Iliad* (University of Texas Press, 1994) and Paul Lack's *The Texas Revolutionary Experience* (Texas A&M University Press, 1992).

Each work asks questions specifically related to Tejanos during the period. More recently, two of the authors included in this anthology, Andrés Reséndez and Raúl A. Ramos, have published important studies analyzing the development of a Tejano identity during this formative era in modern Texas history. Reséndez's book, *Changing National Identities at the Frontier: Texas and New Mexico, 1800–1850* (Cambridge University Press, 2005), offers a broadly analytical comparison between very different frontier provinces of New Spain/Mexico that emphasizes the painful repercussions occasioned by the Mexican War of Independence and the Anglo-American invasion. Raúl A. Ramos's more focused *Beyond the Alamo: Forging Mexican Ethnicity in San Antonio, 1821–1861* (University of North Carolina Press, 2008), traces the evolution of Tejano identity from dominant group to marginalized minority. This book follows the trend of exploring how Tejanos coped with changing circumstances over which they had very limited control and hopes to further research on the members of the Tejano community whose lives and actions are worthy of attention.

The eleven biographies contained in this volume include the lives of the best known Tejanos of the first half of the nineteenth century— Juan Seguín and José Antonio Navarro—and the most obscure—Fr. Refugio de la Garza and Rafael Manchola. The individuals included represent two of the three major areas of pre–Mexican War Tejano settlement—San Antonio and Goliad—and an active public life spanning the time of the birth of Mexican Texas to the eve of the American Civil War. They represent businessmen, clergy, landowners, and military men. Politically, they range from those who remained loyal to Mexico, despite an increasingly arbitrary government intent on repressing local autonomy, to those who as Juan Seguín wrote in his memoirs "embraced the cause of Texas at the sound of the first cannon which foretold her liberty."

The subjects of all the essays are males because in that time and place women had no recognized role in public life. It is an unfortunate fact that throughout the period under study in this volume women could not hold elective office or even vote. Women in the Hispanic world did hold more legal rights than their Anglo-American counterparts, as scholars have made clear over the years, but such rights usually extended only as far as property. Women could sue and accuse, serve as witnesses in their own right, and make contracts. Nevertheless, they were prevented from exercising legal authority over anyone except their minor children. Although on occasion a woman such as Patricia De León enjoyed the privilege of acting as the economic head of her family, she could do so only in the background or as a widow without adult male children. For instance, we know that while Erasmo Seguín was away serving as Texas' representative to the constituent congress, his wife ran the post office in San Antonio with the help of their son Juan, but María Josefa Becerra de Seguín could never be postmaster in her own right. As in the world generally, the women of revolutionary and republican Texas labored under second-class citizenship status. Their stories, therefore, must be told in the realms of social and cultural history and not in works such as this that focus on public service.

The absence of a Tejano representative of East Texas is testament to the work that remains to be done in illuminating the roles of Texans of Mexican heritage from that part of the state. With the exception of Paul Lack's work on the Córdova Rebellion, the story of East Texas Tejanos remains an unaddressed void. Most often the only people of Mexican heritage mentioned in relation to East Texas are members of the Mexican military, most famously José de las Piedras. In fact, Tejanos such as José Ignacio Ybarbo and Juan Mora, as well as Vicente Córdova, played important roles in negotiating between the growing Anglo-American community and the increasingly marginalized Tejanos of the area.

This book excludes mention of the people who lived below the Nueces River and in the Trans-Pecos region. Until 1847, Texas exercised no jurisdiction in the Nueces Strip or in the area of El Paso. The populations of these areas played no direct role in the development of Mexican Texas or the Texas War of Independence. This is not to say that there are no individuals of importance to the history of the Rio Grande Valley or the El Paso areas during the 1820s–40s, only that they and their activities are beyond the immediate scope of this work.

In fact, the present assemblage of prominent Tejanos does not even exhaust the possibilities within the context of Mexican and revolutionary Texas from the San Antonio area. Erasmo Seguín, Juan's father, was in public service as early as 1807; he was part of the delegation sent to bring Moses Austin back to Texas in 1821; and he served as Texas' representative at the Constitutional Convention of 1823/24 in Mexico City that drafted the Constitution of 1824. Francisco Ruiz, who was a revolutionary going back to the Mexican War of Independence, also served as an Indian agent and was a signer of the Texas Declaration of Independence in 1836. José María de Jesús Carvajal became a protégé of Stephen Austin, who sent him to the

United States for an education. Carvajal returned to Texas a convert to Protestantism and a trained surveyor who went on to a transborder revolutionary career beginning in the Texas War of Independence period. Miguel Arciniega, like Erasmo Seguín, began his public service during the late Spanish colonial period, then went on to serve at the local and state levels, becoming land commissioner for one of Austin's colonization contracts and remaining a prominent property owner in San Antonio in the 1840s. There are others.

This volume is the product of a project that began in April 2005, when I invited a group of colleagues to help me celebrate the two-hundredth anniversary of Juan Seguín's birth in October 2006 with a conference on the topic of Tejano leadership in Mexican and revolutionary Texas. The project, as I framed it to them, would examine Texas in the 1820s and 1830s from the Tejano perspective. Delving into the lives of Tejanos who were "movers and shakers," whether or not we remember them today, could and should stimulate a reconsideration of the state's history during the period of its transformation from a remote Mexican frontier outpost to vanguard of American westward expansion.

The participants in the project, although mostly historians in the traditional sense of the word, include public historians, genealogists, and theologians. Two who made presentations but were not able to contribute essays—Adán Benavides and Dora Guerra—represented the library/archival community. All the authors have relied on widely varied sources, in some cases rather abundant and in others relatively scarce. Consequently, the essays offer not only narratives of the lives of a diverse group of individuals but insights into different ways of addressing those lives. Moreover, some of the essays tackle individuals whose importance might seem slight in our time but who carried considerable weight in their own time, even though the documentary evidence for them is not as complete as we would wish.

In the preparation of these essays, some incontrovertible truths have emerged. There is still much archival material out there capable of shedding considerable light on the history of Mexican and republican Texas from alternative perspectives. Despite the bounty of documentation, the possibility of working on some topics is limited by a dearth of direct evidence. There is a real thirst, and therefore a substantial audience, among an increasingly diverse Texas population for information on a broader range of topics centered on Mexican and republican Texas history. Finally, there is a great need for scholars to take on investigating and writing about these topics.

This book owes a great deal not only to the participants in the symposium of October 2006 who went on to prepare the essays that appear herein but to those who made the symposium itself possible. First, the Department of History at Texas State University—staff, faculty, and graduate students—contributed time and effort to making sure the symposium was a success. Funding for the event came from various Texas State University sources including a major grant from the Office of Equity and Access, the Taylor Lecture Fund, Dean Jaime Chahín of the College of Applied Arts, and the Student Diversity Team. Additional support came from the Seguín Family Historical Society and the San Marcos chapter of the American GI Forum, and from Messrs. Federico Garza, Jack Ayoub, and Charles Porter. Finally, a special thanks to Ms. Nina Wright for her efforts to make the symposium a reality.

Jesús F. de la Teja
Texas State University
San Marcos, Texas
March 2010

TEJANO
LEADERSHIP
IN MEXICAN
AND
REVOLUTIONARY
TEXAS

INTRODUCTION

Jesús F. de la Teja

AT THE END OF THE EIGHTEENTH CENTURY, Texas appeared poised finally to develop into a productive province of New Spain. A relative state of peace with the autonomous American Indian tribes of the region based on an acceptance of each others' interests in Texas had allowed the occupation of substantial portions of the countryside around the three areas of settlement: San Antonio, La Bahía (now Goliad), and Nacogdoches. This state of affairs had been made possible, in large part, by Spain's control of neighboring Louisiana, the Indian agents of which had always been more effective in dealing with independent native peoples and whose work for the crown of Spain bore similar fruit. The turbulence produced by the French Revolution and Napoleon's ambition had yet to reach the Texas frontier, although the central parts of Spanish Mexico were already feeling the strains of a mother country under assault.

The unhappy reality of imperial collapse first reached Texas in the form of the Louisiana Purchase. When Napoleon forced the weak king of Spain, Charles IV, to return the vast central portion of North America to France and then sold it to the upstart United States, the growing sense of security and measured progress that Texas had enjoyed during the previous decade came to a resounding halt. It was at about this time that all the men represented in this volume were born or began their public careers. Theirs were to be lives of tested loyalties, contested allegiances, and difficult choices. So, for instance, José Antonio Saucedo, who began his public career shortly before Hidalgo launched his revolt against bad government in September 1810, remained loyal to the Spanish government when a local insurrection briefly brought Hidalgo supporters to power in January 1811 and, later, when the insurgent Bernardo Gutiérrez de Lara and Augustus Magee invaded Texas from Louisiana in 1812. Despite his loyalty to the Spanish crown, Saucedo enjoyed the trust of his fellow citizens, as is evidenced by the respect he commanded later as *jefe político* (political chief, executive officer) of the province in 1823.

Tejanos who sided with the insurgents in 1813 or were compromised by events were killed or fled to Louisiana or Indian-controlled areas or labored under suspicion of disloyalty. Among these were

1

Juan Martín Veramendi, who went on to serve as interim governor of Coahuila y Texas in 1832–33, until he died in a cholera epidemic sweeping the southern United States and Mexico. Another Mexican War of Independence exile was José Francisco Ruiz, who later served as an Indian agent and signed the Texas Declaration of Independence with his nephew José Antonio Navarro, who was a teenager when he fled to Louisiana with the surviving insurgents. Others saw their livelihoods entirely destroyed and retreated to other parts of Mexico. Erasmo Seguín, who was accused of treason to the crown, lost all his property and was forced to take his family, including his son Juan Nepomuceno Seguín, the future War of Independence hero, to Saltillo.

The last years of Spanish Texas consisted of attempts to restore normality in the face of deteriorating circumstances. Military units, whose members and their families constituted a healthy percentage of the population, were withdrawn as the government again shifted resources to other parts of the viceroyalty where the insurrection continued to smolder. With them went Juan Antonio Padilla, a native of Coahuila who would later side with the Texans in their struggles against the national government. Nacogdoches was almost entirely deserted and other recently established settlements were abandoned in the face of Indian attack, floods, and neglect. Control of the border with the United States and the Gulf coast was something of a miracle under the circumstances, for the lack of troops meant that royalist forces at San Antonio and La Bahía could do little more than react to the frequent incursion of pirates, filibusters (military adventurers), and Indian bands fleeing westward-expanding Anglo-Americans across the Sabine River. Spanish control of Texas extended little beyond the immediate confines of the town of San Antonio and the presidio community at La Bahía, where most farm plots went untended, livestock uncared for, and trade reduced to barely a subsistence level.

Under the circumstances Tejanos were challenged by a variety of problems at Mexican independence. First, they faced chronic Indian warfare without adequate military support from the national government—a situation they felt went well back into the eighteenth century, and which prevented safe movement even in the immediate area of the surviving communities. Second, they confronted economic disaster: the Spanish government had been unable to pay the garrisons at San Antonio and La Bahía with any regularity, so that soldiers and their families were destitute, with obvious consequences for the merchants, farmers, and artisans who depended on military payrolls for their business and the soldiers' service for protection. Soldiers were increasingly involved in criminal activity, on the one hand, and on the other they were unequipped to carry out their duties. Third, without safe conditions or economic activity beyond the subsistence level, there was little chance of population growth, particularly on the part of people of means unwilling to take the risks involved to establish themselves on the hostile Indian frontier.

Newly independent Mexico appeared ill equipped to meet the needs of far-off and unproductive Texas. Mexico had lost over a million souls to the War of Independence. Silver production declined by 75 percent between 1809 and 1821 as mines ceased functioning through deliberate destruction, flooding, collapse from inattention, and the unavailability of labor. Similarly, agricultural land went fallow for lack of labor. The tax system relied almost exclusively on import and export tariffs, an inadequate funding situation even if corruption and waste were not rampant and a healthy chunk of available funds not spent on a bloated military hierarchy. Although Texas representatives to the national congresses in the 1822–24 period were gladdened by the political autonomy and new social compact that independence had produced, they were sobered by the knowledge that the national government could do little on its own to improve the lot of Texas and Tejanos. Texas' first representative in Mexico City, the San Antonio native and parish priest Refugio de la Garza, had written home that divisions among Mexicans based on race or status had ended. His replacement at the second constitutional convention, Erasmo Seguín, found that all the good will and exuberance created by independence could not hide the reality that Texas was a burden that the other northern provinces did not wish to take on. In spring 1824, Seguín negotiated an alliance with Coahuila, Texas' poor neighbor to the south, which resulted in the creation of the poorest state in the new Mexican federal union. Although union with Coahuila promised greater local autonomy for Texas in the short term, it would prove to be an unworkable marriage. In the meantime, Tejanos sought solutions to Texas' ills elsewhere.

In stepped the Americans. Already on the eve of Mexican independence Moses Austin had come to San Antonio to ask for permission to establish a colony of Roman Catholic Americans for whom he would serve as agent. Like his biblical namesake, Moses Austin was destined not to enter the Promised Land with his people, a task that fell to his son Stephen, who soon changed his name to Esteban to fit in. He quickly learned Spanish and sent his brother Brown to live with the Seguíns so that he might learn the language and customs of the people with whom he would be working for the rest of his life. Stephen Austin also set about establishing good working relations with other Tejanos.

Instrumental to the success of Austin's early colony was José Antonio Saucedo, whose experience as a public official in the last years under Spain made him ideally suited to navigate the turbulent political waters of the immediate post-independence period. It was Saucedo who kept Austin within the law and offered advice on how to establish rules for the colony. Although Austin employed as his first land commissioner the Baron of Bastrop, a Dutch émigré who had established himself in Louisiana until the Purchase and then moved to Texas, he later employed the services of San Antonio businessmen Gaspar Flores and Miguel Arciniega. He later worked closely with jefe político Ramón Múzquiz, a native of Coahuila who was attempting to establish his economic interests in Texas.

Soon other Anglo-Americans seeking opportunities in Texas joined Austin in the land speculation business. Texas was about land, and Tejanos understood that Anglo-Americans had access to the labor, capital, and business contacts necessary to bring about development. Francisco Ruiz famously wrote that "I cannot help seeing advantages which, to my way of thinking would result if we admitted honest, hard-working people, regardless of what country they come from . . . even hell itself."[1] Of course, the hard-working people from hell were the Anglo-Americans, who were already beginning to raise suspicions, especially on the increasingly contentious issues of land and slaves.

With few people and lots of land, the first order of business for Tejanos was to get the land settled and the Indian frontier defended. Anglo-Americans brought an uncompromising attitude toward native peoples that promised to solve the long-running problem of insecurity for Tejano communities. Tejanos did not have the resources to defeat Apaches, Comanches, and other aggressive autonomous tribes; the Anglo-Americans did. There were not enough Tejanos or migrants from the interior of Mexico to cultivate Texas commercially, but Anglo-Americans were hell-bent on exploiting international cotton demand by expanding production everywhere possible. Tejanos saw incoming promoters of the cotton industry, people whom they referred to as "capitalists" because they had access to financial resources unavailable to Mexicans, as exactly what Texas needed, never mind that they brought slaves to a country that had renounced human bondage.

At every turn then, the vast majority of Tejano leaders favored, promoted, encouraged, and defended Anglo-American immigration. Because these leaders generally backed a policy focused on local autonomy and states' rights favored by advocates of a strong federal system in Mexico, they have come to be known as federalists. At the state congress in Saltillo and later Monclova, federalists such as José Antonio Navarro defended the practice of slavery in Texas as necessary to economic development. Properly regulated under more humane Spanish-Mexican laws, slaves in Texas could serve the interests of development. When the state legislature opted for emancipation, it was the Tejano delegates who presented Austin's plan to allow the practice of indentured servitude. By this ruse, slave owners would manumit their slaves on paper before crossing over into Texas on condition that the bondsmen paid for their freedom with ninety-nine years of labor. For a while this practice kept the doors open to Anglo-American immigration. When the Law of 6 April 1830, with its annulment of empresario contracts and tax provisions, threatened to stop almost all immigration from the United States, Tejanos such as jefe político Múzquiz and Texas representatives to the legislature Rafael Antonio Manchola and José María Balmaceda raised such complaints that Balmaceda was expelled from the legislature and Manchola was censured.

There were some Tejanos who were actively engaged in establishing new communities and economic activities. Martín De León, the only Tejano empresario, founded the town of Victoria and, until his death in the cholera epidemic in 1833, attempted to establish good working relations with American and European immigrants settling in the coastal region. His son Fernando De León and son-in-law Plácido Benavides continued their generally warm relations with the Anglos and identified themselves with the Tejano federalists. Just to the south, in the Goliad area, Carlos de la Garza, a member of an old presidio family, established one of the largest ranching communities in the region. He counted among his friends several of the Irish and Anglo families that moved into the area in the early 1830s.

Clearly, Texas did not lack for Tejano leadership, and it might be argued that without that leadership Anglo-American immigration might well have gone far more slowly. Nevertheless, it would be wrong not to note that there were voices of caution, if not of outright hostility, to the direction of developments in Texas. The De Leóns, who generally had good relations with the new arrivals, had repeated run-ins with Green DeWitt and his colonists over trade, property, and boundary issues. Some Tejanos began to see the growing flood of Anglo-American immigration, unmatched by a similar Mexican migration, as potentially dangerous. Balmaceda, who had previously supported immigration from the United States, by the spring of 1833 was writing, "The political situation of the Mexican part of Texas is very difficult and compromised at present, and we all wonder very much that the state's authorities have not dictated some measures to preserve even the appearance of the laws and respect for the authorities entrusted with enforcing them."[2]

In the Nacogdoches area of East Texas, Vicente Córdova, a leader of the local Tejano community, had to deal with the fact he and his followers were completely surrounded and outnumbered by Anglo-Americans. The East Texas Tejanos focused their displeasure on national and state governments that refused or were incapable of enforcing immigration laws and protecting their interests. By the start of the Texas War of Independence, they were so alienated from both sides that they agreed only to defend their homes, neither taking the government's side against the rebels nor joining in the revolution.

Generally, in 1831–33 Tejanos were still much farther away from rebellion than the growing Anglo-American population, which had less and less reason to conform to Mexican practices. Although they had taken an oath to be good Mexicans, Anglo settlers, in the absence of Tejano neighbors or Mexican authorities, recreated Southern society in Texas. Beyond the Tejano zone along the San Antonio and lower Guadalupe rivers, Anglo-Texan communities increasingly resembled places in Mississippi, Alabama, and Louisiana. Whites ran their affairs in English, and blacks (although technically free) were treated as slaves, with little thought to the fact that they lived in Mexico. In 1834 an inspector from the national government, Juan N. Almonte, wrote that the Anglo-Americans all carried in their back pockets a copy of the U.S. Constitution as if it were the law of the land. Without a counterweight to this flood of immigrants, which had reduced the Tejano population to approximately one-fifth of the province's total, Texas was lost. Nevertheless, many Tejanos tried to balance openly advocating the cause of Anglo-American interests with finding a way to stabilize Mexican politics. When the Anglo-American parts of Texas came together in conventions in 1832 and 1833, the Tejano settlements did not send representatives but separately endorsed the grievances voiced at the meetings.

As the political situation in Mexico deteriorated in 1834 and 1835, Tejanos faced increasingly difficult choices. Juan Seguín, who had assumed the office of jefe político in January 1834, had to announce the news that Stephen Austin had been arrested and taken to Mexico City under charges of sedition. Later in the year he attempted to call a convention in San Antonio of representatives from all the municipalities of Texas to decide on a course of action, given the fighting that had erupted between federalists and the supporters of Antonio López de Santa Anna's reactionary takeover of the national government. If the federalists represented the promoters and defenders of states' rights, the promoters of a strong national government in which the rights and privileges of the military and the church were preserved were called centralists. Centralists had turned to Santa Anna to overthrow the increasingly reform-minded work of acting president Valentín Gómez Farías, and the resulting struggle between federalists and centralists had thrown much of the country into chaos.

In Coahuila the federalists controlled the state legislature sitting at Monclova, while centralists in Saltillo called on Mexico City to support their efforts to brand the Monclova government illegal. For Tejanos, these disputes required taking sides, and most saw Texas as naturally in the federalist camp. A large number of Texians, that is, Anglo-American settlers, wanted no part of the federalist-centralist struggle. Increasingly they had come to see Mexican politics as mired in personality disputes, corruption, militarism, and superstition (as they labeled the Catholic Church). As a result, Tejano federalists found little support among Anglos for their efforts to assist the federalist cause in Coahuila.

Thus, in the fall of 1835, when rebellion broke out in Texas, it may have done so in the Anglo portions of the province, but Tejanos were more than ready to take part for their own reasons. Juan Seguín raised a company of Bexareños (citizens of Béxar) to defend Texas against centralist aggression, and Plácido Benavides did the same in Goliad. By the end of the year more than a hundred Tejanos had joined the Texan army, making them a disproportionately large percentage of the army in comparison with the Texians. As the only Texas-born participants in the struggle, Tejanos were invaluable in providing intelligence and logistical support to the rebellion.

In spring 1836, when the rebellion against centralist rule turned into a war for independence, Tejanos had a new choice to make: assume responsibility for their portion of the fight or remain loyal to Mexico, even if to an increasingly despotic government. Most chose the path of independence. Navarro and Ruiz signed the Texas declaration of independence along with the Mexican nationalist Lorenzo de Zavala. Juan Seguín and his men, including Antonio Menchaca, fought during the Runaway Scrape and at San Jacinto. Not all Tejanos sided with the cause of independence, however. Carlos de la Garza organized a company of men loyal to Mexico and assisted General José Urrea in his coastal campaign. Nevertheless, Garza was unwilling to see his Texian friends persecuted and lent aid to a number of them. Perhaps because of this he was not molested on his property after the war and lived to establish a sizable progeny in the Goliad area. Plácido Benavides, unwilling to cross the line between rebellion against bad government and rejection of Mexico, went home to sit out the rest of the struggle when he found out about the declaration of independence. The former jefe político, Ramón Múzquiz, withdrew to Coahuila, as did an unknown number of Tejanos who refused to abandon their allegiance to Mexico.

In the long run, the problem for the thousands of Tejanos who decided to remain in their homeland after independence was that their few numbers, their mixed racial background, their Catholic heritage, and their Spanish language combined to isolate them within a society that had come to be dominated by Euroamerican, Protestant English speakers. Because of their Mexican cultural heritage, Tejanos were looked upon as Mexicans, and Mexicans were foreigners and the enemy. The De León clan, which had provided assistance to the Texian cause throughout the revolution, was forced to go into exile in Louisiana when newly arrived and uninformed Anglo settlers flooded the area around Victoria. Eventually, those De León family members who survived the exile returned to recover part, but not all, of their estates. For Juan Seguín a brief period of prominence, including service as a senator in the congress of the Republic of Texas and as mayor of San Antonio, was followed by accusations of treason, exile, and an eventual partial reconciliation. In East Texas, Vicente Córdova and many of his followers were forced into rebellion by the ill treatment they received at the hands of the ascendant Anglo-American population, dooming the Tejano population of that part of the republic to marginalization.

By the time of the American Civil War, the Tejano population of

Texas had retreated to a marginalized status that failed to reflect a century and a half of Tejano life in Texas. A few Tejanos hung on in East Texas, but most remained within a Tejano homeland stretching along the San Antonio River valley from Béxar to Goliad. In this region, the landowning elites suffered a steady decline in land ownership, and the laboring class became increasingly subject to discriminatory and segregationist practices. In the mid-1850s, Texans suspicious of "Mexicans" expelled Tejanos from several communities east of San Antonio. That treatment, combined with violence against Tejano freighters, contributed to an episode in Texas history now known as the Cart War. Although some Anglo-Texan statesmen and political leaders denounced the racist actions of their fellow Texans, they had little control over what happened in a countryside increasingly populated by people who could not and would not see Tejanos as legitimate sons and daughters of Texas.

Still, some Tejanos continued to exercise leadership roles, especially in the San Antonio area. Navarro, Menchaca, and Juan Seguín participated in founding the Bexar County Democratic Party, helping to develop a Spanish-language platform. All three men published writings in defense of themselves and their community. Menchaca broke with his erstwhile Democratic allies to support Sam Houston's Unionist position on the eve of the Civil War, Navarro sent two of his sons to serve the Confederacy, and Seguín spent those years in Mexico fighting the French intervention. In other words, whether or not they approved, Tejanos lost control of the world they had been instrumental in bringing into being, and the best they could hope for was to accommodate themselves to the changes.

To the degree that their stories continued to be told after their passing, it was in terms of their support for the ascendant Anglo-Americans who saw the establishment of the Republic of Texas in terms of manifest destiny. Such a perspective, as we learn in the pages that follow, does ill service to the lives of men who saw themselves as Texan leaders in their own right. The recovery of their visions and their stories can serve us well today, as we seek to find that common ground that does justice to the unofficial motto of the United States, E Pluribus Unum—from many, one.

Notes

1.   As quoted in David J. Weber, *The Mexican Frontier, 1821–1846: The American Southwest under Mexico* (Albuquerque: University of New Mexico Press, 1982), 176.

2. Quoted in Jesús F. de la Teja, "The Colonization and Independence of Texas: A Tejano Perspective," in *Myths, Misdeeds, and Misunderstandings: The Roots of Conflict in U.S.-Mexican Relations,* ed. Jaime E. Rodríguez O. and Kathryn Vincent (Wilmington, Del.: Scholarly Resources, 1997), 93.

February 8, 1825, letter from Governor Rafael Gonzales appointing José Antonio Saucedo interim jefe político of the department of Texas. Saucedo had a long career under both Spain and Mexico. After serving in San Antonio's presidio company in the late eighteenth century, he embarked on a business and public service career. As jefe político, he helped establish the rules for Austin's colony and maintained political order during the chaotic years immediately following Mexican independence.

Courtesy Spanish Collection 123/3, p. 34, Texas General Land Office, Austin.

JOSÉ ANTONIO SAUCEDO

AT THE NEXUS OF CHANGE

Raúl A. Ramos

BETWEEN THE YEARS 1823 and 1827, the Mexican province of Texas experienced a rapid series of transformations that permanently shifted the region's social and political relations. Increased Anglo-American immigration and commerce, elevated concern for Texas by the nascent Mexican federal government, and higher levels of engagement with several indigenous groups in the hinterland required an expansive grasp of transnational and intercultural conflicts by provincial officials. From his seat in Béxar, the *jefe político* of Texas, José Antonio Saucedo, observed these tectonic movements while managing the day-to-day business of improving life on the Mexican frontier. Saucedo navigated these complex issues by relying on personal relationships and a culture of social and political brokering gained from a lifetime in the region.

Saucedo's significance came from his time serving as jefe político, a position that functioned as the de facto governor of Texas. The office of jefe político defined the unique administrative status of Texas—not being a state, but requiring local governance as a department. Appointed by the governor, Saucedo carried out executive functions during a critical time in Mexican history. From his desk, the jefe político governed the entire district including Nacogdoches and La Bahía. It is worth exploring the impact of Saucedo's policies and actions since they provide early signs of growing problems for government officials in Texas. Despite these tensions, Saucedo sought to find a balance between the demands of the young Mexican nation and ambitious American immigrants. Before detailing his governance of Mexican Texas, it is useful to examine Saucedo's life trajectory as a Tejano on the frontier and early political actor during the end of the Spanish colony.

At first glance Saucedo seems an unlikely person to hold the top political position in Texas during the Mexican period. He lacked the national political aspirations and personal wealth of other Tejano leaders. This is not to say he did not serve his community, but rather that he entered political service at an older age. In a sense, Saucedo grew into the position during a time that required attention to the subtleties and nuances of living in the borderlands.

Little is precisely known of Saucedo's life owing in no small part
to his modest and seemingly unimportant early years. Working back-
ward from often contradictory census records and references in other
documents, one finds that he was born in Béxar around 1766 to José
Antonio Saucedo and Margarita Angulo.[1] He was married to Manuela Flores, with whom he had two daughters. His extended household also seems to have included two of his aunts, Juana Beralda and
Antonia. The 1793 census also counts an unnamed mulatta slave in
his household, though she may have been tied to his aunt Antonia
since she is listed in Antonia's household in an earlier census.[2] The
same 1793 census also counts three orphaned Indian children in the
household; they do not appear in other early records, but some clues
to their lives appear in later documents. For instance, an 1819 count
lists a José Saucedo with the *calidad* (status) of *Indio* and the occupation of day laborer.[3] His listed age at forty-one comes close enough
to the fourteen-year-old orphan from the census twenty-six years
prior. That the Saucedo family housed and adopted Indian children
appears consistent with research on the complex network of captive
exchange between Spanish colonists and several indigenous tribes
on the frontier.[4] These children may have come to the family as a
result of inter-Indian or Spanish-Indian warfare as far away as New
Mexico and Coahuila. Several indigenous groups, including Comanches, frequented Béxar to trade and receive gifts from Spanish and
later Mexican officials and included among their wares both Indian
and Spanish captives.[5] It is even possible that Saucedo's family took
responsibility for these children after a raid José Antonio may have
participated in as a soldier. The nature of the arrangement remains
speculative since the orphans are not mentioned in his will.[6]

José Antonio Saucedo's father served in the Spanish military approximately thirteen years. He submitted his resignation on 30 June
1779, after claiming that injuries prevented him from continuing
his duties.[7] He concluded his petition by stating that he would have
wanted to live out his days in the service, "since I have not had a
greater love for any other thing in this life." As a second-generation
soldier on the Texas frontier, José Antonio was associated with military service at a time when the military provided civilian settlements
protection against Indian raids. That experience must have served
him well as jefe político, since he was required to make many military
decisions affecting Mexican-Indian relations throughout Texas.

Early on, Saucedo earned a living by farming and becoming active
in the wild horse and cattle market. On several occasions between

1791 and 1793 he submitted requests for licenses to lead groups from Béxar to round up *mesteños* (feral horses) and loose cattle.[8] The licenses prohibited the groups from hunting the livestock, unless required for the group to eat. One permit even went so far as to caution the group against breaking treaties with neighboring Lipan Apaches, making Saucedo responsible for any damages.[9] Later evidence suggests Saucedo's corral in town had a more public function. In one instance, the alcalde ordered disputed cattle held in Saucedo's corral while its ownership was determined.[10] These ventures in the horse and cattle market established elements of Saucedo's trustworthiness and leadership in the community. His *mesteño* business also put him in contact with ranchers from around Texas and gave him firsthand knowledge of the land. All these experiences would serve him later as an administrator.

Saucedo made his first foray into public service in 1799, when his name surfaced in consideration to head the important and potentially lucrative tobacco monopoly.[11] Although Luis Galán received the position over Saucedo, the appointment letter praised Saucedo, who "in no way will remain disgraced for not being chosen for this position; I consider that he will have an honorable destiny, in that Villa [Béxar], and as a consequence more to his advantage." This acknowledgment suggests that Saucedo's importance in the community was on the rise.

As his social status rose, so did Saucedo's wealth. A few clues remain regarding Saucedo's daily life. One glimpse appears through the proceedings of a trial charging Saucedo with whipping his servant, José Vicente Anaya.[12] Although the severity of Saucedo's punishment of Anaya was in question, the facts of the case were not. Saucedo discovered that Anaya had stolen several pieces of silverware. The case, along with census records, suggests that Saucedo lived in a large household. His temper also appears in his own testimony: he minimized the twenty lashings with a leather whip by noting that some "caused him a few superficial scars." The case highlights Saucedo's relative wealth and status in Béxar society.

In 1809 Saucedo gained his first political position as the commissioner for the Barrio del Sur (South Ward) in Béxar, one of the four wards into which the town was divided by the governor as part of a series of good government reforms.[13] Less than a year later, Saucedo requested a leave of absence for an illness he claimed prevented him from carrying out his duties.[14] It is unclear how long Saucedo sat out, though his title changed to secretary of the council in 1811.

On 4 March 1811 the Provincial Junta of Texas ordered he be paid a monthly salary of 60 pesos a month, adding, "even though this Patriot serves the same as all the other commissioners (*vocales*), he has had the honor of serving and fulfilling his duty at his own cost."[15] The junta made mention of his allegiance to the crown during the recently quashed independence revolt in Béxar led by Juan Bautista de las Casas.

Saucedo's support for the royal government in the early stages of the independence movement in Mexico might appear natural given his position, but two years after his appointment another insurrection put Saucedo's patriotism and allegiance to the crown to the test again. Even though he served in the Spanish military and held the seat, his support of the royal government could not be taken for granted. After all, many other Tejanos holding similar political and social positions supported independence. During the 1812–13 rebellion led by Bernardo Gutiérrez de Lara, Saucedo maintained his loyalty to the royal government. On 24 September 1813 Saucedo and Luis Galán submitted a list of "fugitives" and their property to the provincial governor.[16]

Royalist general Joaquín Arredondo rewarded Saucedo's support with several advancements, including alcalde in 1813 and postmaster in 1814, after the previous postmaster, Luis Galán, fell ill.[17] Soon after his appointment to the postmaster position, Saucedo found his office woefully underfunded. He forwarded his concerns to Mexico City, asking for "indispensable expenses for paper, ink, quills, string, and other necessities for this office: In virtue of this need, and because my own resources will not cover these expenses, I hope that you will have the generosity to tell me where I should recover the necessary funds to operate the post office."[18] Saucedo's request highlights just one element of the crown's shift of resources away from the northern provinces after 1810. Frontier governments were left largely to their own devices to continue basic bureaucratic functions.

During this period before independence, Saucedo's importance in Béxar society also rose. He began to play a more frequent role in local affairs. José María Zamora included him in a secret meeting to discuss problems with other *vecinos* (resident citizens of a community), and Juan Martín Veramendi asked him to hold funds in trust during a financial dispute.[19] His financial standing appears in a petition for reimbursement of property lost during the 1813 insurrection. He claimed losses totaling 2,479 pesos, including 1,256 pesos in cash, 32 pesos worth of gold, and 672 pesos worth of debts owed by indentured servants who fled.[20] Felipe Enrique Neri, Baron de Bastrop, swore witness to Saucedo's petition. On the eve of independence, the alcalde Erasmo Seguín requested contributions from about twenty prominent *vecinos* to fund Saucedo's position as secretary of the *ayuntamiento* (municipal council).[21] Through his position, Saucedo oversaw the day-to-day functions of the city, including payment of salaries of soldiers in the presidial company. The relative uneventful cooperation between pro- and anti-royalists in Béxar suggests that most elites had put these differences aside by 1820. Saucedo himself served as a bridge figure for the transition to independence.

Saucedo's importance to Texas and the region reached its peak after independence, when he was appointed jefe político of the province of Texas in 1823.[22] As jefe político, he served as de facto governor for Texas, carrying out the basic functions of managing the province in the name of the actual governor in Saltillo. Perhaps chosen for his skills as a manager or the trust established among notable elites in Béxar, at approximately fifty-seven years of age Saucedo brought seniority and stability to the highest political office residing in Texas.

The issues faced by post-independence Texas required Saucedo to draw from his years of experience in the region. His perspective came from his connection to the military, work as a rancher, relationship to three orphaned Indian children, time holding public office, and involvement in political battles to defend Texas during the insurgency. As a subordinate of the governor of Coahuila y Texas after the two provinces were joined as a single state in 1824, he made frequent and detailed reports of his activities. These reports provide a close look into the multiple concerns Saucedo had to keep in mind on a daily basis. These concerns can be grouped into three areas: regional development, Anglo-American immigration, and Indian relations.

Being the top Mexican government official in Texas made Saucedo's principal task to oversee the smooth management and growth of the province. In 1824 this meant maintaining the lines of authority with existing towns and among the growing Anglo-American population. Outside of Béxar, the two largest administrative centers were Nacogdoches to the north and La Bahía to the southeast. Requests for funds or approval of policy decisions from any of these towns all came to Saucedo's office. In short, Saucedo was the face of the Mexican government in Texas.

Representing Coahuila y Texas mattered even more at a time when the state needed to assert its significance and meaning in the wake of independence from Spain. Saucedo's role in state building came to the fore when he presented the newly ratified Constitution of 1824 to the province. On receiving the documents, Saucedo organized a citywide festival in Béxar. He noted, "The moment the arrival of the documents was publicly announced, all the inhabitants of this town in general and individually dedicated themselves to show their deep feelings by decorating their homes, setting off fireworks, and other demonstrations of rejoicing."[23] The celebration on 26 February 1824 consisted of a military parade, public speeches in the plaza, and a Te Deum mass in San Fernando Church. These ceremonial rituals functioned to replace allegiance to the crown with loyalty toward the Mexican republic.[24]

Beyond announcing the transition to the constitutional government, Saucedo needed to oversee the changes and inform the province of the new federal system. To that end, the governor sent along forty copies of the pamphlet titled "Advantages of the Republican Popular Federal Representative System" for him to disseminate throughout Texas.[25] Saucedo added that it should be distributed to towns and schools around the region in order to consolidate the federal system, "with which we have certainly joined the fortunes of all Mexicans." The new constitution also required new rounds of elections and other changes to municipal governance.

Saucedo took advantage of his position to make social changes at the local level. He kept close tabs on a plan to build schools in Texas and particularly in Béxar. He requested funds for a school building and a teacher to staff it.[26] When the project seemed to fall behind, he continued to encourage the construction, noting that it was one of his "sacred duties."[27] Saucedo considered the broader social benefits of a public school when he noted that it would educate children who wandered the streets and would help families of limited means.[28] Although his attention focused on a school for Béxar, Saucedo consistently referred to the regional project to open public schools in all municipalities. He continued to request funds for buildings and school supplies frequently in his communications with officials in Saltillo.[29]

Several disputes around the distribution of secularized mission lands to indigenous peoples brought Saucedo into that element of the changing social landscape as well. Missions were always meant to be temporary institutions whose lands were to be turned over to Indian converts. The missions began to secularize in 1793, and in 1823 the government decreed completion of the process.[30] During this process, *ayuntamientos* in both Béxar and La Bahía asked Saucedo to adjudicate who should own the lands and what might be their best use.[31] The questions and complaints raised during secularization show signs that the process was vague and open to abuse. In one case, Saucedo received complaints that a dozen Taraname Indian families should be moved off mission land for being poor farmers and ranchers.[32] Fray Antonio Díaz de León vouched for the families and asked Saucedo for more time. In another case regarding mission lands around Béxar, Saucedo requested more guidance from the legislature over the interpretation of decrees, noting his urgency to resolve the multiple claims on the land given the poor condition of these Indians.[33] Saucedo's oversight of mission lands distribution emphasized the execution of government Indian policy in opposition to the desires of local elite families.

In general, Saucedo's position required him to manage funds and policy for the three main towns and their hinterland. Beyond Béxar, La Bahía and Nacogdoches kept him busy between funding military protection, settling land disputes with immigrants, and monitoring Indian relations. As a life-long *vecino* of Béxar and a member of the Tejano elite, Saucedo used individual contacts to maintain the government in these locations. When word of contraband trade reached his desk, Saucedo encouraged Juan Seguín, then alcalde of Nacogdoches, to regain control of imports from the United States.[34]

Confronting contraband trade was related to another duty of his office, paying for the establishment and maintenance of government on the frontier. Saucedo sought to raise funds by enforcing fees and taxes, such as those on tobacco. In one attempt to levy the fee, Saucedo noted potential resistance by settlers in Nacogdoches and by indigenous groups: "If [colonists] have an open mind to the reasonable and fair request, I believe they will see their errors and, like good citizens, will obey the law that benefits the State."[35] At other times raising funds meant collecting import duties or colonization fees from empresarios, and at others it meant making appeals to notable elites to pay for necessary functions.[36] In a letter to Austin, Saucedo wrote, "The extreme lack of public funds that plagues this Province and the severe urgencies that currently surround its government, have obligated the sixth commissioner of this Provincial Department Baron de Bastrop to undertake the shameful journey to your town with the goal of collecting any possible portion of the fees that are due to the Nation."[37] Saucedo's struck an apologetic tone in the letter, suggesting that the request seemed out of the ordinary. Other reports to the governor made frequent mention of lacking sufficient funds, especially to deal with Anglo-American immigrants and with hostile indigenous groups.[38] In most of these cases, he emphasized that funding his government meant the difference between keeping and losing Texas.

Perhaps the most significant transformation under way during Saucedo's tenure, and the most critical issue involving regional development, related to his oversight of the empresario colonization program as it grew between 1824 and 1826. Saucedo's close ties to Stephen F. Austin and his participation as an empresario commissioner for Green De Witt suggests he believed the colonization policy held benefits for Texas. But as the jefe político, Saucedo also witnessed the violations of the law and threats to stability brought on by Anglo-American immigrants and Americans operating across the Sabine River border. He believed these transgressions would erode Mexican authority and power along the frontier and lead to the loss of Texas.

Although the governor and legislature in Saltillo held the power to decide who would be granted an empresario contract, Saucedo had to supervise and enforce the contracts. He seemed well suited to the task, possessing a detailed familiarity with the extensive national and state colonization laws. He took the time to point out potential problems to empresarios and alcaldes in the immigrant areas. In a letter to James Gains, then alcalde of the Sabine district, Saucedo noted the unmonitored settlement of immigrants he called vagrants and criminals among the Anglo-Americans entering his district.[39] Saucedo asked Gains to "make it known to them the error they have committed by settling without permission from this government." Later, he wrote to the alcalde of Nacogdoches, Luis Procela, insisting that he post the colonization laws and ensure that the immigrants "have the prerequisite of being Catholics and industrious."[40] Saucedo continued to issue such warnings in other letters to officials along the frontier. In one letter he suggested that these problems could be solved with increased migration from within Mexico. Writing in support of empresario Martín De León, Saucedo noted that "the benefits to the federal government and particularly to the state that should result from the admission of Mexican colonists over foreigners are noteworthy both for their compliant character as well as their lack of disdain for our laws."[41] Other problems with colonization continued to surface, including questionable claims to lands made by several Anglo-Americans who fought in 1813 with José Bernardo Gutiérrez de Lara.[42] Ultimately, Saucedo held adherence to the law as the measure for success of the colonization laws and as critical to the future of the entire northern frontier.

In Stephen F. Austin, Saucedo found his closest ally in matters impacting the frontier with the United States. Time and again, Saucedo turned to Austin when he sensed that immigrant problems might increase or tensions with indigenous groups could destabilize the border region. Regarding Anglo-American immigrants Saucedo wrote to Austin, "I have to tell them that once they are admitted by the Mexican government they will form one single family with the rest of its sons; they have no reason to presume that I will let them down on my word."[43] Austin lent a hand on several occasions when government funds fell short by advancing the colonization fees to Saucedo. For Saucedo, the successful expansion of the nation-state into the frontier required the full participation of Anglo-American immigrants.[44]

During his tenure, Saucedo monitored several problems that arose in the border areas. He felt that too many immigrants were settling along rivers, coasts, and the border itself, in violation of the colonization laws. In his mind, breaking these rules led to lawlessness in general and the breakdown of stability. By 1826 Saucedo felt the situation was deteriorating. After receiving a report about election problems in Nacogdoches, he commented, "If the empresarios and colonists are not obligated to respect and follow the laws of their adopted nation, then this will be made more difficult after the settlement of greater numbers, and who knows if they will separate from the state and adhere to those of their native nation with all the land they occupy."[45] Saucedo repeated this warning elsewhere in his reports. He noted several instances of empresarios and immigrants securing land grants with no intention of moving to Texas from the United States.[46]

Along with these broken laws, Saucedo warned of a possible conspiracy, or collaboration, between Anglo-Americans on both sides of the border and the indigenous groups in the area. This threat became real when Hayden Edwards and associates launched an insurrection known later as the Fredonian Rebellion. Once again Saucedo turned to Austin for help by authorizing him to form a military unit from his colonists. Saucedo acknowledged that his decision to rely on Anglo-American colonists might make his superiors nervous. In a letter to Governor Joaquín Blanco, Saucedo implored, "For the good of the population, I ask you to have the good will to approve my operations and forgive the liberty I have taken in taking these steps, that without a doubt should improve the happiness and tranquility of this border."[47] Saucedo went so far as to travel to Nacogdoches in winter 1826 to make his point more forcefully in person.

Once in Nacogdoches, Saucedo invoked the power of the state to bring tranquility to the frontier.[48] He directed his 4 January 1827 speech to "the inhabitants of Nacogdoches and the district up to the Sabine River and to all the peaceful Indian tribes that live along the border with the United States of the North." In it he set out the goals to "reestablish order, conserve the territorial integrity of the Mexican Republic, avoid if at all possible the disasters of war, and hear the concerns of those unjustly aggrieved." Through this public notice Saucedo laid out several of the principles that guided his tenure as jefe político. Once again, he believed the government should play the role of partner to colonist concerns. He noted that the government, "with every measure at its disposal, will protect your personal security and that of your interests as long as you remain loyal and refrain from disrupting the common cause that all of us who have the honor of belonging to the Mexican government ought to sustain." Addressing Mexicans, Anglo-Americans, and Indians alike, Saucedo offered to extend the power of the state into the frontier. Garnering the resources to carry through with his promise would prove to be more difficult.

In Nacogdoches, Saucedo's immigration problem intersected threats by indigenous groups because of the access to contraband trade across the border. He faced mounting conflicts with other indigenous groups throughout Texas, especially when a peace treaty with Comanche bands broke down. He believed that indigenous incursions, like Anglo-American insubordination, threatened Mexico's hold on the territory. Saucedo relied on decades of life on the frontier to make policy decisions regarding Indian relations. These decisions attempted to balance military force with a long-established system of gift giving and negotiation.

Saucedo had to respond to indigenous hostilities in the form of both reports of potential violence and actual attacks on people and settlements throughout the region.[49] On hearing of a meeting between Waco and Tahuayacan Indians near Nacogdoches, Saucedo responded by calling for a strong military strike to achieve a wider effect across the entire frontier. He suggested "a decisive premeditated strike that would make them know the superiority of our weapons."[50] Saucedo paired this exhortation with a request for more rifles and manpower for the frontier areas.[51] In a subsequent letter to the military commander of Texas, he went beyond calling for one military strike, instead proposing "to the higher government, if they wish, that in order for this important part of the federation to achieve the peak of abundance that its inhabitants practice without disruption, the most sure method is to exterminate the nations that cause us such damage, putting in effect a campaign from points around New Mexico, Coahuila, and Texas with a thousand cavalry soldiers."[52] In this case he was responding to reports of a meeting between Comanche, Aguaje, Tahuacano, Talmayace, and Waco groups who seemed to be planning an all-out war.

In other instances, Saucedo received word of individual attacks and the resulting reaction by presidial troops. On 24 March 1826 a group of eighty Comanche raiders entered Béxar via Mission Espada.[53] His report noted that the raiders almost captured a little girl but were thwarted by her mother wielding a rifle. In the ensuing moments, the dragoons of the Second Regiment chased the Comanche group but fell short of their objective. Saucedo criticized the soldiers and their horses for not knowing the territory or having the stamina to make a long chase. He used that criticism to request more and better-equipped soldiers for Texas. Despite these problems, Saucedo continued the Béxareño long-held practice of giving monthly gifts to Comanche groups that came in peace. When local funds for these gifts ran low, he asked for additional funds from the government or temporary support from local elites.[54]

In the immigrant Cherokees, Saucedo faced the most politically organized indigenous group on the Nacogdoches frontier. Over the period of his tenure as jefe político, he received contradictory reports on the support or opposition of Cherokee groups, especially of Chief Richard Fields. At one point, Saucedo believed Fields had organized a massive insurrection on the border. Later, Fields denied the charges and signed a peace treaty with Saucedo in 1827. Of that treaty Saucedo noted, "The affection we have shown them and the shelter and protection of our government [have] resulted in the manifestation of their sentiment in favor of the Mexican Republic, which they recognize as mother."[55] Saucedo seemed to suggest that these indigenous groups, much like the Anglo-American immigrants, could eventually become citizens of the new nation.

By mid-1827 Saucedo had stepped down from his position as jefe político, turning over the duties to his longtime second, Ramón Múzquiz.[56] He continued participating in local politics and maintained a connection with Anglo-American colonization by becoming the commissioner to Green De Witt's colony. These empresario commissioner positions carried the additional benefit of paying well for those Tejanos fortunate enough to obtain them. Saucedo died in 1832, just as tensions in the region were starting to push to an all-time high. Many of the problems in the border areas he warned about during his tenure as jefe politico had begun to materialize.

With his health failing him, Saucedo sat down to write his last will and testament.[57] He made mention of his deceased wife Manuela Flores, two daughters, Manuela and Encarnación, and two grandchildren from Encarnación, Francisco and Manuel. The will noted that he owned a stone house on Flores Street and had land at Mission San Juan de Espada. Gaspar Flores oversaw the execution of his will, including a listing of debts owed to and from many *vecinos* in Béxar. His estate gives the impression of deep connections to the people and place.

Saucedo occupied the highest political seat in Texas during a turbulent transition. Several factors put him in this position and permitted him to navigate these changes. Most of these influences emanated from Saucedo's birth. First, he was born male, which gave him access to education, military service, family patriarchy, and, most important, public office. Saucedo circulated comfortably among other elite Tejano men sharing his status. In doing so, he cultivated an idea of honor based on expectations of his gender and class. Second, he was born on the Texas frontier, which allowed him to experience firsthand the widely diverse people and cultures traversing the region. It also gave him a sense of how best to advocate improvement of the region with the new government. Finally, Saucedo was born a creole in time to witness and participate in the formation of the Mexican republic. He understood the political implications of Mexican citizenship. He also sensed the differences that existed between Mexicans and the members of other groups living in Texas. These differences later grew to create new states and new identities—developments that Saucedo intuited but could not control.

Notes

1. Census transcriptions from University of Texas Institute of Texan Cultures at San Antonio. *Residents of Texas, 1782–1836* (San Antonio: University of Texas Institute of Texan Cultures, 1984), 1:69, 75, 135, 227–28, 271, 337, 342. Frederick C. Chabot, *With the Makers of San Antonio* (San Antonio, Tex.: Artes Gráficas, 1937), 65.

2. *Residents of Texas*, 1:135.

3. *Residents of Texas*, 1:271.

4. James Brooks, *Captives and Cousins: Slavery, Kinship and Community in the Southwest Borderlands* (Chapel Hill: University of North Carolina Press, 2002). On adopted Indian servants, also see Jesús F. de la Teja, *San Antonio de Béxar: A Community on New Spain's Northern Frontier* (Albuquerque: University of New Mexico Press, 1995), 122–23.

5. Raúl A. Ramos, "Finding the Balance: Béxar in Mexican / Indian Relations," in *Continental Crossroads: Remapping U.S.-Mexico Borderlands History*, ed. Samuel Truett and Elliott Young (Durham, NC: Duke University Press, 2004), 35–65.

6. Estate of José Antonio Saucedo, 5 January 1832, Bexar Archives Microfilm [BA].

7. Petition to retire, 30 June 1779, BA.

8. Request for license, 16 November 1791, and 21 September 1793, BA.

9. Request for License, Saucedo to Governor, 21 September 1793, BA.

10. Manuel Barrera to Vecinos of Béxar, 11 November 1809, BA.

11. Arispe to Saucedo, 30 October 1799, and 7 December 1799, BA.

12. Case against Saucedo, 8 July 1809, BA.

13. Circular, 5 October 1809, BA.

14. Statement of Alvino Pacheco, 1 March 1810, BA.

15. Acta, 4 March 1811, BA. "Saucedo, José Antonio," *Handbook of Texas*, notes that he served on the council in 1812.

16. "Relación de las Casas de Piedra y Paja, Labores y Ranchos qe. tenían los Ynsurgentes qe. salieron fugitivos de esta Capital," José Antonio Saucedo and Luis Galán to Governor Cristóbal Domínguez, 24 September 1813, Archivo General del Estado de Coahuila, Fondo Colonial, c.27, e.54.

17. Saucedo to Ayuntamiento, 4 May 1814, BA.

18. Saucedo to Benito Armiñán, 10 June 1814, BA.

19. Béxar, 8 November 1814, and 27 September 1815, respectively, BA.

20. "Rasón de lo que perdí en la entrada que los revolucionarios Anglo Americanos y Españoles Iniciaron en esta Capital en el año de 1813," Béxar, 30 November 1818, BA. See also Jesús F. de la Teja, "The Colonization and Independence of Texas: A Tejano Perspective," in *Myths, Misdeeds, and Misunderstandings: The Roots of Conflict in U.S.-Mexican Relations*, ed. Jaime E. Rodríguez O. and Kathryn Vincent (Wilmington, Del.: Scholarly Resources, 1997), 82–83.

21. Erasmo Seguín to Governor, 19 November 1820, BA.

22. The first document I located with mention of his new office was a letter addressed to him as "jefe político de esta Provincia from La Bahía," 15 February 1823, BA.

23. Saucedo to Zambrano, 5 March 1824, BA.

24. On the performance of nationalism, see Andrés Reséndez, *Changing National Identities at the Frontier: Texas and New Mexico, 1800–1850* (New York: Cambridge University Press, 2005), 83–91.

25. Saucedo to Béxar Ayuntamiento, 22 May 1826, BA.

26. Saucedo to Ayuntamiento de Béxar, 23 January 1825, BA.

27. Saucedo to Rafael González, 18 April 1825, BA.

28. Ibid.

29. Saucedo to Rafael González, 18 September 1825, 21 January 1826, and 22 May 1826, BA.

30. Félix D. Almaráz Jr., *The San Antonio Missions and Their System of Land Tenure* (Austin: University of Texas Press, 1989), 2–7.

31. Saucedo to Zambrano, 8 January 1824, 5 February 1824, and 1 June 1824; Saucedo to Rafael González, 30 October 1825, and 12 November 1826, BA.

32. Saucedo to Rafael González, 30 October 1825, BA.

33. Ibid.

34. Not to be confused with Juan N. Seguín of San Antonio, the Nacogdoches Juan Seguín was a cousin of Erasmo Seguín. Saucedo to J. Seguín, 29 July 1824, BA.

35. Saucedo to Rafael González, 18 April 1825, BA.

36. Duties, 18 April 1825; Saucedo to Austin, 18 July 1825; Request funds in Béxar, 21 April 1825, BA.

37. Saucedo to Austin, 22 June 1824, BA.

38. Saucedo to Jefe Político de Coahuila, 8 July 1824, BA.

39. Saucedo to Gains, 8 March 1824, BA.

40. Saucedo to Procela, 14 June 1825, BA.

41. Saucedo to Austin, August 21, 1825, BA.

42. Saucedo to Minister of State, 15 April 1824; Saucedo to Austin, 17 October 1825; and Saucedo to Ayuntamiento de Béxar, 17 November 1825, BA.

43. Saucedo to Austin, 10 July 1824, BA.

44. Saucedo to Jefe Político de Coahuila, 8 July 1824; Saucedo to Austin, 18 July 1825, BA.

45. Saucedo to Rafael González, 19 February 1826, BA.

46. Saucedo to Rafael González, 11 June 1826, and 22 July 1826, BA.

47. Saucedo to Blanco, 9 January 1827, BA.

48. A los habitantes de Nacogdoches, 4 January 1827, BA.

49. In a letter to General Manuel Mier y Terán, Saucedo describes a Comanche attack on Karankawa and Taraname Indians resident in Mission Espíritu Santo at La Bahía. 25 June 1824, BA.

50. Saucedo to Rafael González, 4 October 1825, BA.
51. Rafael González to Saucedo, 22 August 1825, BA.
52. Saucedo to Comandante de Armas, 11 November 1825, BA.
53. Saucedo to Rafael González, 2 April 1826, BA.
54. Saucedo to Zambrano, 13 February 1824; Saucedo to Zambrano, 21 February 1824; Saucedo to Rafael González, 21 April 1825, BA.
55. Saucedo to Arizpe, 15 March 1827, BA.
56. Saucedo to Arizpe, 12 February 1827, BA.
57. Gaspar Flores, Saucedo estate, 5 January 1832, BA.

The Veramendi Palace. Juan Martín de Veramendi enjoyed the comforts of one of the more substantial homes in San Antonio, built by his father Fernando in the 1770s and demolished in the early twentieth century after years of use as a saloon and oddities museum.

Courtesy UTSA's Institute of Texan Cultures, #081-0500, Thomas W. Cutrer.

JUAN MARTÍN DE VERAMENDI

TEJANO POLITICAL
AND BUSINESS LEADER

David R. McDonald

THREE SAN ANTONIO NATIVES born in Spanish Texas attained the office of governor of the Mexican state of Coahuila y Texas: Rafael Gonzáles, Juan José Elguézabal, and Juan Martín de Veramendi. Of these, Veramendi stands out as the only one who rose to power through a lifetime of participation in civil government and business enterprise; González and Elguézabal achieved their status as military men. Unfortunately, Veramendi's tenure as governor was short, lasting less than one year, during 1833, when he and family members died tragically in a cholera epidemic in Monclova. Thus, for Veramendi, the political journey was as important as his political destination.

The heritage of Juan Martín de Veramendi extends back to the Basque region of Spain, where his father Fernando was born in the city of Pamplona around the year 1745; his paternal grandparents were Martín de Veramendi and Benita Olagué.[1] Fernando arrived in San Antonio de Béxar by 1775 and quickly won acceptance by local residents. On 17 April 1776 he married María Josefa Granados, a San Antonio native.[2]

Fernando prospered. By 1783 his family lived in a fine stone house located on Soledad Street on a lot that extended east to the San Antonio River, and he had purchased four tracts of irrigated land.[3] In addition, he gained a seat on the ayuntamiento in 1782. The next year, at the end of April, Veramendi set out for Mexico City in the company of other travelers. Barely a month later he was killed in an Indian attack near present Guerrero, Coahuila.[4] On arrival of news of his death, the church bells sounded, demonstrating the esteem Bexareños felt for him.

Fernando left behind three sons: José María, Juan Martín del Carmen (the subject of this study), and Fernando Ramón, ages six, five, and one, respectively.[5] A daughter, María Josefa, was born posthumously.[6] Veramendi left a detailed will in which he asked parish priest Pedro Fuentes to handle the education of his sons and Juan José de la Santa to manage their property interests.

Veramendi's widow remarried—to Juan Martín de Amondaráin, a Castilian Spaniard—and named him as the manager of her children's inheritance. After her death and the departure of Father Fuentes in 1790, a five-year power struggle ensued over the management of the Veramendi heirs' property. De la Santa charged Amondaráin with mismanagement of and losses to the heirs' property; in addition, Amondaráin attempted to move to Guanajuato, taking the children with him. He remained in Béxar, however, and retained custody of the Veramendi sons through 1796.[7] During these years Juan Martín formed lasting friendships with boys who would become Bexareño leaders such as Erasmo Seguín, José Francisco Ruiz, and José Angel Navarro—in whose house his future wife was born in 1792.

By age twenty-three, Veramendi had attained personal independence. His stepfather was no longer active in Béxar after 1796, and by 1801 Juan Martín had acquired ownership of the Soledad Street house from his siblings.[8] He learned the skills of the merchant trade and began to build on the successes of his father. In contrast, his older brother José María worked as a day laborer (*jornalero*).[9]

The 1804 census indicates that Veramendi shared his household with a brother, a sister, and a slave girl age five years; his occupation was listed as notary (*escribano*).[10] Juan Martín's designation as a notary suggests that his education included knowledge of the proper forms for writing legal documents, which he would subsequently put to good use.

Alcalde Angel Navarro appointed Juan Martín to his first public office of record in 1808.[11] As *síndico-procurador*, Veramendi was responsible for enforcing ayuntamiento rules such as those pertaining to public health. He found a way to combine his municipal duties with his merchant activities, for he dedicated four months of that year to a mercantile journey. By age thirty Veramendi was an experienced merchant. He knew how to obtain large quantities of marketable goods and knew the trade routes between Béxar and Nacogdoches.

By early March 1808 he had assembled fourteen mule loads of goods to take to the military settlement of Trinidad de Salcedo on the Trinity River and to Nacogdoches.[12] The Veramendi caravan included sweets, black and white soap, cowhide footwear, footwear from Córdoba, corn, jars from Guadalajara, guitars, and saddles. Among his personal possessions were some "small gold items." He did not complete his trip to Nacogdoches, however; the military commandant there reported his failure to arrive. When questioned about his tardy return, Veramendi explained that because of an intermittent fever he remained many days in the vicinity of Trinidad del Salcedo and the nearby Bernín ranch.[13] Perhaps so, but Veramendi's trip may have combined legal and contraband trade, which was common along the southeastern area of Texas. With his "small gold items" he could have easily bought a stash of goods from Louisiana traders such as tobacco and cloth for which there was always a market in San Antonio.

In addition to his merchant activities, Juan Martín started a household and became a stock raiser on the eve of the Mexican war of independence. He operated a ranch called San José on Cíbolo Creek, southeast of San Antonio.[14] In 1810 he reported 470 head of cattle, and his 2,142 head of sheep and goats nearly doubled those of any other rancher. The Veramendi sheep produced large amounts of wool for export. Also in 1810, he married eighteen-year-old María Josefa Navarro, younger sister of his friend and neighbor José Angel. By the end of the year, Juan Martín de Veramendi at age thirty-two had all the trappings of success—material, political, and social—and had exceeded the accomplishments of his father. As a result of his marriage, Veramendi joined the Navarro and Ruiz families. Bound by kinship, marriage, and shared political values and economic ideals, this formidable clan exerted a powerful influence on public affairs. Veramendi's tranquility and well-being were about to be severely challenged, however, by the violent struggle for Mexican independence.

Inspired by the initial success of Father Miguel Hidalgo, Juan Bautista de las Casas led a revolt that captured Governor Manuel Salcedo and his officers in January 1811. Veramendi joined a junta led by sub-deacon Juan Manuel Zambrano that plotted a counterrevolt that overthrew Casas on 3 March. After the revolutionary dust had settled, Commandant General Nemesio Salcedo from his headquarters in Chihuahua congratulated the junta for ridding the province of traitors and revolutionaries.[15] Among those commended were Juan Veramendi, Francisco Ruiz, and Angel Navarro. The list of thirty-four names reads like a who's who of San Antonio royalists. Within two years, however, Veramendi and many others who were honored that day would be on the list of traitors to Spain and would be fleeing for their lives.

By the end of October 1811 a semblance of normalcy had returned to Béxar—just as Juan Martín and Josefa Navarro brought their first child into the world. Parish priest Darío Zambrano baptized Ursula María Fructuosa on All Saints' Day, 1 November 1811. Demonstrating his growing political influence, Veramendi arranged for military governor Simón de Herrera to be her godfather.[16] The Veramendis also added an adopted daughter to their family; as godparents, they took in Juana Gertrudis, natural daughter of José Angel Navarro and Concepción Cervantes.[17]

After Hidalgo's defeat, most revolutionary activity shifted to central and southern New Spain. In Texas, however, a crushing attack on royal authority began in summer 1812. Bernardo Gutiérrez de Lara and Augustus Magee led a force of volunteers across the Sabine River, intending to overthrow Spanish rule. Near Nacogdoches, their self-styled Republican Army of the North encountered Juan Martín de Veramendi and sub-deacon Juan Manuel Zambrano, both of whom were on their way to Louisiana with large shipments of wool. In the confrontation that ensued these two prominent royalists lost their wool and mules. Veramendi continued to Nachitoches and remained there pending the outcome of the Gutiérrez-Magee invasion. He was no stranger to Nachitoches; records show that he had loaned money to various individuals there, including "416 pesos to a Mr. [Jean or Pierre] Lafitte."[18]

Gutiérrez and Magee rode south and captured La Bahía. At San Antonio during March 1813, Gutiérrez defeated the royalist forces near Rosillo Creek. Juan Martín's brother-in-law, José Antonio Navarro, observed the surrender of Salcedo and his officers on 30 March and recorded a vivid account of their brutal execution a few days later.[19]

Retribution for the killing of Salcedo was not long coming. In Monterrey, Commandant General Joaquín de Arredondo organized a powerful army and marched toward Texas. On the morning of Wednesday, 18 August 1813, he engaged the Republican Army of the North in a battle that ranged along the Medina River. Francisco Ruiz was among the insurgent combatants; José Angel Navarro fought on the royalist side. By afternoon, Arredondo's well-trained troops had routed the undisciplined opposition. Among the hundreds of refugees fleeing Arredondo's wrath who managed to cross the Sabine were Veramendi's relatives José Francisco Ruiz and José Antonio Navarro.

In San Antonio accused rebels fell daily before firing squads. Rebel property was confiscated, as was the Veramendi house—which was rented to two army officers.[20] In October, General Arredondo issued a general pardon and amnesty for rebels in Louisiana who took part in the insurrection—with certain exceptions for the principal leaders. Among these he listed Juan Martín de Veramendi and Francisco Ruiz, who were "unworthy of receiving any consideration whatever."[21] The general offered a 250-peso reward to anyone who killed Veramendi,

Ruiz, or other principal revolutionaries and doubled the reward for any foreigner who killed them.

Despite his "unpardonable" status of the previous year, by March 1814 Veramendi managed to secure in Natchitoches, Louisiana, for himself and his brother Fernando, a pardon—provided that they were placed under surveillance as being dangerous to the public tranquility.[22] Perhaps Veramendi made the case that being on a trading trip to Nacogdoches, he and his brother were not involved in the battle of Medina or Salcedo's execution. The Veramendi brothers returned to Béxar around the end of the year.

Juan Martín set about to regain possession of his house and to clear his reputation. He gained permission for an audience with General Arredondo. Showing political skills that would later make him a governor, Veramendi met with the commandant general in Monterrey and achieved total vindication. He returned triumphantly with an order from Arredondo that stunned the governor and the officers renting Veramendi's house. They were ordered not only to return the house but also to dismiss the charges that Veramendi had adhered to the revolutionary party. Moreover, as a good patriot, he was not to be further molested in person or property.[23]

Texas had been devastated economically and militarily by years of revolutionary upheaval. The entire eastern frontier of the province and the coast lay undefended, leaving Texas vulnerable to the advance of intruders. Responding to reports in 1818 of foreigners at Galveston, Governor Antonio Martínez sent a military force under the command of Captain Juan de Castañeda to investigate.[24] Veramendi and José Angel Navarro volunteered to go at their own expense.[25] Evidently, they took advantage of this opportunity to combine volunteer service with trade. The expedition left San Antonio on 16 September and by mid-October had crossed the Trinity River.

Castañeda ordered Sergeant José Jiménez to take a contingent of three soldiers and five civilians to carry official correspondence to Natchitoches.[26] Veramendi and Navarro rode with this group, crossed the Sabine, and arrived at the Calcasieu River. Jiménez, who kept a diary of his trip, rode north to Natchitoches, accompanied by Veramendi and Navarro, leaving the others at the Calcasieu camp.[27] On their return, Jiménez then mysteriously took his contingent to Opelousas, an out-of-the-way hundred-mile round trip. According to the diary, they stayed only one day and then began the return trip to San Antonio.

At some point—at the Calcasieu camp, Natchitoches, or Opelousas—illegal traffic with Louisiana traders evidently took place. After their return, an official reprimanded Governor Martínez for giving permission to Veramendi and Navarro to go to Nachitoches, where "they could meet officially with authorities from the United States."[28] Moreover, he accused them of trading mules and horses, their own and those of others, for merchandise. The charges were not prosecuted, however, and Veramendi and Navarro remained citizens in good standing.

In 1820 Veramendi was again elected to the ayuntamiento, this time as a councilman. This was a landmark election, the first held under the articles of the recently reinstated Spanish Constitution of 1812, which provided for the popular, public election of electors who then voted for council members. This implementation of representative elections invigorated the San Antonio community and raised its morale. The introduction of the 1812 constitution marked the rapid transition from Spanish rule to Mexican independence. The next year, on 16 July, Governor Antonio Martínez conducted an oath of allegiance to the Plan de Iguala, which called for Mexico to be organized as a constitutional monarchy.[29]

Veramendi, Erasmo Seguín, and other men from San Antonio, however, were unaware of this development. That spring they traveled to Nachitoches and met Stephen F. Austin, who had decided to carry on his deceased father's colonization plan. The Bexareños escorted Austin to San Antonio, where they first learned about Mexican independence to shouts of *viva la independencia* and other exuberant expressions.[30]

Under the new order, a main concern of Bexareños was to achieve a goal that had been desired and denied since the earliest days of settlement in Texas—the establishment of a port—which was authorized in 1820. The next year, the ayuntamiento designated La Bahía a port of entry and named Veramendi collector of import taxes for goods brought from various coastal locations such as Matagorda Bay and Aransas.[31] Imports from New Orleans increased rapidly, being distributed not only in Texas but also in shipments to Coahuila and Nuevo León. Import duties provided substantial income. Veramendi's report of July 1822 showed a total of 727 pesos collected.[32] At first some of the funds went into the Béxar treasury. Commandant General López, however, instructed the interim customs agent in Béxar that "none of this [import-export] money is to go the [Béxar] ayuntamiento. Because it belongs to the public treasury, it can only be used for the troops.[33]

In summer 1824, while the framework of the Mexican republic was being forged, Texas and Coahuila were joined into one state. Within three months, by decrees at the national and state levels, Texas lost its political autonomy, a traumatic development for Tejanos.[34] Between 1824 and 1827, political leaders in Saltillo wrote a colonization plan and a constitution, providing a political foundation for the new state. Saltillo was designated as the capital, a decision that greatly displeased the people of Monclova, which had been the capital of Coahuila since the earliest days.

During this period of state building, the work of municipal government never stopped, and Veramendi served twice as San Antonio's alcalde, during two political transitions. Electors selected him as the alcalde for the year 1825, the first operational year of the state of Coahuila y Texas.[35] On assuming office, Veramendi immediately faced heated disputes over the ownership of property confiscated in 1813. Decrees issued in 1821 and 1822 provided a legal basis, under certain conditions, for the return of confiscated property to the original owner or for compensation to be paid. Many claims resulted, and Veramendi faced the wrath and ridicule of irate parties. In June, however, he reported that all the disputes had been resolved except one.[36]

Another vexing problem was 11,387 pesos in paper money in circulation, issued by the Bank of Texas, that were now worthless. The bank had been established in the aftermath of independence as a way of providing some cash to the troops when payrolls for Texas ceased. The public saw the bills as receipts for a debt the government owed them and clamored for restitution "in metallic money."[37] Despite Veramendi's efforts, no gold or silver coin was forthcoming.

On leaving office at the end of 1825, Veramendi resumed his merchant career, but Bexareños kept him in mind for public service. In May 1827 the ayuntamiento elected him as a alternate legislator in case a substitute was needed to replace either Miguel Arciniega or José Antonio Navarro, who were Texas representatives in the first state congress. At the same time, Veramendi began acquiring land. In summer 1827 he applied for an eleven-league grant, which the governor approved.[38]

San Antonio leaders must have been impressed with Veramendi's performance in 1825, for they reelected him to serve as alcalde for the year 1828. Juan Martín did not want to serve a second term at that time and rejected the appointment. He appealed to the jefe político and to the governor, saying that his position as alternate legislator prevented him from serving, and requested that his election be annulled.[39] To Veramendi's dismay, Governor José María Viesca ruled against him, saying that having being elected Juan Martín must serve as alcalde until such time as he might be required to substitute for one of the legislators. Thus the reluctant Veramendi served another term and was the first alcalde to serve under the laws of the new state constitution.

The first state congress ended its term in September. The last decree it passed, number 64, declared Monclova to be the state capital.[40] The constitution provided that, with a two-thirds majority vote, the capital could be moved. The transfer, however, would not be effected for four years, until after Veramendi became governor. He completed his second term as alcalde at the end of 1828 and was freed from what were evidently the onerous chores of local government leadership. During the next two years he pursued his merchant efforts. But Bexareños had in mind another political role for Veramendi, and in 1830 they sent their nomination for him as vice-governor to the Saltillo legislature.

The legislature, composed of eight members, met on 3 January 1831 and elected José María Letona as governor. For vice-governor, Veramendi and Ignacio de Arizpe entered a runoff. When the ballots were counted, Veramendi won by a unanimous vote.[41] He remained in Béxar and tended to his mercantile business and other interests. There was little for a vice-governor to do at the capital, and no record has been found of his being sworn into office that legislative session.

A few months before Veramendi's appointment as vice-governor, James Bowie arrived in San Antonio. Already a legend in Louisiana, Bowie crossed into Texas in February 1830 with the intent of becoming a citizen and seeking his fortune.[42] In San Antonio, Bowie met Veramendi, and they evidently sized each other up as influential men who could work together toward mutual interests. Bowie became enamored with Ursula Veramendi, age nineteen, and must have seen the possibility of a marriage that would provide him with both a desirable mate and entrance into a respected, influential family. On 25 April 1831 Bowie and Ursula married in what was said to have been the most elaborate social event in years.[43]

Veramendi and Bowie cooperated in at least one enterprise. Bowie's expedition to find the fabled San Saba silver mines failed, but during the trip he observed fur-trapping opportunities.[44] As a result, Veramendi (and no doubt Bowie) prepared a plan to exploit the otter and beaver resources Bowie had seen. Veramendi petitioned the governor for fourteen years of exclusive rights for his company, and for military escort to trap these fur-bearing animals.[45] The government never approved the proposal, and Veramendi's interests soon turned to his land dealings.

Juan Martín arrived in Gonzales in fall 1831 and began the final process of gaining title to five of the eleven leagues conceded to him in 1827. During November, land commissioner José Antonio Navarro awarded him possession of five leagues of land, approximately 22,000 acres; three leagues were located on springs that were tributaries of the Guadalupe River (one of which is the present Comal Springs), and two leagues were on the San Marcos Springs.[46] Veramendi intended to take his remaining six leagues at a site near Refugio mission, but he died before being able to obtain title to them.[47]

Governor José María Letona died in September 1832. Two months later, the legislature sent for Veramendi to come to Saltillo and take charge of the state government. He arrived on 18 December and was sworn on the twenty-fourth.[48] On 1 January 1833 Veramendi addressed the legislature.[49] His presentation was optimistic and he spoke in upbeat generalities, but Veramendi also noted the difficulties that the state and nation faced. For the duration of his tenure Veramendi was always referred to as the "vice-governor," apparently because of a constitutional article that called for a new election if the outgoing governor had served less than two years, as was the case with Letona. Nevertheless, they chose to call on Veramendi rather than hold a new election, which perhaps caused Veramendi to continue to be designated vice-governor.[50] In any case, he exercised the full state executive power.

Veramendi came into office in a legislative environment that was decidedly favorable to Texas, one supported by a majority block of representatives from Monclova and Parras.[51] On 2 March 1833 the legislature took under consideration petitions from San Antonio, Goliad, and Parras to remove the capital from Saltillo to Monclova.[52] On the ninth, the assembly voted, and the measure passed with a vote of seven to three, the three Saltillo members voting against it.[53] Veramendi signed the measure into law on the same day.[54]

The next day, the fourth state congress held its last session in Saltillo. Eager to facilitate the move, the ayuntamiento of Monclova

provided thirty mules with harnesses and fifteen carts to transport the equipment of state government. After a transition of only
twenty days, on 1 April the Monclova state legislature opened its first
session.[55]

In its first four months under Governor Veramendi, the Monclova
legislature was concerned with such issues as retail trade, officials'
salaries, military funding, funding for schools, and establishing wells
along the road to Chihuahua. By summer, however, a fearful threat in
the form of cholera arrived in Coahuila that demanded the government take preventive measures. On 13 August Veramendi sent an
order to the jefe politico of Saltillo to put into effect a plan to quaran-
tine persons who developed cholera symptoms.[56] If the jail was filled,
he ordered the official to expropriate individual houses in which to
place and contain the sickened persons.

Symptoms of cholera, a water-born disease, soon appeared in
Monclova. For hundreds death was imminent. Infected water flowed
through the town, having somehow entered the upper reaches of the
acequia that provided much of the town's water supply.[57] During
the early days of September the entire Veramendi family fell ill and
died at the height of the epidemic. The first victim was María Josefa
Navarro, Veramendi's wife.[58] On the seventh the governor expired
at six o'clock in the morning.[59] The epidemic ravaged Monclova for
thirty-one days, resulting in a total of 458 deaths.[60] In an attempt to
contain the epidemic, the dead were buried in great haste. The Veramendis, like hundreds of others, were interred in a mass grave in the
cemetery of the old Royal Hospital.[61]

News of Veramendi's death arrived in Béxar by 26 September, and
the church bells tolled for him as they had for his father fifty years
before. The estate inventories fill nearly two hundred pages and illus-
trate Veramendi's success as businessman and his dedication to civic
leadership. The net value of his property, which was to be distributed
among eight minor heirs, totaled 30,378 pesos.[62] His library contained
more than thirty books, demonstrating the practical and intellectual
scope of his interests. The works included *Medicine without a Doctor,
Don Quijote* [*La Quixotita*], *French and Spanish Grammar, Rights of Man,
Diary of Santa Elena, El Periquillo Sarniento, Life of Napoleon, Lesson in
Geography, Daily Exercise,* and the New Testament.[63]

To date, the life story of Juan Martín de Veramendi has come
down to us in a highly abbreviated form, one that is joined with and
subordinated to the story of James Bowie. As is the case with most
prominent Tejanos of his generation, no account of his life has been

published other than a brief sketch in the *New Handbook of Texas*, an unjustified neglect that this essay only begins to correct.[64] Veramendi left a legacy of confidence to his fellow Tejanos—the affirmation that leaders among them had the capacity to serve at the highest levels of state government and to excel in business. Therefore, Veramendi's legacy as seen by Mexican historians needs to be reassessed. Vito Alessio Robles's three-volume work of the history of Coahuila y Texas is a monumental accomplishment, one indispensable for a comprehensive understanding of Texas history. Alessio Robles, however, took a jaundiced view of Veramendi. Basing his view on the memoirs of Antonio Menchaca, Alessio Robles concluded that Veramendi's vice-governorship was a creation of Anglo-American colonists, that he was little more than a tool serving their interests, and that he was not very Mexican to boot. In addition, he concluded that it was James Bowie who was responsible for the transfer of the state capital from Saltillo to Monclova. In the first instance, he wrote "that the [Anglo] American colonists, having gained complete rights during the five years of their residence, now used them to advance their interests and schemes. The [Anglo] Texans succeeded in 1830 in having a Texan elected as vice-governor, Juan Martín de Veramendi, of Spanish descent, who was entirely disconnected [*enteremente desvinculado*] from Mexico."[65]

In the second instance, he quoted from the Menchaca memoirs: "On February 7, 1833, Bowie and seven North Americans arrived in Saltillo. The next day he met with Veramendi and was introduced to the members of congress. When his dealing with the principal legislators was sufficient to gain assurances of success, he explained the purpose of his visit . . . and gained their support to change the congress from Saltillo to Monclova."[66]

Alessio Robles's interpretation of Veramendi and Bowie is seriously flawed. He relied solely on the memoirs of Antonio Menchaca as the source for his analysis and accepted them without question. Menchaca's memoirs are certainly a valuable historical source, as Timothy Matovina's essay in this book makes clear, but they should be used with caution and corroboration in this case, since he dictated his recollections about Veramendi and Bowie more than thirty years after the fact.[67] The evidence compiled for this study does not support Menchaca's account regarding Veramendi or Alessio Robles's interpretation.

Regarding the first allegation, that Anglos engineered Veramendi's vice-governorship for their purposes, as noted above, the 1831 legislature elected him by a unanimous vote. Although Anglos such as Stephen Austin or Bowie may have influenced the Bexareños' nomination of Veramendi, they could hardly have determined the legislators' decisive vote in Saltillo. Regarding moving the capital from Saltillo to Monclova, at best Menchaca greatly exaggerated Bowie's role. As noted above, Bexareño legislators initiated the move to Monclova in 1828. Then, in 1833, with their own Juan Martín de Veramendi as governor, supported by a favorable legislature, they were positioned to accomplish that long-sought goal. The Monclova and Parras legislators did not need Bowie to influence them; they already wanted the capital moved to advance their own interests. Alessio Robles presents other ramifications concerning the move to Monclova that are beyond the scope of this brief study. Nevertheless, credit for the change in capital cities should be given to the efforts of Veramendi, his fellow Bexareños, and members of the fourth legislature, not to James Bowie.

This study affirms that Juan Martín de Veramendi was not a lackey of Anglo-American colonists but rather a political and business leader whom his fellow Tejanos valued, respected, and grieved for at his untimely death.

Notes

1.   No. 62. Causa Mortal de D.n Fern.do Beramendi Nat.1 del Reyno de Nabarra, 28 April 1783 [Veramendi Will], Bexar Archives Microfilm [BA].

2.   John O. Leal, comp. and trans., "San Fernando Church Marriages, 1742–1780" (unpublished manuscript), no. 104.

3.   Veramendi Will, 396–97.

4.   Ibid., 394.

5.   John O. Leal, comp. and trans., "San Fernando Baptismals," [SFB] Book 1775–1793 (unpublished manuscript). José María's baptismal record, 52, no. 880; Juan Martín's, 52, no. 785; Fernando's, 68, no. 1106.

6.   SFB, Book 1775–1793, 76, no. 1205.

7.   Bexar census records of 1790, 1792, 1793, 1795, and 1796 list the Veramendi children as living in Amondaráin's household. *Residents of Texas, 1782–1836*, trans. Carmela Leal (St. Louis: Ingmire Publications, 1984), 1:65, 82, 122, 202, 241.

8.   Fredrick C. Chabot, *With the Makers of San Antonio*, facsimile ed. (San Antonio, Tex.: Artes Gráficas, 1937), 251.

9.   *Residents of Texas*, 1:330.

10.   Bexar census [1804], BA. The brother would have been Fernando

Ramón; the sister, María de los Dolores. (Note: *Residents of Texas*, 1:390 inaccurately translates this entry.)

11. Angel Navarro to Governor, 30 December 1807, BA.

12. Juan Martín de Veramendi, merchandise declaration, 8 March 1808, BA.

13. José Guadiana to Antonio Cordero, 3 August 1808, and Simón de Herrera to Antonio Cordero, 14 August 1808, BA.

14. *Residents of Texas*, 2:69–70.

15. Nemesio Salcedo to [Manuel Salcedo], 13 October 1811, BA.

16. SFB, Book 1793–1811, 1 November 1811, n.p., no. 1125.

17. SFB, Book 1812–1825, 28 December 1812, 9, no. 69.

18. Listing of property losses. María Josefa Navarro to Baron de Bastrop, 20 November 1818, BA; Jack Jackson, *Los Mesteños: Spanish Ranching in Texas, 1721–1821* (College Station: Texas A&M Press, 1986), 531.

19. David McDonald, trans., and Timothy Matovina, ed., *Defending Mexican Valor in Texas: the Historical Writings of José Antonio Navarro, 1853–1857* (Austin: Statehouse Press, 1995), 48–49.

20. Maríano Varela to Joaquín de Arredondo, 25 October 1815, BA 55:882.

21. Joaquín de Arredondo to Christóbal Domínguez, 10 October 1813, BA. Translation in Mattie Austin Hatcher, *The Opening of Texas to Foreign Settlement, 1801–1821*, University of Texas Bulletin no. 2714 (Austin: University of Texas, 1927), 342–43.

22. Antonio Saucedo, List of Pardoned Insurgents, 8 March 1814, BA.

23. Draft of Governor Mariano Varela to Joaquín de Arredondo, 25 October 1815, BA.

24. Joaquín de Arredondo to Antonio Martínez, 16 May 16, 1818, BA; Antonio Martínez, [manifest of the forces of the expeditionary division], 16 September 1818, BA.

25. Joseph María Zambrano and Baron de Bastrop to Governor, 16 September 1818, BA.

26. José Jiménez, "Diario de las novedades," 5 January 1819, BA.

27. [Inspector Antonio Puertas] to [Antonio Martínez], n.d (document fragment), BA.

28. Ibid.

29. 16 July 1821, BA.

30. Stephen F. Austin, "Journal of Stephen F. Austin on His First Trip to Texas, 1821." *Texas Historical Association Quarterly* 7 (April 1904): 286.

31. Antonio Martínez to La Bahía alcalde, 11 November 1821, BA.

32. Customs report, July 1822, BA.

33. Gaspar López to interim Béxar custom agent, 27 February 1822, BA.

34. Andrés Tijerina, *Tejanos and Texas under the Mexican Flag, 1821–1836* (College Station: Texas A&M University Press, 1994), 98–101.

35. Election report for 1825, BA.

36. Veramendi to José Antonio Saucedo, 6 June 1825, BA.

37. Veramendi and ayuntamiento to Governor, *Quaderno de Oficios Borrador*, 5 January 1825, BA.

38. Bexar County Deed Records, Spanish Transcripts, vol. C-1, 64–65. One league equaled 4,428 acres.

39. Governor Viesca to Jefe Político, 25 January 1828, BA.

40. H. P. N. Gammel, ed. and comp., *The Laws of Texas, 1822–1897* (Austin: Gammel Book Company, 1898) 1:217.

41. "Actas del Tercer Congreso Constitucional del Estado Libre de Coahuila y Téxas," box 2Q229, vol. 706, 1371–1372, University of Texas at Austin, Center for American History [CAH].

42. Thomas McKinney to Stephen F. Austin, *The Austin Papers*, 3 vols. (vols. 1and 2; Washington, D.C.: American Historical Association, 1924, 1928; vol. 3, Austin: University of Texas Press, 1927), 2:331–32.

43. Chabot, *With the Makers of San Antonio*, 244.

44. Jefe Político to Governor [Letona], 18 December 1831, BA.

45. Veramendi to Governor, 23 May 1832, FJPB, c22, 1832, expediente 44, Archivo General del Estado de Coahuila [AGEC].

46. Bexar County Deed Records, Spanish Transcripts, vol. C-1, 64–76.

47. Veramendi to Ramón Múzquiz, 22 September 1831, Spanish Collection, box 126: 24, 250–251, no. 894, Archives and Records Division, Texas General Land Office, Austin.

48. "Coahuila y Texas Constitutional Actas," 24 December 1832, box 2Q229, vol. 709, 41–42, CAH.

49. "Actas del Quarto Congreso Constitutional del Estado Libre de Coahuila y Texas," 1 January 1833, box 2Q229, vol. 707, 1637, CAH.

50. "Coahuila y Texas Constitutional Actas," box 2Q229, vol. 709, 36, CAH.

51. Tijerina, *Tejanos and Texas*, 134.

52. "Actas del Quarto Congreso Constitutional del Estado Libre de Coahuila y Texas," 2 March 1833, box 2Q229, vol. 707, 1678, CAH.

53. Ibid., 1681; Vito Alessio Robles, *Coahuila y Texas desde la consumación de la independencia hasta el tratado de Paz de Guadalupe Hidalgo*, 2d ed. (Mexico: Editorial Porrúa, 1979), 1:442.

54. Gammel, *Laws of Texas*, 1:317.

55. Actas del Quarto Congreso Constitutional del Estado Libre de Coahuila y Texas," 1 April 1833, box 2Q229, vol. 707, 1687–88, CAH.

56. BA 158:141–42.

57. Lucas Martínez Sánchez, speech to Bexareño Genealogical Society, 7 May 2005, San Antonio, Texas.

58. Lucas Martínez Sánchez, *Monclova: Hechos Históricos del Siglo XIX* (Monclova: Colegio de investigaciones Históricas del Centro de Coahuila, 2004), 63.

59. Ibid.; "Coahuila y Texas Constitutional Actas," box 2Q229, vol. 709, 54–55, CAH.

60. Sánchez, *Monclova: Hechos Históricos*, 62–63.

61. Ibid., 64.

62. Veramendi estate inventories, Veramendi estate, 615, BA; Veramendi family tree, in Alvin and Angie Gerdes, eds. and comps., "A Navarro Family Heritage: Their Kith and Kin" (San Antonio, Texas: privately printed, 1997). The eight heirs were José Marcos, María Josefa, Juan Martín, José Primo (nickname, Pepe), María Antonia, Eufemia, Teresa, and Fernando. Their ages ranged, respectively, from sixteen to two years.

63. José J. Fernández de Lizardi's picaresque novel *El Periquillo Sarniento* [The Mangy Parrot] is considered by many to be the first Hispanic-American novel. It is a sardonic account of life in the Mexican capital.

64. For a chapter that focuses on Veramendi as vice-governor and governor, see Sánchez, *Monclova: Hechos Históricos*, 51–65.

65. Alessio Robles, *Coahuila y Texas*, 1:424–25 (my translation). He cites Frederick C. Chabot, ed., *Memoirs of Antonio Menchaca* (San Antonio, Tex.: Yanaguana Society, 1937), 21.

66. Alessio Robles, *Coahuila y Texas*, 1:441–42 (my translation). He again cites *Memoirs of Antonio Menchaca*, 21.

67. *Memoirs of Antonio Menchaca*, Introduction, n.p.

Page from Rafael Manchola's land grant record. Manchola's widow, María de Jesús De León, continued the process of obtaining the league of land that her husband petitioned for in her father's colony. The location was finally established on Coleto Creek in Victoria County.

Courtesy Spanish Collection 100/4, p. 6, Texas General Land Office, Austin, Texas.

RAFAEL ANTONIO MANCHOLA

TEJANO SOLDIER,
STATESMAN, RANCHERO

Andrés Tijerina

MEXICAN AND TEXAS history books have neglected Rafael Antonio Manchola. Even books that have recently begun to be published
on Tejano history have tended to mention Manchola only in passing.
Tejano history is a developing field, and Tejanos are now beginning
to be seen as having played important roles in Texas history. A few
Tejanos have attracted their own biographers. But not Manchola.

Tejano history books do recognize that the Tejanos of the Mexican
independence era and the Texas Revolution faced serious challenges.
This was the generation of Tejanos who had to transition from Spanish colonial to independent Mexican status. Tejanos had to contend
with royalist military campaigns, filibustering expeditions from the
United States, and the Mexican army. Most important, these were the
Tejanos who had to develop the political strategies necessary to find a
place under new governments, first Mexico and then Texas.

Rafael Antonio Manchola participated in all of these challenges
facing Tejanos of this turbulent period. He was a member of prominent families by birth and by marriage. He served as a military commander of a presidio, and he valiantly led his troops to protect his
community and patrol the frontier. His major contribution, however,
was in developing the intellectual and political strategies during the
fluid transformations of municipal government, the state congress,
and the federalist constitution of the national government of Mexico.
His *memorias*, or declarations, represent a milestone in the radicalization of Tejano politics on the eve of the Texas Revolution. He was
a ranchero, a cavalry commander, an alcalde, a state deputy, and a
courageous Texas leader.

Born in 1800, Rafael Antonio Manchola assumed the command
at La Bahía del Espíritu Santo in 1822, where he owned a ranch and
quickly attained social prominence. At twenty-four, he married
María de Jesús "Chucha" De León, the fourteen-year-old daughter
of the famous empresario Martín De León. According to Carolina
Crimm, De León's biographer, "It was an excellent match for Chucha, but it was even better for promoting Don Martín's political connections, since the Manchola family were influential at La Bahía."[1]
The marriage brought Manchola into the De León family with its

45

connections to the Aldrete, Garza, and Benavides families as well. As a fellow rancher, he served his empresario father-in-law in administering land grants, conducting family business, and preserving the public order.

Manchola later took command of the mounted militia at the presidio of Nuestra Señora de Loreto in 1826. He served off and on in that position until 1831. These were violent years on the Texas frontier, and Manchola found himself in almost all of the major military events of the period, from pursuing marauding Indians to riding out on military excursions.

One of his first assignments as presidial commander was in response to the tense situation that had developed between the De León colony and neighboring Green DeWitt's colony. In 1826 Martín De León had become involved in a dispute over livestock with an Anglo colonist in Gonzales. Later that year, jefe político José Antonio Saucedo ordered De León to confiscate some contraband goods that Anglo colonists had hidden in DeWitt's colony. The Texas military commandant also ordered Manchola, as commander of the presidio, to escort De León with an armed troop. When the Anglo colonists heard that the Tejanos were coming and that De León had supposedly vowed to return with DeWitt's head, the Anglos prepared themselves to resist. An armed conflict was averted only by the deterrence of Manchola's troops as De León negotiated the matter.[2] These incidents were only the beginning of a long series of conflicts between Anglos and Tejanos in that region. For years Tejano authorities repeatedly arrested Anglos with illegally acquired property, contraband goods, or rustled livestock. Indeed, the point of contact between Tejano and Anglo-American settlements was nowhere closer than between Victoria and Gonzales. Manchola found himself involved in maintaining the public order and soon developed a negative impression of the Anglo colonists of Texas.

Manchola began to feel that Anglo-Americans were generally undesirable in society—or, as one Mexican diarist in 1828 wrote, they were a "lazy people of vicious character." Manchola also probably concurred with the diarist that, when he encountered a kind or courteous Anglo, it was "a very rare thing among individuals of his [Anglo-American] nationality."[3] If these sentiments reflected those of Manchola, it was probably because he was particularly upset at DeWitt, whom he contemptuously described as being "drunk in the streets constantly." He felt that the Anglo-American was an "adventurer" or opportunist, and that his activities were "fraudulent." In one report to a state authority at this time, the Goliad leaders said, "Let us be honest with ourselves, Sir, the foreign empresarios are nothing more than moneychanging speculators caring only for their own well-being and hesitating not in their unbecoming methods."[4]

As militia commander, Manchola was involved in other critical situations that brought him into direct contact with the most important leaders of the time in Texas. One major assignment was as troop commander in the government campaign against Haden Edwards's Fredonian Rebellion in 1826/27. Anastacio Bustamante, commandant general for the eastern interior provinces and later president of Mexico, had to spend several days in Goliad during the rebellion. Colonel Mateo Ahumada and Texas jefe político Saucedo also went from Béxar to Goliad, where they spent several days in January 1827 before they moved on to San Felipe and then to Nacogdoches. At Goliad, Colonel Ahumada ordered Manchola to accompany him with Manchola's cavalry troops as a combined force to quell the rebellion.[5]

Indeed, in these disputes the Anglo-Americans alienated Manchola at a critical time in his career and in the development of the government of Texas. As military commander he had personally observed many illegal activities among the Anglo colonists. After the DeWitt incident, Manchola wrote a report to his commander, Colonel Ahumada at Béxar. Manchola wrote, "I have been told verbally that Gren DeWitt [sic] has said that *if I had arrived by day instead of by night as I did he would not have let me come near;* and I consider him . . . to be very capable of it because of his total lack of respect for our authority, which is completely scoffed at by him as well as by his colonists and those of the Brazos and the Colorado, all of whom need to be forced to live an orderly life and to stop the libertine way they live now." Manchola heavily underlined key phrases for emphasis. He went on to recommend that military detachments be stationed in the Anglo colonies to guard the rivers and bays for contraband activities. He added:

No faith can be placed in the Anglo-American colonists because they are continually demonstrating that they absolutely refuse to be subordinate, unless they find it convenient to what they want anyway, all of which I believe will be very detrimental to us for them to be our neighbors if we do not in time, clip the wings of their audacity by stationing a strong detachment in each new settlement which will enforce the laws and jurisdiction of a Mexican Alcalde which should be placed in each of them, since under their own colonists as judges, they do nothing more than practice their own laws which they have practiced since they were born, forgetting the ones they have sworn to obey, these being the laws of our Supreme Government.[6]

Manchola's recommendations may well have been responsible for the assignment of Colonel José de las Piedras to East Texas with a detachment of two hundred men the following summer. The Mexican garrison was stationed among the Anglo-American colonies specifically to enforce the colonization laws of Mexico. Manchola's direct communication with his political and military commanders as their reporter in the field could hardly be ignored.

To complement his military work, Manchola had a successful political career at the municipality level as well as at the state level. He served as alcalde of Goliad in 1831 and is credited with changing the name of La Bahía to Goliad, when he served as a state legislator earlier. He petitioned the state of Coahuila y Texas to change the name to Goliad, an anagram for the famous Father Miguel Hidalgo, the heroic giant of Mexican independence. The constitutional congress of Coahuila y Texas approved the name change on 4 February 1829, and Governor Viesca issued Decree no. 73 to comply. Ramón Múzquiz, then jefe político of the department of Béxar, forwarded the decree on to Goliad on 8 March 1829. In the legislature, Manchola had also played a key role in establishing the ayuntamiento of Guadalupe Victoria in 1929.[7]

His most influential role in politics, however, was as a state deputy of the state congress of Coahuila y Texas. In 1828, Manchola served as a state deputy in the Coahuila y Texas legislature after being elected by the District Electoral Assembly of Texas. As state deputy during this critical time, Manchola served with Béxar deputy José María Balmaceda. Together, Manchola and Balmaceda represented the interests of the department of Texas at the state level, and they collaborated with the liberal political faction of Governor Viesca, State Senator José María Viesca, and national leaders as well. Balmaceda had only recently retired as a military officer in Béxar in 1827. He had served as *regidor* (council member) on the ayuntamiento and was described as a leading merchant and "principal citizen" of Béxar. He had served as a state deputy along with Manchola between 1828 and 1830. Balmaceda and Manchola took advantage of their alliance with the Viesca group in the state legislature to secure important offices and committee positions. A review of their terms in office reveals that Balmaceda and Manchola attended the legislature for all except two months of the entire one-year period between January 1829 and February 1830.[8]

Despite his wariness regarding Anglo-American colonization, Manchola advanced a Tejano political agenda that included colonization, tax exemptions, and liberal laws—positions Balmaceda supported. In describing the Tejano legislators Stephen F. Austin said, "The people of this place are unanimously hostile to the present [Bustamante] administration, and they are more friendly to the North American emigration than they ever were."[9] The Tejanos took this political position in full knowledge that it would put them in direct opposition to the national administration of centralists in Mexico City.

They would pay a price for their stance against the centralist national powers. Manchola and Balmaceda were initially attacked in the state legislature for their liberal stances by a block of conservative representatives from Saltillo. They had Balmaceda publicly denounced by citizens in that capital city. In article 4 of the Plan de Jalapa, a movement led by Anastacio Bustamante to overthrow the federalist government of President Vicente Guerrero, Balmaceda and another liberal deputy were formally reprimanded, and subsequently they were expelled from the legislature by Decree no. 149 on 18 September 1830.

Balmaceda and Manchola opposed Decree no. 149 by issuing a call for public support. The Tejano deputies requested that the ayuntamientos of Texas write to affirm their support against the Saltillo "anarchists." In response, the ayuntamientos of Béxar, Goliad, and San Felipe immediately proclaimed that only the appropriate constituents would determine the merit of a deputy.[10] The congressional session ended before this particular dispute became any more critical. But this was one of the major events at the state level in the commitment of Tejanos to the liberal federalist standard. The events surrounding Decree no. 149 almost automatically committed the incoming Texas deputies, Stephen F. Austin and Manuel Múzquiz, to the liberal Viesca faction and against the conservatives in Saltillo and Mexico City. Not only had Manchola helped develop the political philosophy of the liberal Tejanos and Viescas, he took his stand in the legislature and in the national debate.

One of the most important political actions taken by Manchola occurred in 1832, when events in the Anglo colonies reached a boiling point over the heavy-handed manner of Mexican army commander

Juan Davis Bradburn. Colonel José Antonio Mexía was ordered to Anahuac to prevent revolutionary activities there. Mexía was a liberal who was supporting the Plan de Veracruz, Antonio López de Santa Anna's federalist revolt against the Bustamante regime, when he decided to investigate the situation among the colonies. The colonists convinced him that their actions were directed only at Bradburn and not against the Mexican government. They affirmed their support of the latter, especially Mexía's liberal party. While Mexía was in Texas, Colonel José de las Piedras declared in favor of the Plan de Veracruz and joined Mexía.[11] Mexía and De las Piedras left Texas later that summer, taking their combined armies to join the struggle against centralism in Mexico. With them they took all of the national army troops that had been sent to enforce the Law of 6 April 1830.

These events tended to place Manchola and other Tejano leaders in something of a quandary. No one complained more bitterly about the unruly Anglo-American colonists than Manchola, but even he recoiled at the harsh restrictions of the central government in the Law of 6 April 1830. The Tejano perplexity only increased as Anglo colonists began to act unilaterally in response to national events.

Mexía's visit sparked a wave of liberal enthusiasm among the colonists, who were greatly encouraged to declare also for Santa Anna. But when they attempted to induce Tejanos to do likewise, the Tejanos declined. The colonists proceeded unilaterally to declare for Santa Anna in July. In August, when Tejanos declared themselves in favor of the Plan de Veracruz, the colonists went one step further and called a convention for October in San Felipe. They felt it appropriate under the circumstances to draft a list of demands from the government which they supposed, by now, to welcome liberal pronouncements.

The convention was called by Horatio Chriesman and John Austin. Settlers from all of the Anglo colonies met on 1 October 1832 and drew up their list of demands. They petitioned the government for repeal of the exclusion article in the Law of 6 April 1830. As mentioned earlier, they petitioned the government for school land grants, and they provided for a permanent troop to guard their frontier against Indians. They also requested land grants and customs privileges in the colonies.

Just as the convention adjourned, Rafael Antonio Manchola arrived with José María Jesús Carvajal as the only Tejano delegates to the convention. In a last-minute appeal for Tejano support, the colonists appointed Manchola as commissioner along with William H.

Wharton to transmit the resolution to the government authorities. Manchola agreed to do it although other events in Mexico City precluded any need for his commission.[12] Nevertheless, Manchola and Carvajal took the Anglo colonists' grievances and added their own as a stronger resolution, which they submitted to the ayuntamientos of Goliad and Nacogdoches.

The resolution was drawn up by Manchola with some contribution by Carvajal. Formally submitted to jefe político Ramón Múzquiz, the resolution is perhaps most revealing of Tejano sentiments of the time. It was generally a statement of the social contract and concluded with an implicit threat of the secession of Texas from Coahuila:

> If the people who are ruled by despots are permitted the natural right of revolutionary measures against their oppression then those people, who by their own consent live under the divine republican system, have also had conceded to them by the political compact the right to petition as a primary measure which they may use toward remedying the evils which afflict them, whether those evils originate from the inertia of the laws, by the ignorance of the Legislators, or by the ineptitude of their governing officials.[13]

In a classic Mexican phrase of protest, the resolution exhorted, "Basta ya" [Enough]:

> We have had enough of these legislators who insult through their very capriciousness the sacred charter such as those who passed the unconstitutional Decrees Numbers 5, 149, and 183; We want no more of legislators such as the one who disregarded the sacred rights of this community for no other reason than to protect the false pretensions of two colonization empresarios. Bring to an end this administration of justice so defective and so backward as this semi-Gothic one which we are practicing. In a word, let the laws be complied with, let's be republicans, let's be men, let's defend our rights, or let's not exist at all.

The resolution added statements supporting all of the arguments of the resolutions from Béxar and Nacogdoches. It protested an earlier conflict with the Powers and De Witt colonies, citing the illegal aspects and activities of these colonies. It spoke of Don Esteban Austin as the only "true empresario." Citing the many times Goliad had submitted pleas for rectification of these evils, the resolution described the Tejano attitude toward the colonization program:

Ah, Sir! If this outrage had been committed against any other people, they would have seceded in an instant from such an unjust and impolitic government, but such has not been the conduct of Goliad, for she will always be obedient, but never again will she allow such odium on her social rights. And let it not be said that because of this, colonization is not desired, far from such an absurd idea, only an effort to correct the defects in the laws [is desired].

And mixing sublime courtesy with deadly advertence, it stated their position most respectfully:

Finally, Sir, these inhabitants confide in the goodness of Thy Honor, having heard the representation of the Illustrious Ayuntamiento . . . that the constitutional laws and the remedies which our grievances decry shall be dignified with a response; for their inattention will force Tejanos to the hard but necessary task of demanding of the Honorable Assembled Chambers of the union the compliance of the Second Article of Decree No 35 of the General Constituent Congress of the year 1824.

Unfortunately, Manchola was not able to see the effects of his resolution, nor was he able to see the other unfolding events of the Texas Revolution, because he died in the cholera epidemic that swept through Texas later in 1833. But his sentiments and his philosophy were memorialized and exposed to all the policymakers of Texas and northern Mexico. His writings were not the philosophical musings of a sequestered thinker. They were the articulated discourse of a statesman and military commander in the field. In his official correspondence and his candid *memorias,* Rafael Antonio Manchola left the literary remains of one man's impassioned effort to synthesize constitutional theory with the challenging circumstances on the Texas frontier. Throughout his brief political career as statesman at the municipal and state levels, Manchola strongly supported the admission of Anglo-Americans into Texas and he adamantly defended democracy. Manchola not only developed the state laws for introducing Anglo-Americans into Texas as colonists, but he actively protested the anti-immigration Law of 6 April 1830. He wrote the municipal ordinances for Texas' first democratically elected ayuntamientos, and he chartered them. As mentioned above, Tejano leaders found themselves in a dilemma of supporting Anglo-American immigration while pressing for more controls on Anglo-American smuggling and rebelliousness. Manchola's major contribution to Texas, however, was in initiating the infrastructure for radicalism of Tejano politics, which ultimately became the rallying call of Anglos and Tejano leaders alike.

Like the American patriots of 1776, Tejanos underwent first a radicalization of politics as Manchola and others grew frustrated in the face of centralist measures like the Law of 6 April 1830. In her book *From Resistance to Revolution,* Pauline Meier explains that "in America, too, alternatives to force were being foreclosed. Colonists began to reject petitions as a way of opposing their grievances." In their *memorias,* Tejanos began to reveal subtle warnings of their turn to stronger action. The Mexican phrase "Basta ya" was followed with their warning that they wanted to "Bring to an end this administration."[14] As mentioned earlier, Texas history books have tended to depict the Tejano leaders as a two-dimensional landscape for powerful Anglo-Texans like Stephen F. Austin and William B. Travis. But in these documents lies the literary record of the transformation of men like Manchola from radicals to revolutionaries. He did not live to ride with Juan N. Seguín in the battles of the Texas Revolution, but Manchola's words provided the philosophical thrust to advance from petition to action.

Although history books have yet to give Manchola his due in the story of Texas, his local community finally erected a marker to acknowledge his role as early founder. On 15 July 2006 an official Texas State Historical marker was dedicated in memory of Rafael Antonio Manchola in the Courthouse Square Historic District in downtown Goliad.

Notes

1. Ana Carolina Castillo Crimm, *De León: A Tejano Family History* (Austin: University of Texas Press, 2003), 83.

2. Ethel Zivley Rather, "DeWitt's Colony" (M.A. thesis, University of Texas at Austin, 1902), 108–13.

3. José María Sánchez, "A Trip to Texas in 1828," trans. Carlos Eduardo Castañeda, *Southwestern Historical Quarterly* 29 (April 1926): 249–95.

4. Goliad Ayuntamiento to State Congress, 15 January 1833, Nacogdoches Archives, Texas State Library and Archives, Austin [NA].

5. Gregg Cantrell, *Stephen F. Austin: Empresario of Texas* (New Haven, Conn.: Yale University Press, 1999), 184, 188; Mateo Ahumada to Francisco Ruiz, 10 December 1826, Center for American History, University of Texas at Austin Bexar Archives [BA].

6. Rafael Anto. Manchola to Mateo Ahumada, 29 October 1826, BA.

7. "Actas del congreso constitucional del estado libre de Coahuila y Texas" (typescript), 29 January 1829, University of Texas at Austin, Center for American History [CAH]; Cosme Garza García, *Prontuario de leyes y decretos del estado de Coahuila de Zaragoza* (Saltillo: Oficina Tipográfica del Gobierno, 1902), 37.

8. "Actas del congreso," 1829–30 passim; Stephen F. Austin to Samuel M. Williams, 6 December 1832, in Eugene C. Barker, *The Austin Papers,* vol. 2, Annual Report of the American Historical Association for the year 1922 (Washington, D.C.: Government Printing Office, 1928), 2:897.

9. Austin to Samuel M. Williams, 28 December 1830, *Austin Papers,* 2:568.

10. Leona Vicario: Permanent Deputation to Béxar Ayuntamiento, 4 September 1830, BA; J. P. Kimball, trans., *Laws and Decrees of the State of Coahuila and Texas in Spanish and English. To Which Is Added the Constitution of Said State: Also: The Colonization Law of the State of Tamaulipas, and Naturalization Law of the General Congress* (Houston, Tex.: Telegraph Power Press, 1839), 160.

11. Carlos E. Castañeda, *Our Catholic Heritage in Texas, 1519–1936* (Austin: Von Boeckmann-Jones, 1936–58), 6:235.

12. Eugene C. Barker, *The Life of Stephen F. Austin, Founder of Texas, 1793–1836: A Chapter in the Westward Movement of the Anglo-American People* (Austin: University of Texas Press, 1969), 351.

13. Nacogdoches Ayuntamiento to State Congress, 30 January 1833, and Goliad Ayuntamiento to State Congress, 15 January 1833, NA. This passage was previously published in Andrés Tijerina, *Tejanos and Texas under the Mexican Flag, 1821–1836* (College Station: Texas A&M University Press, 1994).

14. Pauline Maier, *From Resistance to Revolution: Colonial Radicals and the Development of American Opposition to Britain, 1765–1776* (New York: Knopf, 1972), 213.

I am responsable to Mr. Placido Venavides to the value of a kaga of powder containing twenty five pounds, which has been disposed of by an order of the Provisional Government of Texas to sustain the war. I certify it as the principal judge of this Municipality, and as a witness, my hand

John Joseph Linn

I certify that this is a correct Translation

W. H. Patton

Translation of the receipt given by John Joseph Linn to Plácido Benavides for a barrel of powder to be used in the war effort. Like numerous other Tejanos, Benavides supported the war not only through military service but by providing goods on credit to the provisional government.

Courtesy #2009/1-2-1, Republic Claims reel 7, 312 [304-033], Texas State Library and Archives Commission.

PLÁCIDO BENAVIDES
FIGHTING TEJANO FEDERALIST
Stephen L. Hardin

A SINGLE DECISION can alter the rest of a person's life. Plácido Benavides, alcalde of Nuestra Señora de Guadalupe Victoria, could not have foreseen the terrible consequences of his choice, but he knew he had reached a personal crossroads. He was a staunch federalist, a supporter of the liberal principles heralded in the Mexican Constitution of 1824. With growing distress, Benavides watched Antonio López de Santa Anna emerge as a dictator; watched as he centralized the national government; watched as he discharged state militias; watched as he crushed a federalist revolt in Zacatecas. Now, in June 1835, the tyrant's minions were riding toward Victoria to arrest José María Jesús Carvajal, Benavides's brother-in-law and political ally. He could watch no longer. It was time to act. Exercising the prerogative of free men, Benavides said "no" to authority—and it would cost him everything.[1]

Benavides intended to greet the centralist cavalrymen properly. He polled his constituents. Thirty Victorianos (citizens of Victoria) volunteered to stand against the centralists. The ferryman received instructions to alert citizens when the solders hove into view. Just as Benavides had anticipated, the horsemen ferried across the Guadalupe River and boldly entered the town's central plaza. The detachment's commander demanded an immediate audience with the alcalde. Benavides, like a Tejano Cincinnatus, was tending his cornfield when the officer dispatched a townsman to summon him. Wiping dirt from his hands, Benavides presented himself to the captain and enquired how he might be of service. The captain presented a warrant for Carvajal. On reading the order, the alcalde informed the captain that he would not surrender Carvajal or any other citizen. He was, Benavides insisted, a "constitutional officer, and not at all amenable to the [centralist] military."[2]

The captain discovered himself in no position to debate the matter. On Benavides's signal, his militiamen blocked off the corners of the plaza and leveled muskets at the dismounted cavalrymen. As armed militiamen closed in, the captain saw resistance would be hopeless. According to one witness, "The officer, seemingly in dread of precipitating a crisis, ordered his men to saddle their horses. . . . This was the end of the affair."[3]

The wily border captain had again defended Victoria and its citizens. Yet, by resisting centralist authority, he had earned a place on Santa Anna's hit list. As the hoodwinked horsemen rode out of Victoria, Benavides knew that this incident was but the opening act of a dark drama. Even as he accepted the congratulations of his fellow Victorianos, he realized that their lives would never be the same.[4]

The road that brought Benavides to this uncomfortable juncture had been long and circuitous. Like many of the state's heroes, he was not originally a Tejano. A native of Reynosa, Tamaulipas, Benavides was born in 1810. His godfather was Captain Enrique Villareal. The association proved vital. Villareal paid for the boy's education and in 1828 dispatched the young man to Texas. There, Benavides accepted the position as secretary to Fernando De León, commissioner of the De León colony and the son of empresario Martín De León.[5]

The twenty-two-year-old secretary did not arrive alone. Three married brothers—Ysidro, Nicolás, and Eugenio—traveled north with him. They claimed lands south of Victoria. Plácido's duties kept him in town, where his talents impressed the empresario. As secretary, Benavides oversaw correspondence, recorded business transactions, and mastered the inner workings of a borderland colony. No job could have better groomed him for a leadership role. Lettered and respectable, Benavides also assumed responsibilities as the colony's teacher.[6]

Benavides grew comfortable in Victoria and made plans to sink his roots there. He began construction of a house—and what a house it was. The structure was a *torreón,* a circular defensive bastion. It had gun slits on the first floor and a heavy, reinforced door. Because of Comanche and Apache raids, such strongholds dotted the northern frontier. A distinctive Victoria landmark, the structure became recognized as "Plácido's Round House."[7]

There seemed to be no task Benavides could not master. In 1832, Victorianos elected him alcalde. He performed the duties of that position so well that he won reelection in 1834. Late in 1832, Benavides also won the hand of eighteen-year-old Agustina, the daughter of Don Martín and Patricia De León. Their union produced three daughters: Pilar, Librada, and Matiana. The young man was affable, diligent, and, most of all, ambitious. He likely would have succeeded in any circumstance, but joining the colony's most prominent family certainly boosted his social standing. Well entrenched in Victoria society, he assumed a high profile. After the death of his father-in-law in 1833, Mexican officials recognized his talents and authorized Benavides to assume the duties of colonial administrator.[8]

Of all his accomplishments, perhaps the greatest was his almost instinctive talent for tactics. A native of the northern borderlands, he had never known a time when Indian raids did not threaten his people. Assisted by his brother-in-law, Silvestre De León, he commanded the Victoria militia in numerous forays against Coco and Tonkawa camps. On other occasions, however, the Tonkawas proved useful allies. In 1834 Captain Benavides mustered a company of Tejano and Anglo settlers that clashed with Karankawas at Green Lake in what is now western Calhoun County. Local Tonkawas probably augmented the force. Although the Karankawas offered a dogged defense, Benavides's motley force routed them.[9]

In 1832 and 1833 the De León Colony became increasingly embroiled in the issues concerning their Anglo-American neighbors. José María Jesús Carvajal, a young surveyor who had married Don Martín's daughter María de Refugia, became a community lighting rod. Fluent in the English language, Carvajal increasingly involved himself in the interests of the American colonists. He, like many Mexican federalists, supported American immigrants for the economic benefits they provided Texas. Moreover, Carvajal sincerely admired the Anglo settlers and they genuinely trusted him—so much so that in May 1831 he had won election to an Anglo-American caucus to petition the Mexican government for redress from the abuses of centralist commander Juan Davis Bradburn. The following November, Carvajal won appointment to the civil government at San Felipe de Austin. He also helped the American residents of Liberty establish their town council. As a bilingual surveyor, he traveled the region befriending both Tejanos and Anglos. Victoria was a federalist bastion, and the majority of its residents sided with American settlers on issues of common interest.[10]

Nonetheless, many citizens condemned Carvajal for his ties with the American colonists. Although they may have agreed with Anglo settlers on a purely political basis, many Victorianos still found them irresponsible in their demands. Some recalled the numerous American filibustering expeditions into Texas between 1800 and 1820. Could Tejanos trust these people to remain loyal to Mexico? So long as that question remained unanswered, many citizens castigated Carvajal for being too friendly with the Americans. Such associations might bring centralist wrath down upon their heads. When news of the Anahuac Disturbances of 1832 reached Victoria, Carvajal supported the Anglo protestors. He insisted that the excesses of Bradburn and his garrison had justified the violence employed against them. Few in Victoria agreed. Only Fernando De León and Plácido Benavides stood with their beleaguered brother-in-law. By bucking popular opinion, Benavides proved himself a firm defender of federalism, a loyal friend, and a man of unassailable character.[11]

As the relationship between Anglo settlers and Mexican officials steadily deteriorated, Tejanos debated their role in a struggle that most thought inevitable. The dispute separated communities and even families. Late in 1834, Carvajal moved his family to San Antonio de Béxar. In February 1835 citizens elected him representative for the Béxar district to the state congress in Monclova. Meeting in March 1835, the Monclova congress ignored President Santa Anna's orders to disband state militia companies. It also authorized the sale of some 1.2 million Texas acres to speculators. The proceeds provided for the raising of a federalist army that would resist centralist forces.

In June 1835 General Martín Perfecto de Cos arrived in Saltillo at the head of a centralist army. In his pocket, he carried arrest warrants for every member of the Monclova congress. Carvajal rode hell-for-leather to Béxar, where he halted his journey just long enough to collect Refugia and their children. Then, with his family in tow, he made his way to Victoria. With all his plans crumbling around him now that Cos had declared him a traitor, could he still rely on the support of hometown friends and family?[12]

Whatever their political persuasion, few Victorianos were willing to hand one of their own over to a centralist firing squad—certainly not Plácido Benavides. On 21 June, Colonel Domingo Ugartechea, the centralist military commander in Béxar, received orders from General Cos to arrest Carvajal for treason. Carvajal bolted before Ugartechea could apprehend him, so the colonel dispatched a company of cavalry to Victoria to seize the fugitive. As related earlier, Benavides ambushed the company and booted them back to Béxar without their quarry.[13]

In September 1835 news arrived in Victoria that shattered the community's tranquility. American empresario Stephen F. Austin had returned from his eighteen-month stint in a Mexican dungeon a changed man. He had always favored accommodation with the Mexican government, but now he insisted that war was the only viable course. Intelligence also arrived that General Cos was marching toward Texas with orders to quell rebellion and execute dissidents. Carvajal was certainly on his arrest list and, now that Benavides had defied centralist authority, he likely was too. The time to choose sides had finally arrived.[14]

Even within the De León family, members came down on opposing sides. Benavides, Carvajal, and Fernando De León went whole hog for the federalist Constitution of 1824. Silvestre De León could not decide; he opposed Santa Anna's centralist regime but mistrusted Anglo hotspurs. He finally announced lukewarm support for the federalist cause. Félix De León, however, refused to take arms against his countrymen and resolved to sit out the coming hostilities on his Mission Valley ranch. The family matriarch, Doña Patricia, clearly announced that she had no wish to hear her children labeled bandits and fervently opposed the actions of Carvajal and Benavides.[15]

Even so, Benavides did not go out of his way to pick a fight. When centralist troops arrived in Victoria to retrieve a three-pound cannon citizens employed for Indian defense, the alcalde handed it over without quibble. Ordnance of such a miniscule caliber did not warrant bloodshed. Yet the American residents of Gonzales refused to surrender their six-pound gun and, on 2 October 1835, issued a challenge to centralist soldiers to "Come and Take It." The subsequent skirmish ignited the long anticipated conflict.[16]

Now that the rebellion had begun in earnest, Benavides determined to strive manfully in the federalist cause. After the "Come and Take It" fight, he rode to Gonzales with Irish Victoriano John J. Linn. The pair had hatched a daring scheme. They proposed leading a force to capture General Cos, who had arrived in Texas and was then marching from Goliad at the head of a centralist army to reinforce Ugartechea. Few of the American volunteers in Gonzales expressed any enthusiasm for their plan. Consequently, Benavides and Linn joined Benjamin Fort Smith's company, which marched out of Gonzales intent on capturing Goliad.[17]

Riding ahead of Smith's company, Benavides arrived in Victoria to discover another unit with the same notion. George M. Collinsworth and a group of Matagorda volunteers were already in Victoria, and they intended to attack Goliad as well. Several Victorianos joined Collinsworth's expedition, with Captain Benavides commanding a company of some thirty Tejanos. Consequently, he was one of the leaders of the federalist unit that stormed Presidio La Bahía on 10 October 1835.[18]

Shortly after the capture of Goliad, General Stephen F. Austin, commander of the ad hoc "Army of the People," dispatched orders for Captain Benavides to join him in the drive on Béxar. On 14 October he departed Goliad at the head of twenty-six mounted rancheros. The company served as mounted scouts throughout the siege of Béxar, the two-month campaign to drive the Mexican army out of San Antonio.[19]

It was during one of these scouting sorties that Benavides tarnished his reputation. He joined his company with James Bowie's and patrolled the area south of Béxar in search of enemy mounts. They found no horses but detained a local herder on information provided by one of his Tejano neighbors. The informant insisted that the herder had concealed the animals, but the suspect steadfastly disavowed any knowledge of their whereabouts. Samuel C. A. Rogers, one of Bowie's volunteers, recounted what transpired next:

> Benevidas prevailed upon Colonel Bowie to hang the Mexican till he was not quite dead and he would tell us. We tied the Mexican's hands behind him and put a rope around his neck and brought him to a tree. . . . Then they pulled the Mexican up and held the rope until he nearly quite [quit?] kicking. We then let him down and with our guns cocked [and] pointed at him, [explained] that we would shoot him to pieces if he didn't tell us where the horses were. I remonstrated with Colonel Bowie and told him I didn't [participate] in such cruelty. I didn't have anything more to do with it. They had to hang the Mexican three times before he would tell.[20]

The responsibility for this atrocity must fall on the expedition commander, James Bowie, yet one cannot ignore that Benavides suggested it. His instigation of this lamentable incident seems at odds with everything historians know about his character, but Rogers had no reason to fabricate the episode. Benavides's involvement implies a complex disposition of loyalties among Tejanos. Combat dehumanized its practitioners; in the name of military expediency, men committed deeds they never contemplated as civilians.[21]

Still, to attribute this incident solely to the reduction of humanity engendered by war fails to consider the part class played. Tejano society consisted of the rich and the poor. Military commandants, government officials, successful financiers, and large ranch owners constituted the ruling elite. In stark contrast were the mixed-blood *peones*, common laborers who lived out their day in drudgery and service to the *patrones*. One of the leading oligarchs, Plácido Benavides—or more properly, *Don* Plácido, since his status as an alcalde and landowner entitled him to the honorific—did not hesitate to abuse a herdsman, a creature clearly his social inferior.[22]

Historians will probably never know if the herdsman was a civilian agent of the centralists or, as Rogers believed, an innocent who surrendered his own horses to save his life. It is certain that the episode illustrates the plight of many Tejanos caught in the swirl of changing politics and shifting loyalties. Benavides's actions in this instance do not require modern readers to admire them, but they should understand that he mirrored the prevailing attitudes of *his* time and place.

On 5 December Benavides's unit joined Colonel Francis Johnson's Second Division and fought as infantry during the storming of Béxar. Benavides and his men received commendation for their daring attack on the Veramendi house. Benavides's performance so impressed the members of the provisional government that they afterward offered him the rank of first lieutenant in the regular army.[23]

With victory at San Antonio, many Texians believed the war won and returned home to enjoy Christmas with their families; Benavides knew better. He rejected an offer to join William Barret Travis's Legion of Cavalry, which carried with it a regular army commission. Toward the end of December, Benavides rode south from Béxar with Colonel José María Gonzales's "division of observation." An unswerving federalist, Gonzales had long resisted Santa Anna's centralist regime. Now commanding a Tejano spy company, Benavides received orders to "scour the country between San Antonio and the Rio Grande." Colonel Gonzales, however, intended to do far more than that. He planned to raise, organize, and command the Tamaulipas federalists. Headquartered in the Rio Grande settlement of Camargo, Benavides acted as a liaison between federalist authorities in Matamoros and Scottish adventurer Dr. James Grant. While performing his duties, Benavides made many useful contacts that kept him well informed of the enemy's designs.[24]

In February 1836 the De León family called on Benavides to save Carvajal a second time. By then Captain Benavides had returned to his home range, where he was serving under Major Robert C. Morris at San Patricio. Word came from Victoria that the centralists had captured his brother-in-law and imprisoned him in the infamous Casamata in Matamoros. Morris authorized a putative "spy mission," but from the start Benavides viewed it as a rescue attempt. Arriving in Matamoros, Benavides and his men found the town swarming with centralist troops. Indistinguishable from the local population, Benavides made his way to the prison, where he employed his mother-in-law's gold to bribe the guards. Securing Carvajal, the small party attempted a getaway. The centralists, however, discovered Carvajal's escape and sounded the alarm. The centralists pursued them and captured twenty-two of his men, but with his brother-in-law safely in tow Benavides made it back to San Patricio.[25]

While Benavides had been in Matamoros, the federalist alcalde had warned him that Santa Anna was planning to lure the Texians south of the Rio Grande, a better position from which to launch a surprise attack. Benavides warned Major Morris of Santa Anna's intentions. In a letter dated 6 February, Morris informed Colonel James Walker Fannin of Benavides's "disagreeable intelligence." Receiving the letter at Refugio, Fannin was intent on conducting the Matamoros expedition. Benavides's warning may have caused Fannin to reconsider. At any rate, Fannin abandoned the Matamoros scheme and marched his army to Goliad.[26]

Benavides also dispatched vital information to Béxar. He sent courier Blas Herrera with a letter warning that Santa Anna was on the march toward San Antonio at the head of a large force. Béxar resident Antonio Menchaca recalled that Herrera arrived in town at 1 A.M. on 11 February and that Colonel James Bowie declared Benavides's communiqué one of "grave importance."[27]

Shortly thereafter, Benavides and his spy company briefly joined Dr. James Grant's forces at San Patricio. Grant did not fight for Texas independence or the Constitution of 1824, but for a republic of northern Mexico. Recent evidence also indicates that Grant was an agent of the United Kingdom and acting on its behest. Did Benavides endorse Grant's schemes for a republic of northern Mexico? Was he aware of Grant's true motives? Given the lack of documentation, historians cannot answer those questions.[28]

Benavides's alarms had been accurate and timely; sadly, the Texians failed to heed them. On 16 February 1836 Santa Anna crossed the Rio Grande on the Camino Real and drove toward Béxar with the bulk of his army. On 23 February the "Napoleon of the West" arrived in San Antonio and began a bombardment of the Alamo, which, after a thirteen-day siege, fell on 6 March. On 17 February General José Urrea forded downriver at Matamoros with 320 infantry and 230 dragoons. Barreling up the Atascosito Road, his mission was to retake Goliad. Urrea's spies had informed him that rebel commanders Frank Johnson and James Grant had assembled their forces in and around the village of San Patricio. The centralist general drove rapidly northward to the Nueces River to strike before the Texians could shake off their lethargy.

Blithely unaware of Urrea's approach, Grant, Benavides, and a detachment of mounted volunteers were out rounding up wild mustangs, leaving Johnson in San Patricio with about sixty men.[29] At 3 A.M. on 27 February, Urrea struck, using a bucketing rain as cover. The centralists fell upon the rebels with such swiftness and surprise that they never had an opportunity to rally. By dawn Urrea had captured nearby Fort Lipantitlán and secured the town; his men had killed twenty Texians and captured another thirty-two. Only eight, including Colonel Johnson, managed to escape. Urrea lost one man killed and four wounded.[30]

Meanwhile, Benavides and his company accompanied Dr. James Grant's detachment. Traditional accounts place the number of Grant's men at twenty-six, but General Urrea later claimed it included as many as fifty-three. Yet the twenty-six men whom historians normally listed failed to include Benavides's rancheros. A month earlier, Frank Johnson reported the presence of forty-seven Tejanos in ranks. If Urrea counted correctly, Benavides commanded as many as twenty-seven men that morning, which constituted half of Grant's unit.[31]

In San Patricio, Urrea had learned that Grant and his contingent would be returning to town. He, therefore, prepared a trap for the unwary Texians at Puerto de Los Cuates de Agua Dulce. The centralist commander could not have selected a better setting for an ambush. As its name implies, Los Cuates—the Twins—was a site where the trail forded two branches of Agua Dulce Creek, about twenty-six miles south of San Patricio. Mottes, or thick clusters, of oaks sheltered the crossing, and Urrea split his force into six squadrons and concealed them in the woods.

On 2 March—the same day that delegates at the town of Washington declared Texas independence—Grant's detachment stumbled into Urrea's trap. Benavides, Grant, and Ruben R. Brown rode about half a mile ahead of the rest of the men, who were driving several hundred head of wild horses. As the main body passed between two large mottes, more than sixty centralist dragoons swept out of the timber. Grant looked back and saw that enemy troopers had already cut off his command. Benavides wanted to rejoin his men but, "being better mounted" than Grant or Brown, they "told him to go on & save himself if he could." Someone had to warn Fannin of Urrea's advance.

As a native of the region with intimate knowledge of the countryside, Benavides had the best chance of getting through to Goliad.

As Benavides galloped off toward Presidio La Bahía, Grant and Brown charged to the aid of their comrades. As they drew near, however, it became apparent that most of their party were already dead. A centralist lancer killed Brown's horse, but he quickly mounted another. At that instant, the herd stampeded, breaking through the cordon of enemy cavalrymen. Seeing that they had no chance of helping their friends, Grant and Brown attempted to escape amid the swirl of mustangs. The centralists observed them and gave chase. After a seven-mile chase, the dragoons overtook the pair, killed Grant, and captured Brown.[32]

Thus ended the ambush at Agua Dulce Creek. General Urrea reported that his men killed forty-two rebels, captured three, and witnessed five escape. That accounted for forty-five of the fifty-three men he claimed his men engaged. Benavides and as many as four others managed to get away, but the majority of his company of federalist Tejanos died alongside their Texian comrades. If Urrea's numbers are correct, more Tejanos—perhaps as many as twenty-four—died at Agua Dulce than in any other battle of the Texas Revolution.[33]

As good as his word, Benavides raced to Presidio La Bahía (which the rebels had renamed Fort Defiance) in Goliad and alerted the garrison of the enemy's approach, but what he learned there shook his world. The declaration of independence changed everything. He was a Mexican fighting *against* centralist tyranny and *for* the Constitution of 1824. As a federalist and a man of principle, he would not help strip Texas from Mexico. He explained his quandary to Colonel Fannin, who amicably discharged him from the Texian army. Benavides returned to Victoria, where he proclaimed his neutrality and sought to sit out the rest of the war.

A humane act thwarted his peaceful intentions. Late in March, Benavides was inspecting his ranch when he came upon the wounded Isaac D. Hamilton, the quartermaster of the Alabama Red Rovers. On 19 March General Urrea had overtaken Fannin's command on its march toward Victoria, and the battle of Coleto ensued. Outnumbered and outgeneraled, Fannin surrendered the following day. Mexican soldiers escorted their prisoners back to Presidio La Bahía. Then, on 27 March, acting upon Santa Anna's orders, they gunned down 342 unarmed Texians. In the chaos, several of Fannin's men escaped the massacre, among them Isaac Hamilton. Seriously wounded and starving, he stumbled onto Benavides's ranch. He knew Hamilton, for they had served together at Goliad. Benavides felt obligated to help a wounded man, whatever his political affiliation. He placed Hamilton in his cart and pledged to take him to safety.[34]

Yet an approaching centralist cavalry patrol prevented him from honoring that pledge. Benavides could now do nothing to save Hamilton. Indeed, he might not have been able to save himself had the centralists believed he was assisting a condemned rebel escape. Benavides opted for self-preservation. He called out that he had captured one of the rebels, coolly demanded a receipt for his prisoner, and handed Hamilton over to Urrea's lancers. Hamilton, incensed by what he could only interpret as reprehensible deceit, was "placed on a bare backed horse and was most cruelly beaten through the prairie until we arrived at Victoria." There he awaited the firing squad.[35]

Hamilton did not, however, meet his expected fate. He was one of those fortunate Texians saved by the intercession of Francita Alavez, the "Angel of Goliad." Hamilton subsequently escaped and made his way back to the Texian lines. He never forgave Benavides and frequently related the "treachery of the Mexican who betrayed him" to all who would listen. Many did. According to one of Hamilton's descendants, "Family tales picture Isaac thereafter as embittered, and under driving compulsion to find and kill Plácido." He even went so far as to commission a new rifle, "which he told friends he was going to use in killing this Mexican, when he found him." The rancor of Hamilton and others of his ilk poisoned the atmosphere for Benavides and other Texas Mexicans.[36]

Yet that was not the only incident that colored Texian attitudes. With news of Fannin's defeat at Coleto Creek, many Tejanos who had earlier proclaimed their devotion to the federalist cause now sought to demonstrate their loyalty to Santa Anna's centralist government. Henry Reilly, in Victoria at the time, later described the harrowing escape of Doctor Benjamin Harrison, reputedly the son of President William Henry Harrison:

> The inhabitants [of Victoria] became extremely insulting to the few Americans who remained, and as soon as they ascertained Fanning's [sic] defeat, they, headed by the second Alcalde, bound Dr. Harrison's hands behind him, in conjunction with two other Americans, and commenced butchering them; they began on the others first, and by the time they had finished their damned work, Dr. H had succeeded in separating

his hands, and immediately ran into the Guadaloupe timber which is uncommonly thick and secreted himself.[37]

No less an authority than General José Urrea verified that Victoria's citizens were in league with the centralist forces: "The [Victoria] inhabitants—Mexican, French, and Irish—had been in communication with me, and when I arrived they had arrested six of the enemy who were in the town. Two hours after our arrival a party of twenty was seen down the river making their way towards Victoria. I issued orders to cut them off from the woods along the banks of the Guadalupe, and these having been carried out, they were all killed or taken prisoners."[38]

Few today remember the Victoria massacre, but Texians at the time would have learned the particulars and abhorred them. Although many Victorianos had fought alongside Texians in the early battles, most of them had demonstrated little enthusiasm for Texas independence. When the political and military tides turned against them, many had been quick to proclaim their neutrality or even join the enemy.

After the Texian victory at San Jacinto, Brigadier General Thomas Jefferson Rusk established his headquarters at Victoria. With rumors rife of another enemy offensive, he sought to place the country in a state of readiness. Local citizens made his job challenging. On 8 June 1836 he learned that some were "driving on toward the Nueces [River] from five hundred to one thousand head of cattle. It is very important that they should be prevented from passing the Nueces." Important, indeed, since Rusk needed those beeves to feed his men. Wishing to keep their cattle out of Texian bellies, Tejano ranchers drove them toward Mexican-controlled territory. Their actions made Rusk aware that most Victorianos did not support the Republic of Texas or the army that sought to preserve it.[39]

Rusk well understood that the sovereignty that Texians had achieved in eighteen minutes at San Jacinto could be lost just as quickly. "[The Mexicans] have had their pride much mortified in their contest with us," he asserted, "and can any one be so blind as to believe that they will acknowledge our independence[?] . . . I can trust there is no one who has any thing to do with the Govt. who entertains the opinion that the Independence of Texas is secure." Time was fleeting. As Rusk expressed it, "We have but a short period to organize upon this frontier a sufficient force to meet the enemy in another Campaign where beyond doubt he will come with redoubled numbers." Later that month Rusk admitted that he had taken some "pretty high handed steps," which he believed justified "by the circumstances."[40]

One of Rusk's highhanded steps had a profound effect on Benavides and his extended family. In June 1836, Rusk ordered the detention and evacuation of all local Tejanos suspected of sympathy with Mexico. Many prominent Victorianos, among them the De León and Benavides families, found themselves exiled to New Orleans.

One document intimates that Tejanos resisted the order to leave their homes. General Rusk explained the tense situation to a Texian merchant, Phillip Dimmitt:

> I understand that some of the Mexican families near the point[41] are pretending that they have no order to remove. A special order was issued to the Citizens of this place and a general order to all the Citizens to remove east instantly. I have sent down the De Leon [and] Carabajal [*sic*] familys and have sent men with them to see that they meet on Board the vessels. I shall detach more to day and send at least the men on board with directions to report themselves to the Cabinet for their dispositions. I shall leave Cavalry here and in advance and have them expressly to see my orders as to the removal of the families as such Strictly complied with. [A]s you will be near the vessels and the Steam Boat when they arrive[,] I will thank you to render what assistance may be in your power in getting them all on board & off.[42]

On 27 June General Rusk issued a proclamation that announced that neutrality would no longer remain an option for Tejanos: "He that claims a home and a habitation in Texas—must now *fight for it, or abandon it,* to some one who will." This policy boded ill for Benavides and other Mexican federalists of his sort. Clearly, the new order was establishing hegemony.[43]

On 20 July a Texian in Velasco reported the evacuations and the reasons behind them: "Gen. Rusk has ordered the Mexican families on the Guadalupe and La Baca [rivers], and those who were likely to afford information to the enemy to retire upon the Rio Grande, or take themselves off to the Colorado. Carbajal [,] De Leon, and some others, intend making a summer sojourn in New Orleans. Health to them!"[44] At first glance, his final sentiment appears to drip with sarcasm, but perhaps not. New Orleans was an notoriously unhealthy city, infamous for its yellow fever epidemics.

It would be fashionable to denounce General Rusk as a racist thug who engineered a Tejano "Trail of Tears." Yet such an assessment would be shrill and more than a little disingenuous. Documents do not indicate that Rusk was an evil man, merely a commander with a distasteful duty to perform. He earnestly believed that the Mexicans were about to launch another offensive. On the frontier at Victoria, Rusk and his paltry 350-man force acted as their country's first line of defense. He well understood that the local Tejanos had never supported Texas independence and could not allow the town's clandestine agents to further an invading enemy's military and political objectives. His concerns were perfectly justified. Just months earlier, Victorianos had supplied vital intelligence to General Urrea. Moreover, local Tejanos had participated in, or approved of, the murder of helpless prisoners of war. There was but one way to assure security: evacuate *all* civilians. Rusk knew his actions were ruthless, but he believed that conditions justified them.

Similarly, Benavides had believed himself justified back in December when he proposed stringing up the suspected centralist agent. Neither man was a brute. Under normal circumstances Rusk and Benavides, both educated and civilized gentlemen, might have enjoyed each other's company over a glass of sherry. This, however, was war—by definition, a time when inhumanity reigns. Rusk expressed sympathy for the displaced civilians and instructed his men to treat evacuees with deference. Regrettably, the Texian soldiers did not obey his orders. Fernando De León later complained that Rusk's men had abused his family, even "taking the ear rings and jewelry from the persons of helpless females." General Rusk's intentions may have been honorable, but that likely made little difference to Plácido and Agustina Benavides, their girls, and the other Victorianos forced from their homes.[45]

Plácido Benavides never saw Victoria again. In 1837 he died in Opelousas, Louisiana. Nor was his beloved Agustina ever able to return home; she followed her husband to the grave five years later. Plácido's brother Ysidro did come back sometime before 1842, and Doña Patricia De León, who had taken in her orphaned granddaughters, returned in 1846 and resumed her place as a respected matron of Victoria society. To this day, her descendants continue to inhabit the area.[46]

On 6 and 7 August 1840 some six hundred Comanche warriors tore through Victoria. The marauders caught the town by surprise, killing fifteen citizens in the streets. The death toll would have been higher, but residents took refuge inside the vacant Round House. The warriors noted this formidable bastion and sought a softer target, the port town of Linnville. Three years after his death, Plácido Benavides's sagacity and prescience again saved the community he had loved so well.[47]

Notes

1. For Santa Anna's transformation from a liberal federalist into a reactionary centralist, see William C. Davis, *Lone Star Rising: The Revolutionary Birth of the Texas Republic* (New York: Free Press, 2004), 62, 74, 90, 95, 105, 108, 113, 121, 143.

2. John J. Linn, *Reminiscences of Fifty Years in Texas* (New York: Published for the Author, D. and J. Sadlier, 31 Barclay Street, 1883; reprint ed., Austin: State House Press, 1986), 38.

3. Ibid.

4. Linn is the source for this description, but he was notoriously careless about noting exact dates. Professor Ann Carolina Castillo Crimm places it late in June 1835 and I concur. Ana Carolina Castillo Crimm, *De León: A Tejano Family History* (Austin: University of Texas Press, 2003), 142–43.

5. *Handbook of Texas Online*, s.v. "Benavides, Plácido."

6. Ibid.

7. Willard B. Robinson, "Colonial Ranch Architecture in the Spanish-Mexican Tradition," *Southwestern Historical Quarterly* 83 (October 1979): 140. Benavides constructed his Round House on the Calle de los Diez Amigos (the modern Main Street). The house was located at 302 Main, where Fossati's Delicatessen currently sits.

8. Roy Grimes, ed., *300 Years in Victoria County* (Austin: Nortex Press, 1985), 70.

9. Hobart Huson, *Refugio: A Comprehensive History of Refugio County from Aboriginal Times to 1953* (Woodsboro, Tex.: Rooke Foundation, 1953–55), 1: 41.

10. Joseph E. Chance, *José María de Jesús Carvajal: The Life and Times of a Mexican Revolutionary* (San Antonio, Tex.: Trinity University Press, 2006), 20–23; see also *Handbook of Texas Online*, s.v. "José María Jesús Carbajal."

11. For a lucid explanation of the Anahuac Disturbances of 1832, see Margaret Swett Henson, *Juan Davis Bradburn: A Reappraisal of the Mexican Commander of Anahuac* (College Station: Texas A&M University Press, 1982).

12. Chance, *José María de Jesús Carvajal*, 32–33.

13. Crimm, *De León*, 142.

14. Gregg Cantrell, *Stephen F. Austin: Empresario of Texas* (New Haven, CT: Yale University Press, 1999), 297–328.

15. Ibid., 144.

16. Linn, *Reminiscences*, 105, 107. Artillerymen categorized their guns by the weight of the projectiles they fired. Six-, eight-, and nine-pounders constituted the majority of field artillery. One might occasionally see a twelve-pounder, but it was the heaviest caliber gunners deployed on the battlefield. Although the heavier guns were a nightmare to transport (especially in Texas where roads were primitive), they provided advantages that the lighter ones did not. The heavier the shot, the greater was its range, accuracy, and impact. As early as the Napoleonic Wars, three- and four-pound cannon were becoming obsolete. In 1835, Benavides understood that Victoria's teeny ordnance was of little or no military value, at least not against Indians, where superior mobility was crucial. He was, therefore, perfectly content to let the centralists have it. For more on the use of field artillery, see Rory Muir, *Tactics and the Experience of Battle in the Age of Napoleon* (New Haven, CT: Yale University Press, 1998), 29–50.

17. Linn, *Reminiscences*, 106–7; Hobart Huson, *Captain Philip Dimmitt's Commandancy of Goliad, 1835–1836: An Episode of the Mexican Federalist War in Texas, Usually Referred to as the Texas Revolution* (Austin: Von Boeckmann-Jones, 1974), 11.

18. Stephen L. Hardin, *Texian Iliad: A Military History of the Texas Revolution* (Austin: University of Texas Press, 1994), 14–17.

19. Alwyn Barr, *Texans in Revolt: The Battle for San Antonio, 1835* (Austin: University of Texas Press, 1990), 18, 45, 67, 71.

20. Samuel C. A. Rogers, "Reminiscences, 1810–1892," Archives and Manuscript Collection, box 2R166, University of Texas at Austin, Center for American History [CAH].

21. Joanna Bourke, *An Intimate History of Killing: Face-to-Face Killing in 20th Century Warfare* (n.p.: Basic Books, 1999), 173–185. Professor Bourke concludes, "Servicemen of all ranks were unperturbed by most of these acts of lawless killing." One may reasonably suppose that it was much the same among nineteenth-century combatants.

22. Arnoldo De León, *The Tejano Community, 1836–1900* (Albuquerque: University of New Mexico Press, 1982), 2–5; for other aspects of class divisions in Tejano society, see Andrés Anthony Tijerina, *Tejanos and Texas under the Mexican Flag* (College Station: Texas A&M University Press, 1994), 10.

23. Huson, *Refugio*, 1:291.

24. Stuart Reid, *The Secret War for Texas* (College Station: Texas A&M University Press, 2007), 116, 169; James Robinson to Stephen F. Austin, William H. Wharton and Branch T. Archer, January 23, 1836, in *Diplomatic Correspondence of the Republic of Texas*, ed. George P. Garrison (Washington, D.C.: American Historical Association, 1907–11), 1:64–65.

25. Crimm, *De León*, 156; Chance, *José María de Jesús Carvajal*, 38–39. These historians relate the same basic story but differ in one detail. Crimm states that Benavides rescued two of his brothers-in-law, Carvajal and Fernando De León. According to Chance, however, De León had managed to bribe the guards himself and had escaped earlier.

26. Robert C. Morris to James W. Fannin, 6 February 1836, in *The Papers of the Texas Revolution*, ed. John H. Jenkins (Austin: Presidial Press, 1973) 4:274–76; *Handbook of Texas Online*, s.v. "Robert C. Morris"; Stephen L. Hardin, *The Alamo 1836: Santa Anna's Texas Campaign* (Oxford: Osprey, 2001), 7–8, 52–56.

27. Antonio Menchaca, *Memoirs*, ed. James P. Newcomb (San Antonio, Tex.: Yanaguana Society, 1937), 22–23.

28. For more on Dr. Grant's clandestine activities, see Reid, *Secret War for Texas*.

29. Historian Stuart Reid argues that Grant's foray was not a "mustanging" expedition but rather a final effort to establish contact with his federalist allies. Even at this late date, he still appeared committed to his dream of a republic of northern Mexican states. Ibid., 129.

30. Hardin, *Alamo 1836*, 53.

31. Reid, *Secret War for Texas*, 143.

32. Ruben R. Brown, "Expedition under Johnson and Grant," in James M. Day, comp., *The Texas Almanac, 1857–1873: A Compendium of Texas History* (Waco, Tex.: Texian Press, 1967), 218–24.

33. For a breakdown of the casualty list, see Reid, *Secret War for Texas*, 215.

34. Stephen L. Hardin, "Efficient in the Cause," in *Tejano Journey, 1770–1850*, ed. Gerald E. Poyo (Austin: University of Texas Press, 1996), 65–66.

35. Isaac D. Hamilton vertical file, CAH; see also Lester Hamilton, *Goliad Survivor: Isaac D. Hamilton* (San Antonio, Tex.: Naylor, 1971).

36. *Handbook of Texas Online*, s.v. "Alavez, Francita"; Isaac D. Hamilton vertical file, CAH.

37. *Morning Courier and New York Enquirer*, 28 July 1836. I am grateful to Gary Zaboly for bringing this source to my attention.

38. José Urrea, *Diario de las operaciones militares de la división que al mando del General José Urrea hizo en la Campaña de Tejas* (Victoria de Durango: n.p., 1838), 25–26; for the English translation, see Carlos E. Castañeda, ed., *The Mexican Side of the Texas Revolution* (Dallas, Tex.: P. L. Turner, [1928]; reprint edition, Austin: Graphic Ideas, 1970), 238.

39. Thomas Jefferson Rusk to James Smith, 8 June 1836, in Jenkins, *Papers of the Texas Revolution*, 7:73–74.

40. Rusk to David G. Burnet, 13 June 1836, in ibid., 7:135–40; Rusk to Thomas Jefferson Green, 15 June 1836, in ibid., 7:159–60; Rusk to James Morgan, 14 June 1836, in ibid., 7:150.

41. The "point" in question was probably Dimmitt's Landing, where he had established a wharf and warehouse. It was a transshipment site between ocean vessel and wagon trains to the interior on the west bank of the Lavaca River near its mouth at northeastern Lavaca Bay. From Victoria, Dimmitt's Landing would have been the nearest seaport.

42. Rusk to Philip Dimmitt, 22 June 1836, in ibid., 7:232.

43. Rusk, [Proclamation to the People of Texas], Guadaloupe-Victoria, 27 June 1836, broadside, cited in Joseph Milton Nance, *After San Jacinto: The Texas-Mexican Frontier, 1836–1841* (Austin: University of Texas Press, 1963), 12.

44. Fairfax Catelet to editor of the *Arkansas Gazette* [Little Rock], 26 August 1836, in Jenkins, *Papers of the Texas Revolution*, 7:495–96.

45. Fernando De León, Petition to the Legislature, December 1849, Records of the Legislature, Archives Division, Texas State Library, Austin.

46. Huson, *Refugio*, 1:398; Ana Carolina Castillo Crimm, "Finding Their Way," in Poyo, *Tejano Journey*, 121; see also her *De León*, 183–90.

47. Gilbert Onderdonk, "Incidents of Comanche Raid 68 Years Ago," manuscript, Regional Archives, Victoria College, Victoria, Texas.

San Fernando Cathedral, as it looked when Father Garza was parish priest at San Antonio and before the replacement of the nave with a French Gothic structure in the 1870s when the church was elevated to the status of cathedral. Father Garza's tenure proved increasingly turbulent over the course of the twenty years he served as pastor between 1820 and 1840. *Courtesy The San Antonio Light Collection, UTSA's Institute of Texan Cultures, #L-0010-A, Courtesy of the Hearst Corporation.*

FATHER REFUGIO DE LA GARZA
CONTROVERTED RELIGIOUS LEADER
Robert E. Wright, O.M.I.

FATHER REFUGIO DE LA GARZA, who pastored San Antonio throughout the Mexican period and most of the Republic of Texas years, became a historical symbol of the Mexican Catholic clergy and indeed of the Mexican Catholic Church of those times. Often referred to erroneously as one of "the two priests in all of Texas" during the Mexican period, he has been made to represent an allegedly corrupt clergy and a Catholic Church that purportedly neglected or abandoned its people. This depiction is deeply embedded in Texas tradition, going all the way back to 1840, the year that Father Garza was forced to resign as the pastor of San Antonio by the new Catholic Church authorities on their arrival from the United States. His story thus provides an important and indeed crucial vantage point from which to assess the religious situation among Tejanos during those eventful years. That story is in need of major revision.

José Refugio Guadalupe de la Garza was born on 22 November 1775 in San Antonio, just a few years after it had become the new capital of Spanish Texas.[1] The very names given him by his apparently poor parents declared their strong Hispanic Catholic piety. Devotion to Saint Joseph, the husband of Mary the mother of Jesus, was so prominent in New Spain at that time that almost all male infants were given the name José as a prefix to their identifying given names. More significant, the infant's other two given names, Refugio and Guadalupe, were two of the most popular titles of the Virgin Mary in northern New Spain: Our Lady of Refuge and Our Lady of Guadalupe. Refugio was the second of seven children, and the names of most of his siblings confirmed the same pious attitude of his parents.[2]

Refugio came from a long Presidio del Rio Grande lineage on his father's side, with strong San Antonio connections. His paternal grandmother, Margarita Menchaca, was a great granddaughter of Diego Ramón, the first commander of the Presidio del Rio Grande. She married Refugio's grandfather, José de la Garza, in the 1740s. When José died in 1748 while Margarita was pregnant with their third child at Rio Grande, she promptly married José Salinas, a native of that place and himself a grandson of Diego Ramón. Sometime during the 1750s the new couple moved to San Antonio.[3] One can imagine the incentive for the move: Margarita's uncle Toribio de Urrutia was presidio commander at San Antonio de Béxar, and her brother Luis Antonio Menchaca had transferred there and was doing well. Luis Antonio began building the large Menchaca ranching enterprise in the San Antonio valley, and in 1763 he succeeded his uncle as presidio commander.[4] It was thus in San Antonio that Refugio's father Mariano, having arrived as a young boy with his mother Margarita and his stepfather, met and married Josefa Flores.[5]

Refugio's father Mariano died with apparently few assets when the boy was only thirteen years old.[6] Before Refugio was fifteen he had left San Antonio, probably to begin training for the priesthood for the new Catholic diocese of Linares (Nuevo León).[7] Financial support for his studies may well have come from the better-off Menchaca side of the family. When Refugio received the tonsure, a rite admitting him as a candidate for the priesthood, on 24 May 1793, it was at the hands of the bishop of Nuevo León in Monterrey, who probably ordained him in 1800 or 1801, around the typical age of twenty-five at that time.[8] Further research in Mexican church records is needed to determine where Father Garza worked as a priest between his ordination and 1820, a long span of two decades in his life about which nothing is known.[9] During this time his mother Josefa Flores died a poor woman in 1809 at the age of fifty-six, with almost no possessions other than her home in San Antonio. She was preceded in death by three of her children.[10]

In January 1820, at age forty-four, Father Garza returned to the place of his childhood, San Antonio, but now as its permanent pastor.[11] For the next two decades Father Garza blessed and confessed, married and buried, baptized and perhaps chastised the families of most of the Tejano leaders chronicled in this book. Since the chaplaincies of the local military companies, the presidio company of Béxar and the Alamo company, were vacant on his arrival, he also initially ministered to those soldiers and their families.[12] Additionally, a Franciscan priest was still serving the increasingly mixed Indian-Hispanic communities at the missions just south of the town.[13] The other Hispanic settlements in present-day Texas—at La Bahía, Refugio, and those along the Rio Grande—also had their own priests.[14] Father Garza thus joined the clerical ranks in Texas just as the era of Mexican independence was about to dawn. It would be his task to shepherd the sometimes divided townspeople through the years of newly achieved national independence and political formation, the tide of

Anglo immigration into Texas, and the Texas Revolution and its immediate aftermath.

A younger contemporary, Juan Seguín, later testified that in Father Garza's first years as pastor, when Seguín was barely a teenager, the priest "fulfilled his responsibilities with much scrupulosity, propriety, care and dedication to divine worship; he made significant repairs and improvements in the parish church, which gained him the appreciation and respect of everyone."[15] Soon he was giving religious instruction to Anglo-Americans converting to Catholicism as fiancés of Mexican women.[16] On 28 January 1822 his fellow Tejanos elected him the first representative of Texas to the Mexican national constitutional congress, which he reached almost two months later.[17] One can only conjecture why he was chosen other than for the local respect he had earned: he was well educated; during his training and earlier years in ministry he had probably come to know other important persons in Mexico; his clerical status might carry more weight, especially as he was representing such a marginal province. After Agustín de Iturbide, who had himself proclaimed emperor in May 1822, dissolved the congress in the fall, Garza remained there as a member of the select Junta Nacional Instituyente, and again as a member of the congress when it was reconstituted in spring 1823.[18]

Through Garza's efforts in Mexico City, the national government took actions of major consequence for Texas. From the beginning Garza and the San Antonio ayuntamiento were concerned about urgent local issues such as Indian demands and hostilities, the disorderly and potentially threatening influx of Protestant Anglo-Americans,[19] much-needed financial resources, and trade concessions.[20] Garza successfully advocated the national decree that brought about the final secularization of the missions in the province of Texas, allowing their lands to be distributed among Tejanos.[21]

Less recognized, but of even greater importance, was Garza's key role in getting an acceptable national colonization law passed and Stephen F. Austin's contract confirmed. On Austin's first visit to San Antonio in August 1821, he had noted in his diary that Father Garza had expressed a desire to be appointed the pastor of the new colony that Austin was planning.[22] In Mexico City, Father Garza was a member of the five-to-six-person committee responsible for the national colonization decree in both the congress and the Junta Instituyente. Austin himself pointed out the particular importance of that committee to his project. Since Father Garza had been appointed to this very select committee precisely because he was the deputy from Texas, which everyone recognized was the most obvious and desired territory for colonization, it stands to reason that neither the colonization law nor the confirmation of Austin's grant (the only grant made under this 1823 law) would have resulted as they did if Father Garza had not been supportive of those measures.[23]

As a member of the Commission on War and Maritime concerns, Garza was also well placed to address the defense and trade concerns of Texans. He successfully brought about an exemption from import duties for seven years for the province of Texas.[24] He also argued for the establishment of forts along the Indian frontier and the opening of another port for trade on the Gulf coast. But those goals could not be accomplished at that time since attention was focused upon national concerns in the rapidly shifting political landscape of Mexico City.[25] What Father Garza helped accomplish, however, were major milestones in Texas history: the end of the mission system and the privatization of the mission lands mostly into the hands of Tejanos; the confirmation of Austin's grant and the colonization provisions that allowed Austin not only to continue his colony but also to have a crucial head start of more than three years on other would-be Anglo empresarios; and the exemption from import duties for seven years. And yet even the most recent Texas history surveys fail to recognize Refugio de la Garza as the historic first Texas deputy to the Mexican national congress and his major accomplishments on behalf of Texas. Only the outside foreign lobbyist, Stephen F. Austin, is noted in connection with the actions of that first congress and its successor, the Junta Instituyente. This demonstrates the continuing challenge of extricating ourselves from the strong Anglophile heritage of Texas historiography.[26]

During Father Garza's absence in Mexico City, a long-awaited new chaplain for the Béxar military company, Francisco Maynes, finally arrived in San Antonio in November 1822.[27] Maynes also assumed the pastoral care of the Alamo company families. In May 1824 Father Garza returned to his pastorate, having been replaced as the Texas deputy in the national congress by Erasmo Seguín.[28] The San Antonio parish, San Fernando, now included the newly incorporated former mission villages stretching along the river below the town center.[29] For the first time in 106 years there were no longer Franciscans to share in the pastoral care of the local population. But in exchange there was Father Maynes, who remained as military chaplain during almost the entire Mexican period.[30] As the local pastor, Father Garza remained influential in San Antonio politics, and thus in Mexican Texas. It was apparently through his mediation that a heated division in the community in late September 1824 over accepting the abolition of Texas' *diputación provincial* (provincial assembly) by the legislature of the new state of Coahuila y Texas and removing the provincial archives to Saltillo was prevented from exploding into violence.[31] In late 1832, Austin still considered Father Garza one of the half-dozen leading men in San Antonio.[32]

In his 1839 affidavit on Father Garza's character, Juan Seguín declared that on the priest's return from Mexico City in 1824 he "began to dissociate himself almost entirely [*desentenderse casi enteramente*] from the duties of his occupation."[33] Seguín's negative testimony in the political context of 1839 is problematic and is discussed later in this essay. A contemporary assessment of Father Garza's ministry as pastor in the mid-1820s was provided by Father Juan Nepomuceno de la Peña. Father Peña arrived in San Antonio in late December 1824 as the newly appointed ecclesiastical vicar for Texas and remained in the area through at least July 1825. Exercising limited authority over church affairs in Texas, Father Peña took seriously his responsibility to inspect all the church records.[34]

Some later Texas historians have characterized Peña's observations as evidence of a "characteristic negligence" by Father Garza.[35] An analysis of the vicar's comments and of the still extant church registers he inspected requires that this charge of negligence be carefully delimited. Those records indicate that Father Garza was indeed lax in keeping certain permanent church records properly up to date. He also apparently failed to see to it that San Fernando Church itself was kept clean and secure and that the liturgical items stored in it from the former missions were given proper care. But the vicar's entire record of proceedings from December through July do not provide any basis for charging Father Garza with a much more serious neglect in the actual pastoral care of the community.[36] That accusation would come much later, in a very different context.

Like most diocesan priests in the frontier settlements of northern Mexico, Garza sought to improve the limited financial resources that such a parish usually provided its pastor. On his arrival in 1820, there had been no funds in the church account, thanks to unpaid loans made by the previous lay administrator during the hard times of the previous decade.[37] Father Garza had to borrow decent liturgical items from the consolidated San Antonio missions.[38] No surprise that he joined the scramble to acquire the secularized mission lands he had been so instrumental in bringing about, obtaining acreage at the former Mission Concepción as part of his growing property.[39] Within a few years he developed a sizable ranching operation, raising goats, sheep, cattle, and oxen. As his material resources grew, his dependents also increased, giving him a household full of women, men, and children, relatives and otherwise.[40] Garza also benefitted from speculating in land as foreigners increased in the 1830s. In 1834 he sold to John McMullen for $1,100 a large tract of eleven *sitios* of land that he had bought eighteen months earlier for less than a third that amount from the agent of the former San José mission Indians.[41]

As the local pastor, Father Garza was also invariably a member of various civic commissions for the town's welfare. Typically, as pastor he had an important say in who was appointed as the public school teacher. In early 1828 he helped prepare—in fact, actually wrote out—along with Juan Martín Veramendi and another man, a local school ordinance that fully promoted the state religion of Catholicism.[42] In early 1831, Veramendi, Ramón Múzquiz, Father Garza, and Father Maynes were ex-officio members of the public health commission activated to address one of the recurrent cholera epidemics.[43]

In November 1828 a major fire gutted and greatly damaged San Fernando Church. In his criticism of Father Garza a decade later, Juan Seguín charged that the fire was ultimately due to the priest's carelessness: "I say due to his carelessness, since the custody of the church was left in charge of a very young careless and unruly boy."[44] Work began on rebuilding the church, which went slowly since funds were still hard to come by. The reconstruction had progressed sufficiently by September 1830 to celebrate its progress along with the twentieth anniversary of the Mexican 16 September *grito* (Hidalgo's 1810 call for Mexican self-rule) for independence.[45] Important repairs, however, especially to the roof, were still needed.[46]

To this day, Texas historians usually characterize the Mexican period as one of great neglect or abandonment of the Mexican people by the Catholic Church. This is mainly explained, they assert, by a near absence of priests in Texas during those years. A typical allegation from a recent textbook on Texas history: "The Church had all but given up its work in the Far North during the period, and the two priests responsible for Texas Catholicism during the period had earned disgraceful reputations."[47] Contrary to this ingrained negative description, as late as mid-1834 there was a Catholic priest in almost every Texas settlement with a significant Tejano or other Catholic population. San Antonio actually had two priests, Fathers Garza and

Maynes, and Goliad, Nacogdoches, and San Patricio also each had a resident priest. The people of Victoria and the brand-new Refugio colony were the only Catholic settlements in the old province of Texas that had to make do with visits by priests from elsewhere. Along the future Texas side of the Rio Grande, all the Mexican settlements also each had a resident priest, with the sole exception of Socorro, where there were priests available nearby in Ysleta and San Elizario.[48]

The church during the Mexican period did not collapse. It endured through difficult times. It was primarily the Texas Revolution and its aftermath that laid prostrate the church institutions in the old province of Texas. Just before the revolution, in September 1834, Father Maynes died a victim of the cholera epidemic.[49] The following month, as political tensions were beginning to boil over in East Texas, Father Antonio Díaz, the highly respected Franciscan pastor of Nacogdoches who had served in San Antonio at the beginning of the Mexican period, died from a pistol shot while traveling alone with an Anglo stranger. According to the Tejanos, it was murder. The official report belatedly emitted by Anglo authorities in East Texas six months later said it was suicide.[50] During the Texas Revolution itself, the pro-Mexico pastor of Goliad was arrested by the Anglo-Texans and marched off to East Texas. The Irish pastor of San Patricio opted to retreat with some of his people to Matamoros when armed conflict reached his community.[51]

At the end of the revolution the only surviving Catholic community other than Nacogdoches in the former province of Texas was San Antonio. Goliad, Refugio, San Patricio, and to a lesser extent Victoria, all located in the principal theater of conflict and afterward a "no-man's land" between Texan and Mexican raiders, suffered continual depredations in the first years of the Texas Republic and consequently remained practically abandoned. The church property in those towns was heavily damaged or expropriated by the triumphant Anglos—as was also the case in Nacogdoches.[52] In a mere eighteen months the Catholic community in Mexican Texas had suffered drastic reversals. It is essential to remember, however, that this was not the whole picture for what is now Texas. Along the Rio Grande, the same communities as before continued to be staffed with priests from the Mexican church up to 1850 and beyond—even though they in turn were buffeted by international conflict in the later 1830s and the 1840s.[53]

Father Garza, the sole priest left in his parish in the old province of Texas by the end of the Texas Revolution, had witnessed much bloodshed. In late 1835, after the battle near Mission Concepción and before the Texan capture of San Antonio, the "old Padre" served as a messenger between Austin and General Martín Perfecto de Cos.[54] After the battle at the Alamo he, Ramón Múzquiz, and Francisco Ruiz's son were asked by Santa Anna to accompany him to identify the bodies of the slain Texan leaders.[55] A Mexico loyalist, Father Garza continued to serve as pastor in San Antonio during the first few years of the fragile Texas Republic. He and others secretly hoped and plotted for Mexico to reassert its sovereignty over the territory. That put the priest decidedly on the opposite side of the political and existential fence from people like Juan Seguín. To the Anglo-Texans and their Tejano allies, Father Garza was a dangerous political influence and indeed a threat.

Why did Father Garza remain loyal to Mexico if he had initially been favorable to the new Anglo colonies? It would have been surprising had he done otherwise. For one thing, the new colonies had been specifically envisioned as Catholic and loyal to the new Mexican nation and its religion. One can only conjecture, but important factors probably included the alleged murder of Father Díaz, the deepening political rift between the settlers and the Mexican government, and increasing differences between Anglos and Tejanos. The emergence of an increasingly public and anti-Catholic Protestantism before the revolution and its triumph afterward in the Texas Republic could only have reaffirmed Father Garza's nationalist sentiments. He witnessed or heard how unruly Anglo volunteers desecrated the Catholic churches and mistreated the Catholic priest at Goliad, and how the new Anglo authorities expropriated the Catholic churches to their own uses. He was also probably much less heavily involved in commerce than the Seguíns and other pro-settler Tejano elites, and thus less economically tied to the new order.

This political tension must have had something to do with Father Garza's downfall. Catholic Church authorities in the United States and Rome were receiving pleas from English-speaking Catholics in the Republic of Texas who felt deeply the absence of English-speaking pastors and indeed of Catholic clergy in general in the new republic, as Anglo Protestants and their ministers asserted themselves. Therefore church authorities in the United States sent two priests, Fathers John Timon and Juan Francisco Llebaría, on a fact-finding mission with a view to reestablishing the Catholic clergy in Texas under American jurisdiction. By this time the former Goliad pastor, Father José Antonio Valdez, was living on a ranch a few miles from

San Antonio, evidently retired from ministry at the age of fifty-two as Goliad remained depopulated. The church visitors arrived in Houston in early 1839 while the Texas Congress was in session and thus were able to be informed about church affairs in San Antonio by none other than Juan Seguín and José Antonio Navarro.[56] There is no direct report of what Navarro said, leaving Seguín as our primary witness.

Since Father Llebaría spoke Spanish, it was he who interviewed Seguín. Asking about the number and quality of priests in the Republic of Texas, Llebaría reported that Seguín responded:

> In all of [the Republic of] Texas there were only two who currently live in San Antonio de Bexar, and whom he knew very well, and that they were still very close friends since they had been raised together. As regards their qualities, he added that he would not discuss them, if there were not any spiritual necessity or usefulness for them or for the faithful. Nevertheless, after his Excellency learned our commission and saw the powers we have from Monseigneur [Bishop Blanc of New Orleans], then he told me that he would only declare what was public knowledge and which he could confirm by oath if necessary, the good of Religion forcing him to that.[57]

This statement alleges that Seguín and the two priests were close friends, having all been raised together. But Valdez had probably left San Antonio for seminary studies in the interior of Mexico before the end of 1803; that was before Seguín was born in 1806.[58] Similarly, Garza was twenty-one years old and no longer in San Antonio when Seguín was born. Seguín and the two priests may or may not have been close friends, but they were certainly not raised together. Be that as it may, the intriguing note in this report is that Seguín decided to comment upon the priests only when he learned that a new church authority for Texas was being proposed. With that, he leveled his criticism against both, who were well known for their strongly loyalist positions toward Mexico. In a written affidavit, after his praise of Garza's initial two years of ministry in San Antonio, Seguín wrote:

> Since the year 1824, when he returned from Mexico City where he had been sent by his parishioners as their Deputy at the General Congress, he began to dissociate himself almost entirely from the duties of his occupation. One is ashamed to see the filthy condition of the church since it was burned due to his carelessness (I say due to his carelessness, since the custody

of the church was left in charge of a very young careless and unruly boy). As regards his ecclesiastical and moral life, even though he has been somewhat circumspect about it, almost all the people of Bexar are aware that he has lived all the time he has been pastor with different lovers, from whom he has had as illegitimate children Concepción, José de Jesús, and Dorotea. He is an intelligent and literate person.[59]

The testimony about Garza's lovers and offspring was damning enough in the eyes of church officials and Anglo-Americans. But even more serious for Father Garza's personal reputation as a pastor was what Llebaría reported that Seguín said, but did not write, about Garza's "almost complete disassociation from the duties of his occupation":

> These two priests neglect and entirely abandon everything regarding the worship of God; they only say holy Mass at most once a week, never wanting to administer any sacrament, to such an extreme that, if there is someone dying who wants to be fortified with the last aids of our holy Religion, that person must be carried by others to the pastor's house—and that is not because of any impossibility on the part of the pastor, since he knows well how to take a spade and work the ground and make his house servants do the same.[60]

Seguín's accusations triggered Father Garza's downfall. The allegation about mistresses and children can be demonstrated to be true.[61] The charge of laxness in his material administration is also quite credible, based on the vicar's comments in 1825, the observations in 1839–40, and the extant record books.[62] But the accusation that Garza neglected and even abandoned his spiritual duties must be weighed cautiously. Seguín certainly exaggerated in writing that Garza "dissociate[d] himself almost entirely from the duties of his ministry." Either Seguín or Llebaría also was overly negative in alleging that Father Garza "only say[s] holy Mass at most once a week, never wanting to administer any sacrament." The fact that attendance at Mass was obligatory for all Catholics on Sundays and many holy days would not have allowed Garza to restrict himself to Mass "at most once a week." And the extant burial records demonstrate that Garza regularly continued to provide priestly ministry to his parishioners. Those records, which go up to the January 1840 funeral of Francisco Ruíz, carefully note in each entry that everyone who died received on their deathbed the sacraments appropriate to their condition. They also note any exceptions due to sudden death or other special circumstances.[63] It may well be that Father Garza, now in his old age, was far from zealous in the performance of his ministry, but it must be recognized that he took care of at least the bare essentials.

From this point on, the die was cast against Garza. The church authorities in the United States immediately arranged to remove the two Tejano priests in San Antonio from ministry as soon as a new church jurisdiction could be established there.[64] In the meantime, a priest from Kentucky who visited San Antonio in early 1840, having been forewarned about Garza, reported in a telling statement that "all Americans, whether Catholic or Protestant, and many Mexicans" were calling for Garza to be removed. Since the Kentucky priest probably did not speak Spanish, and even such Anglo allies as Seguín and Navarro did not speak English, the information about Tejano attitudes must have come from the anti-Garza Americans. The Kentucky priest did acknowledge, however, that Father Garza had his supporters—"a dozen families," he was told.[65]

When the new church administrator, Father Jean Marie Odin, arrived from the United States at the end of July 1840 to establish the new jurisdiction, he made short work of dismissing both Father Garza and Father Valdez. In his August correspondence Odin described San Fernando Church as still missing "half" of its roof ever since the 1828 fire, which allowed swallows and bats to foul the interior. The liturgical vestments were soiled and rotting. He also charged both priests (inappropriately, in Father Valdez's case) with a great spiritual neglect: there was no spiritual aid given to the dying, "not a word of instruction, no catechism, a mumbled Mass every Sunday, no visitation of the sick, two priests living in the midst of a multitude of women and children." Odin alleged that for five years—an intriguing date going back to the outbreak of the Texas Revolution—no one had gone to confession in San Antonio. The "mercenary" priests, he said, dealt only with what could profit them, charging such extortionate fees for baptisms, marriages, and funerals that the majority of the Tejanos were forced to go without the sacraments or sell their only horse in order to pay for their spouse's burial. "And yet," he concluded, "the monsters had a few partisans."[66]

Most of these accusations must have come from the small number of Protestant and Catholic Anglo-Americans in town. The charge of extortionate fees forcing the poor Tejanos to go without the sacraments has the familiar ring of the highly prejudiced stereotypes typical among Anglo-Americans, especially Protestants, at this time.[67] Several of these accusations are demonstrably based solely on hearsay and indeed can be proved false. Father Odin never witnessed Father Garza say Mass, since he and his companion received permission from Garza to celebrate the only Sunday Mass the day before he dismissed the priest. The parish burial records demonstrate that dying persons did receive all the appropriate rites offered by the church, including confession; that the usual fee collected for burial expenses was one peso rather than the twenty-five or more that the Americans told Odin; and that very poor persons were buried free of charge. There probably were alienated individuals, especially the few Anglo Catholics in San Antonio, who refrained from confessing to the loyalist and uncelibate Father Garza since the Texas Revolution, but this was not the case with the Tejanos he confessed on their deathbed.

For only two of his accusations did Father Odin claim that he was a personal witness. He was so disturbed to see women and children in Garza's household when he paid him a visit the day he arrived that Odin hardly exchanged a word with Garza before taking his leave. Odin reported that, on his next visit to Garza's residence four days later for the purpose of dismissing him, Father Garza told two women who came to ask him to go baptize a child in danger of death that he would do it when they came back with two pesos.[68]

The charges against Father Garza have continued to be magnified in their retelling up to the present, as often happens in such cases.[69] As Carlos Castañeda, the pioneer Mexican American historian, pointed out, Garza and Valdez were not even given an opportunity to defend themselves against the accusations that stemmed from prejudiced witnesses:

> The picture of their derelictions has been painted in darker and more somber colors perhaps than the facts warrant, and unfortunately reflect on the character of the Spanish and Mexican clergy of Texas as a whole, and on the pioneer Spanish and Mexican Catholics of Texas for tolerating such conditions. Guilty as they were,[70] the accused men were not given a hearing or an opportunity to present any kind of defense. Timon [in 1839] condemned them forthwith and solicited their removal and deprivation of Faculties on the evidence of prejudiced witnesses. When confronted with the order of Canonical deposition [in 1840], the two clerics meekly obeyed the Holy See.[71]

Castañeda's complaint that the very negative portrait of the two priests has been made to represent all the Mexican clergy is well taken. As already noted,[72] Texas history surveys and textbooks usually condemn Fathers Garza and Valdez as bad priests and indeed often as the only priests "in all of Texas" during the Mexican period. Those histories give no recognition to other Mexican priests who served in Texas during the Mexican period who were praised by their contemporaries, such as the Franciscans José Antonio Díaz de León and Miguel Muro and the diocesan priests Francisco Maynes (a Spaniard), José Trinidad García, and Ramón Ortiz.[73]

Contributing to the question of political bias in the accusations about Father Garza is the fact that three days after his removal as pastor he was arrested for corresponding with Mexican military leaders and sent to the town of Austin. Once there, however, he was promptly returned to San Antonio.[74] Father Odin reported that Garza's eight-day absence proved favorable. He alleged that during that brief time the local Tejano community had become so attached to their new young Spanish pastor whom Odin had brought with him that nothing would make them let go of him. This was no small thing, since the vast majority of the community were Catholic Tejanos.[75] Whereas Odin's first reports from San Antonio said that Father Garza had only "a few partisans," by the time the new church regime was breathing more comfortably eight months later Odin acknowledged that on his arrival the two priests "were still surrounded by a profound respect" among the Tejanos because of their priesthood. "Judge what had to be my awkward situation in such a critical position," he wrote, since in addition the two men "had been raised in the area and were related to many families of the place."[76]

As Timothy Matovina has observed, "The lack of evidence that Tejanos protested against Odin's removal of their two priests is striking." One should note, however, that at this time the Seguín faction was in the political ascendency in San Antonio.[77] A few days after Father Garza's return to San Antonio the Anglo mayor, who bridged the Tejano and American communities, became upset with Odin when the latter ended a local practice popular with the Anglo sector, the ringing of the San Fernando Church bells for all funerals including those of Protestants, asserting that it was contrary to church policy. In reaction the mayor initiated a petition calling for Father Garza's reinstatement as pastor, but Juan Seguín managed to halt its circulation among the Tejano population.[78] Another factor was that Father Garza was by then almost sixty-five years of age, a very old priest for those times, whereas Odin and his Spanish colleague were much younger. Without discounting political factors, the Tejano population may indeed have opted for a young zealous Spaniard in place of their old lackadaisical native pastor.

Ten months later Father Garza was still in San Antonio carrying on a secret correspondence with the military officers at the Rio Grande presidio.[79] He probably remained in town until its two-day occupation by General Rafael Vásquez in March 1842. Garza attempted to have General Vásquez install him again as the San Antonio pastor. When instead the Mexican troops withdrew to the Rio Grande, Garza probably departed with them.[80]

In September of that year, General Adrián Woll commanded another Mexican military incursion into San Antonio. This time the forward scouts for the Mexican forces were none other than fifty-two San Antonians commanded by Juan Seguín. Viewed as a traitor by Anglo-Texans for sitting out the Vásquez raid, Seguín had been forced to flee to Mexico.[81] Father Garza also accompanied the troops of General Woll as not only the claimant to the pastorate of San Antonio but also the chaplain of the Rio Grande company. Thus Seguín and Father Garza now found themselves in the same Mexican nationalist cause, albeit perhaps not with the same fervor. When Woll withdrew from San Antonio a week later, Father Garza left with him, but he was captured in the rear of the column by the pursuing Texan vanguard. He managed to escape when Woll came to the rescue.[82]

The still hopeful Father Garza remained as the aged pastor and chaplain of Guerrero (the former Presidio del Río Grande) in Coahuila "while things take a different aspect," as he wrote his compadre in San Antonio in 1844.[83] That different aspect turned out to be an eternal one; sometime before December of the following year, he died in Guerrero, his reputation ruined for posterity.[84] It was in those very months that the U.S. Congress approved the annexation of Texas, sealing its loss to the Mexican republic. Fittingly, both Father Garza and any hopes for the reclaiming of Mexican sovereignty over Texas expired at the same time.

Notes

1. San Fernando Baptisms 1761–1793, 208, Catholic Archives of San Antonio [CASA]; David J. Weber, *The Spanish Frontier in North America* (New Haven, Conn.: Yale University Press, 1992), 211.

2. For the Garza-Menchaca family history, I am indebted to the late Gloria Cadena of San Antonio for her genealogical charts. Two of

Refugio's siblings, Gertrudis de la Candelaria and María de Jesús Dolores, bore Marian names (the Virgin of Candelaria, Mary of Jesus, and Our Lady of Sorrows or Dolores), and two others had the names of the most famous Jesuit saints, Ignacio and Francisco Xavier.

3. José Salinas will, 16 May 1787, Wills and Estates 103, Bexar County Archives, San Antonio; for the 1749 birth at the Presidio del Rio Grande of her son José Antonio de la Garza, during whose gestation Margarita's first husband died, see San Fernando marriage investigations, 123–29 (8 June 1773), CASA; for the confirmation of Margarita's young daughter Antonia at San Fernando Church in 1759, providing an end date for the family's move to San Antonio, see San Fernando Combined Register 1731–1760, 242–55, confirmation no. 235, CASA. José Salinas and Margarita Menchaca had their third child in 1752; Salinas bought a lot and stone house in San Antonio in 1761. Frederick C. Chabot, *With the Makers of San Antonio* (privately published, 1937), 194.

4. For the Ramón, Urrutia, and Menchaca family relationships and careers, see Jack Jackson, *Los Mesteños: Spanish Ranching in Texas, 1721–1821* (College Station: Texas A&M University, 1986), 56–57, 63–65.

5. Researchers have been unsuccessful in ascertaining Refugio's maternal lineage through his mother Josefa Flores; there were several women by that name in San Antonio during those years.

6. Burials 1761–1801, San Fernando Parish and Presidio of San Antonio de Béxar, 29 June 1789, CASA. The burial entry states that he made an "extrajudicial" last testament.

7. Only his younger siblings are listed in his mother's household in the Béxar censuses from 1790 through 1797. *Residents of Texas, 1782–1836* (San Antonio: University of Texas Institute of Texan Cultures, 1984), 1:66, 76, 129, 200, 245, 275; *The New Handbook of Texas*, s.v. "Garza, José Refugio Guadalupe de la"; L. Randall Rogers, *Two Particular Friends of Stephen F. Austin* (Waco, Tex.: Texian Press, 1990), 75, surmised that Refugio spent much of his youth with relatives at the Presidio del Río Grande in Coahuila but provided no evidence for this.

8. Libro de Gobierno Arzobispado Año de 1792, 11 verso, Archivo Histórico de la Arquidiócesis de Monterrey.

9. Rogers, *Two Particular Friends*, 86, asserts that Garza served as the military chaplain at the presidio of San Juan Bautista on the Rio Grande from 1808 to about 1816. But that presidio's extant church records from 1776 through 1828 have no entries by Garza (photostats in the possession of Gloria Cadena, San Antonio).

10. Her burial entry stated that she had not made a will since she was poor (San Fernando Burials, 5 May 1809, CASA). Although it gave her age as fifty-three, much earlier censuses in 1790 and 1792 placed her birth in 1752 (*Residents of Texas*, 1:66, 76). There is a will in her name, however, dated 3 May 1809, which described her very meager possessions (Wills and Estates 42, Bexar County Archives).

11. On 2 November 1819 he was named *cura propio* of Béxar by the diocesan authorities (Libro de Gobierno Arzobispado 1818–1832, 24 verso, Archivo Histórico de la Arquidiócesis de Monterrey). Although he arrived in San Antonio before 24 January (Governor to Refugio Garza, 24 January 1820, Bexar Archives microfilm [BA], roll 63, 795–96), he did not take possession of the parish until 26 January (Governor to the mission alcaldes, BA). The following day he received the parish records (San Fernando Baptisms 1812–1825, CASA). This latter account is quoted in P. F. Parisot and C. J. Smith, O.M.I., *History of the Catholic Church in the Diocese of San Antonio, Texas, 1685–1897* (San Antonio, Tex.: Carrico and Bowen, 1897), 53.

12. Garza's entries in the Alamo Company baptism register, CASA, are from 9 February 1820 to 13 January 1822. A loose leaf inserted in the San Fernando baptism register at the place where Garza began his parish entries in 1820 (see previous note) records an 8 February 1820 baptism "hayandose vacante de Ministro capellan la compañia del Alamo," followed by three other baptisms in February and March 1820; the rest of the reverse side is left blank. These entries are other than those written into the San Fernando and Alamo Company registers. The Alamo Company marriage and burial registers are not extant, with the exception of a few burial entries in 1825. There are no extant chaplaincy registers for the Béxar Company in the Catholic Archives of San Antonio. Those records were probably taken with them by the military when they withdrew from Texas after the Texas Revolution. Only a careful reading of scattered entries in the other church registers reveals that they existed.

13. Marion A. Habig, *The Alamo Chain of Missions: A History of San Antonio's Five Old Missions*, rev. ed. (Chicago: Franciscan Herald Press, 1976), 103–8.

14. Robert E. Wright, O.M.I., "The Hispanic Church in Texas under Spain and Mexico," *U.S. Catholic Historian* 20 (Fall 2002): 26–27. In the El Paso district a single Franciscan cared for both Socorro and Ysleta.

15. Juan Seguín affidavit (my translation), 5 January 1839, enclosed in FitzGerald to Blanc, 17[?] February 1839, New Orleans Archdioc-

esan Archives. Translated in Jesús F. de la Teja, ed., *A Revolu-
tion Remembered: The Memoirs and Selected Correspondence of Juan N.
Seguín* (Austin: State House Press, 1991), 172. This contradicts
Carlos E. Castañeda's very negative assessment of Garza's ministry
at this time, for which Castañeda cited no supportive evidence,
evidently relying upon observations about Garza's later ministry.
Carlos E. Castañeda, *Our Catholic Heritage in Texas* (Austin: Von
Boeckmann-Jones, 1936–58), 6:307.

16.   Refugio de la Garza to Antonio Martínez, 27 April 1821, BA.

17.   Antonio Martínez to Cavildo en Sede Vacante, 30 January 1822, BA;
Refugio de la Garza to Ayuntamiento de San Fernando de Béxar,
27 March 1822, BA, announcing his 22 March arrival in Mexico City.

18.   Eugene C. Barker, *The Life of Stephen F. Austin* (Nashville, Tenn.:
Cokesbury Press, 1925), 69, 76.

19.   Refugio de la Garza to Ayuntamiento of San Fernando de Béjar,
27 March 1822, and Ayuntamiento to Refugio de la Garza, 1 [May?]
1822, BA.

20.   Refugio de la Garza to Ayuntamiento of San Fernando de Béjar,
30 April 1822, BA.

21.   Castañeda, 6:318–21; Refugio de la Garza to Ayuntamiento of Béjar,
8 August 1822, BA; Diputación Provincial of Texas to Jefe Político,
22 October 1823, BA.

22.   "Journal of Stephen F. Austin on His First Trip to Texas, 1821," *Quarterly of the Texas State Historical Association* 7 (April 1904): 298.

23.   Barker, *Life of Stephen F. Austin*, 63, 71, 72–76. Barker observed that
Austin must have been "in close relation with" the committee members (71).

24.   Andrés Reséndez, *Changing National Identities at the Frontier: Texas
and New Mexico, 1800–1850* (New York: Cambridge University Press,
2004), 27; Barker, *Life of Stephen F. Austin*, 205, noted the 29 September 1823 decree.

25.   De la Teja, *Revolution Remembered*, 108; Barker, *Life of Stephen F. Austin*, 205–6; Refugio de la Garza to Ayuntamiento of San Fernando de
Béjar, 30 April 1822, and 8 August 1822, BA.

26.   Ironically, although in his wider survey David J. Weber, following
Castañeda (see note 21 above), did note Garza's work in the congress that brought about the secularization of the missions, Weber
charged the priest with "abandoning" his parishioners in order to be
their deputy in Mexico City. Weber, *The Mexican Frontier, 1821–1846:
The American Southwest under Mexico* (Albuquerque: University of
New Mexico Press, 1982), 54. In reality, the Texas governor arranged

for the local Franciscan and then the newly arrived military chaplain Father Maynes to take care of the San Antonio parish in Garza's absence.

27. [Trespalacios] to López, 27 November 1822, BA.

28. For Garza's return, see the San Fernando Parish registers. For Seguín's arrival at the congress in December 1823, see Barker, *Life of Stephen F. Austin*, 135.

29. Jefe Político to José León Lobo Guerrero, 5 February 1824, and José María Sambrano to Refugio de la Garza, 1 June 1824, BA; Parisot and Smith, *History of the Catholic Church*, 55.

30. For Maynes's continuation as chaplain of the Béxar Company, see "Libro de Govierno y Vicita" 1825, bound into the back of the Combined Mission Register, 4 verso, CASA, where he is not identified by name (the folio in which he was identified, 6–6 verso, is missing from the document). For his continuation as Alamo Company chaplain also, see Alamo Company Baptisms for the years 1824–25. The continued presence of Father Maynes in San Antonio as chaplain of the Béxar Company until his death in 1834 (see below) has been ignored by Texas historians. This is true even for those whose studies focused specifically on the Catholic Church in San Antonio or Texas during the Mexican period (Fitzmorris, Castañeda, and Matovina). This is due largely to the fact that the church registers of the Béxar Company were not extant in San Antonio.

31. Charles A. Bacarisse, "The Union of Coahuila and Texas," *Southwestern Historical Quarterly* 61 (January 1958): 347–49. Andrés Tijerina, *Tejanos and Texas under the Mexican Flag, 1821–1836* (College Station: Texas A&M University Press, 1994), 99–101, reports the same incident but presents a significantly different outcome and makes no mention of Father Garza.

32. Barker, *Life of Stephen F. Austin*, 412.

33. Seguín affidavit, 5 January 1839 (my translation).

34. "Libro de Govierno y Vicita" 1825.

35. Castañeda, *Our Catholic Heritage*, 6:316. Jesús F. de la Teja and John Wheat, "Bexar: Profile of a Tejano Community, 1820–1832," *Southwestern Historical Quarterly* 89 (July 1985): 26, relied upon Castañeda in writing of Garza's "carelessness and negligence in the running of the parish" as manifested by the vicar's record.

36. "Libro de Govierno y Vicita" 1825 and the sacramental registers of San Fernando Church, CASA.

37. José Dário Sambrano to Antonio Martínez, San Fernando de Béxar, 28 January 1820, BA.

38. Antonio Martínez to Párroco, 26 July 1820, BA.

39. Félix D. Almaráz Jr., *The San Antonio Missions and Their System of Land Tenure* (Austin: University of Texas Press, 1989), 21.

40. *Residents of Texas*, 2:257, 302, 334. Most of the laborers noted were probably on his ranch, not in his town household.

41. Carlos Eduardo Castañeda, *A Report on the Spanish Archives in San Antonio, Texas* (San Antonio, Tex.: Yanaguana Society, 1937), 72, 73. In September 1836, Garza sold a *suerte* (farming tract of approximately 50 acres in the San Antonio area) of land to S. Rhode Fisher for $300 cash and the balance by note (76). A league of land, as the Anglo-Americans came to call the *sitio*, was a unit of area equivalent to one square league, or approximately 4,428 acres.

42. I. J. Cox, "Educational Efforts in San Fernando de Béxar," *Quarterly of the Texas State Historical Association* 6 (July 1902): 37, 39, 43–45, 52–63; summarized in Timothy M. Matovina, *Tejano Religion and Ethnicity: San Antonio, 1821–1860* (Austin: University of Texas, 1995), 17–18.

43. Tijerina, *Tejanos and Texas*, 48–50. In 1834 there was a serious outbreak of cholera; there were so many deaths that the church bells were ordered not to toll, so as not to add to the gloom. Matovina, *Tejano Religion and Ethnicity*, 20; Castañeda, *Our Catholic Heritage*, 6:355.

44. Seguín affidavit.

45. Castañeda, *Our Catholic Heritage*, 6:351–53.

46. For example, a will in late 1832 offered 40 pesos toward the repair of one of the ceiling vaults if the testator would be permitted to be buried within the church—something generally prohibited for several decades. Anastacia Sambrano will, 26 November 1832, Wills and Estates 123, Bexar County Spanish Archives.

47. Robert A. Calvert, Arnoldo De León, and Gregg Cantrell, *The History of Texas*, 3d ed. (Wheeling, Ill.: Harlan Davidson, 2002), 74. For recent similar statements, see Randolph B. Campbell, *Gone to Texas: A History of the Lone Star State* (New York: Oxford University Press, 2003), 114; *New Handbook of Texas*, s.v. "Religion" and s.v. "Mexican Americans and Religion"; Arnoldo De León, *Mexican Americans in Texas: A Brief History*, 2d ed. (Wheeling, Ill.: Harlan Davidson, 1999), 26–27. Even Carlos Castañeda, the great pioneer Mexican-American historian and devout Catholic, titled his chapter (*Our Catholic Heritage*, 6:307–55) on the church in Texas during the Mexican period "The Agony of the Church in Texas"—in spite of the fact that the chapter itself described a much wider and active church presence before an alleged collapse in 1834. Three decades later, David J.

Weber laid out a similar thesis, likewise leading to a "collapse" of the church throughout the northern frontier, in his *The Mexican Frontier, 1821–1846: The American Southwest under Mexico* (Albuquerque: University of New Mexico Press, 1982), 69–82.

48. Wright, "Hispanic Church in Texas," 25–27.

49. C. E. Castañeda, trans., "Statistical Report on Texas, by Juan N. Almonte, 1835," *Southwestern Historical Quarterly* 28 (January 1925): 193. Almonte noted the recently deceased "vicar" (assistant pastor) in the Béxar department, without giving his name; Almonte erred in identifying him as a vicar rather than a military chaplain. Almonte also erred in stating that Maynes's death left only one priest in the department of Bexar; there were still three, plus another priest at Nacogdoches. Jack Jackson manifests the continued unawareness of Father Maynes's long presence in his puzzlement over who this "vicar" may have been, in Jack Jackson, ed., and John Wheat, trans., *Almonte's Texas: Juan N. Almonte's 1834 Inspection, Secret Report & Role in the 1836 Campaign* (Austin: Texas State Historical Association, 2003), 241 n.27.

50. Parisot and Smith, *History of the Church*, 55–59; Castañeda, *Our Catholic Heritage*, 6:336–40. Parisot, Castañeda, and Jackson and Wheat, *Almonte's Texas* (242 n.28) conclude that Father Díaz was murdered. I have since come across some contemporary correspondence on this matter previously unknown to historians. It reveals that the diocesan authorities in Saltillo were incensed that they first received official notice of Father Díaz's death, with no information as to its cause, in a request for a new priest sent by the Anglo jefe político in Nacogdoches supposedly on 24 February 1835, by ordinary (not express) mail, postpaid, which did not arrive in Saltillo until 3 October. By then the church authorities had already received rumors of what had happened. They immediately notified the Franciscan leader in Zacatecas and received a response from him within two weeks. The Franciscan said that he too had received rumors of the incident "painted in the ugliest colors" and, seeking information from trusted sources, had learned in a letter written 24 February (an intriguing coincidence of dates) that Father Díaz had been assassinated. He added that he had previously received an anonymous warning that the "Protestant priests" in the new colonies were plotting against the lives of the Catholic priests, who should be withdrawn. He had also been informed that "neither the Authority of the town of Liberty, where [the Father] was requested to perform a marriage, and even less the one in Nacogdoches, made

any effort to discover the truth of what happened. They merely accepted the word of a foreigner who, days afterwards, gave the notice that the Father had killed himself" (my translation). The Franciscan painfully admitted that he had suspected that the warning to withdraw the priests was a ruse to have them abandon the region, leaving only the Protestant ministers, and therefore had not acted upon it. "Documentos de lo acontecido en Nacogdoches," annexed to *Representación que dirige . . . al Exmo. Sr. Presidente . . . sobre la anulación de las leyes de diezmos y demas contrarias a las libertades de la Iglesia Mexicana, el Ilustrísimo Señor Don Fray Jose Maria de Jesus Belaunzaran, Obispo de Monterey* (México: Imprenta de Luis Abadiano y Valdes, 1836).

51. Wright, "Hispanic Church in Texas," 30.

52. Castañeda, *Our Catholic Heritage*, 7:24–25, 45, 73; *Diamond Jubilee, 1847–1922, of the Diocese of Galveston and St. Mary's Cathedral* (privately printed, 1922), 36, 44, 54; Frederick Law Olmsted, *A Journey through Texas; or, a Saddle-Trip on the Southwestern Frontier* (New York: Dix, Edwards, 1857), 262–63; Kathryn Stoner O'Connor, *The Presidio La Bahia del Espiritu Santo de Zuniga, 1721 to 1846* (Austin: Von Boeckmann-Jones, 1966), 234–35; Joseph Milton Nance, *After San Jacinto: The Texas-Mexican Frontier, 1836–1841* (Austin: University of Texas Press, 1963), 50–52, 56–67.

53. Wright, "Hispanic Church in Texas," 31–32.

54. Rena Maverick Green, ed., *Samuel Maverick, Texan: 1803–1870* (San Antonio, Tex.: privately printed, 1952), 33–34.

55. Castañeda, *Our Catholic Heritage*, 6:292.

56. Ibid., 7:6–26.

57. Llebaría to Etienne, 11 January 1839 (my translation), Catholic Archives of Texas [CAT].

58. *New Handbook of Texas*, s.v. "Valdez, José Antonio" and "Seguín, Juan Nepomuceno."

59. Seguín affidavit (my translation).

60. Llebaría to Etienne, 11 January 1839 (my translation). Whether Seguín actually said it or not, Llebaría's report of this conversation accused both Tejano priests equally of gross pastoral neglect. But the final criticisms were only about "the pastor," presumably Father Garza since he was the only priest still functioning as pastor. Seguín had to have been the one who told the visiting priests that Father Valdez lived five miles outside San Antonio. So it was probably Llebaría himself who inappropriately branded Father Valdez with the same pastoral neglect in San Antonio as that charged against Father

Garza. The historical record argues that Valdez was a conscientious pastor wherever he ministered.

61. For children named Concepción, José de Jesús, and Catarina (not Dorotea) in Father Garza's own household at various times between 1826 and 1832, see *Residents of Texas*, 2:208, 257, 302, 334. This alone would not prove they were his children, but the way they were listed indicated that he was at least their legal guardian. More conclusive is the 28 December 1845 marriage of Francisco Lazarín and Concepción de la Garza, recorded as the daughter of Don Refugio de la Garza, deceased, and Ramona Martínez, in San Fernando Marriages, CASA. I thank Eileen Treviño Villarreal for this last reference and other information on Father Garza's descendants. See also the dismissal of an alleged mistress by Garza in 1821 after the governor asked church authorities to investigate (Gov. Martínez to José Antonio de la Peña, and Peña's reply to the governor, 22 November 1821, BA). For an accusation in 1826, denied by Garza, of scandalous relations with a woman in his household, see Refugio de la Garza to Juan José Sambrano, 12 June 1826, BA.

62. For Father Odin's observations in 1840, see below. The San Fernando Parish baptism and marriage registers do not have entries after 1835 and 1833, respectively. Recognizing that priests or their sacristans often initially kept sacramental records on loose leaves or in small coverless notebooks and only transferred them into the permanent registers weeks or months later, letting five or even seven years pass without making those permanent entries was certainly a serious fault in proper administration.

63. San Fernando Burials, 1817–1860, CASA.

64. Timon to Bishop Blanc, [January 1839], CAT; Bishop Blanc to Bishop Belaunzarán, 15 January 1839, and Bishop Belaunzarán to Bishop Blanc, 21 February 1839, New Orleans Papers, University of Notre Dame Archives, photostats in New Orleans Archdiocesan Archives. For the same conclusion as to Garza's fate being sealed among foreign church authorities who "already believed the worst" from the time of this interview with Seguín, see James Talmadge Moore, *Through Fire and Flood: The Catholic Church in Frontier Texas, 1836–1900* (College Station: Texas A&M University Press, 1992), 21–22 (quotation), 39–41.

65. Haydon to Bishop Blanc, 13 March 1840, CAT.

66. Odin to Bishop Blanc, 24 August 1840 (my translation), CAT. See also Odin to Bishop Rosati, 27 August 1840, and Odin to Etienne, 28 August 1840, CAT. The second and third letters were mostly

copies of the first, with some variations. Although Odin stated in these letters that both priests were responsible for the pastoral care of San Antonio, it is significant that the letters described only the dismissal of Father Garza from his pastorate. Even more to the point, in Odin's earlier letter from San Antonio right after the priests' dismissal, as reported by Timon in a November letter to the Roman authorities (my research has not yet found Odin's original letter), Odin described only Father Garza as serving the parish and pastorally negligent, while referring to Father Valdez solely as "another scandalous priest of the vicinity" (my translation): Timon to Cardinal Fransoni, 27 November 1840, CAT. Odin himself wrote a little later in the same manner to Rome, stating that "I also found at San Antonio the old pastor of Goliad" (my translation). Odin to Cardinal Fransoni, 15 December 1840, CAT. These two letters of Odin correspond much more closely to Seguín's written affidavit of January 1839.

67. Weber, *Mexican Frontier*, 76; Angélico Chávez, "Doña Tules, Her Fame and Her Funeral," *El Palacio* 57 (August 1950): 232–34.

68. Odin to Bishop Blanc, 24 August 1840, CAT. Odin was told that funeral fees were from $25 to $150, whereas the fee for almost all the burials in 1839 was one peso (dollar). Three burials for which more elaborate ceremonies were requested were charged one more peso. The funeral of Lieutenant Colonel Francisco Ruiz on 20 January 1840 was a great exception, with a fee of 10 pesos for being buried inside the church, a forbidden practice, with special ceremonies. One person in 1839 was buried with no fee (San Fernando Burial Register, 1817–1860). The fact that there were women and children in the priests' households, something deemed improper among the U.S. Catholic clergy, did not of itself indicate improper sexual relations on their part. Often the Mexican clergy on the northern frontier took in widowed female relatives and their children or unrelated orphans, something viewed as quite normal by Mexican society at that time (Moore, *Through Fire and Flood*, 41). Odin himself acknowledged that this was the case in San Antonio (Odin to Bishop Blanc, 24 August 1840). This practice, in fact, is what provided a cover of legitimacy for those who had mistresses or their own offspring living with them.

69. Parisot and Smith, *History of the Catholic Church*, 59, wrote that Garza and Valdez "utterly neglected the care of their flock." Castañeda, *Our Catholic Heritage*, 7:307, wrote that "both sadly neglected their spiritual duties—saying Mass only occasionally, never preaching, and

seldom, if ever, visiting the sick or comforting the afflicted." This is repeated by De la Teja and Wheat, "Béxar," 26.

70. For the reasons already given, I would strongly qualify this judgment.

71. Castañeda, *Our Catholic Heritage*, 7:26.

72. See note 47.

73. For Díaz and Muro, see Castañeda, *Our Catholic Heritage*, 6:331, 334–36, Jackson and Wheat, *Almonte's Texas*, 152, and "Documentos de lo acontecido en Nacogdoches." For Maynes, see William Stuart Red, *The Texas Colonists and Religion, 1821–1836* (Austin: E. L. Shettles, 1924), 33, and "Libro de Govierno y Vicita" 1825, 5 verso. For García in Laredo, see Robert E. Wright, O.M.I., "Popular and Official Religiosity: A Theoretical Analysis and a Case Study of Laredo-Nuevo Laredo, 1755–1857" (Ph.D. diss., Graduate Theological Union, Berkeley, 1992), 518–30, 573–81. For Ortiz in El Paso, see Mary D. Taylor, "Cura de la Frontera, Ramón Ortiz," *U.S. Catholic Historian* 9 (Winter/Spring 1990): 67–85. And even for praise of Father Valdez, his ministry hampered by his poor health, see Sister Mary Angela Fitzmorris, "Four Decades of Catholicism in Texas, 1820–1860" (Ph.D. diss., Catholic University of America, 1926), 25.

74. Joseph Milton Nance, *Attack and Counter-Attack: The Texas-Mexican Frontier, 1842* (Austin: University of Texas Press, 1964), 10 n.9.

75. Odin to Bishop Blanc, 24 August 1840, CAT.

76. Odin to Etienne, 11 April 1841 (my translation), CAT. On his initial trip to San Antonio, Odin had written that his non-Mexican fellow travelers told him that "people have no confidence in them [Garza and Valdez], still the poor Mexicans like them, though I hope there will be no great difficulty in removing them" (Odin to Timon, 14 July 1840, CAT). Four months past the priests' dismissal, he admitted that indeed Father Garza "enjoyed some credit among the Mexicans, who have an extreme veneration for the priesthood" (Odin to Cardinal Fransoni, 15 December 1840, CAT).

77. Matovina, *Tejano Religion and Ethnicity*, 42. Matovina, ibid., 43, and Moore, *Through Fire and Flood*, 40, make the same suggestion about political motives.

78. Seguín was the senator noted by Odin as siding with him in this incident (Odin to Bishop Blanc, 24 August 1840, CAT); he was probably the "one of the most respectable" Tejanos who halted the petition to reinstate Father Garza (Odin to Bishop Rosati, 27 August 1840). For Seguín as senator for Bexar County until October 1840, see De la Teja, *Revolution Remembered*, 40, 176. Ironically, earlier that same year Father Garza had joined Seguín's father and Cornelius

Van Ness in posting bond for Seguín in a court action against him by the city. 27 March 1840 bond, Juan N. Seguin Papers, Daughters of the Republic of Texas Research Library.

79. Garza note enclosed in Mariano Arista, Monterrey, to Ministro de la Guerra, 20 June 1841, typescript in H. E. Bolton Papers, Part 1, no. 471, Bancroft Library. See also Green, *Samuel Maverick*, 151.

80. Matovina, *Tejano Religion and Ethnicity*, 42, reports the attempt to be reinstalled as pastor. In *Texas Reports, Volumes 12–16 (1854–1856)*, reel 3, 152, the Garza heirs said that he moved to Mexico at the time of "the troubles of 1842." Interestingly, a court summons for early March had been issued a few weeks prior to the Vásquez raid for Father Garza "if to be found in your county." Anderson Hutchinson summons for Refugio de la Garza, 12 February 1842, Smith Papers, Daughters of the Republic of Texas Research Library, San Antonio.

81. Joseph Milton Nance, trans. and ed., "Brigadier General Adrian Woll's Report of His Expedition into Texas in 1842," *Southwestern Historical Quarterly* 58 (April 1955): 525, 527; Nance, *Attack and Counter-Attack*, 12, 37–38, 52–54.

82. Nance, "Woll's Report," 548–49. John Henry Brown, a young participant in the battle of the Salado against Woll, wrote fifty years later that Woll reinstalled Father Garza as pastor of San Antonio. Brown, *History of Texas, from 1685 to 1892* (St. Louis: L. E. Daniell, 1893), 2:227, 230. Woll may indeed have done this, knowing full well it was only a momentary gesture of recognition to the loyalist priest, since Woll never intended to occupy the town much longer than a week (523, 542). Matovina, *Tejano Religion and Ethnicity*, 117 n.51, noted that Father Calvo, the priest who was the San Antonio pastor since 1840, performed baptisms one day during Woll's occupation of the town. This does not necessarily contradict Brown's statement; Calvo could have easily performed the baptisms privately and kept the parish registers during the brief occupation.

83. Refugio de la Garza to Domingo Bustillo, 21 September 1844, Bustillo Collection, Daughters of the Republic of Texas Library, San Antonio.

84. The 28 December 1845 marriage of his daughter recorded him as deceased (San Fernando Marriages, CASA). When asked to testify in 1857, one of the witnesses to Father Garza's misplaced will, said to have been made in Guerrero and later taken to Monterrey with the rest of the Guerrero military company's records, said that Garza died in 1844 or 1845, naming as his heirs "Jesús Garza, Jesús' brother Ygnacio Flores, and the girls Catarina and Guadalupe Garza." *Book of Wills, 1866–1883*, 142–144, Bexar County Spanish Archives.

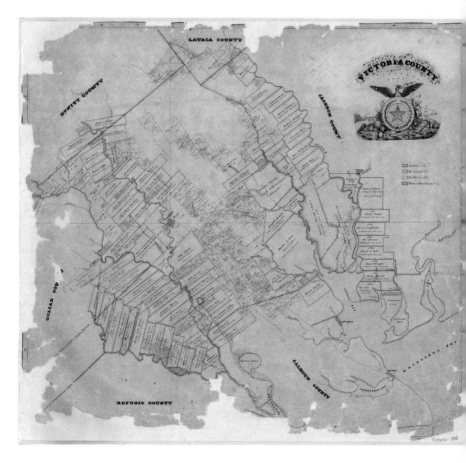

Earliest surviving Victoria County survey map. This 1858 map illustrates the work done by Fernando De León as land commissioner for his father's colony. For his work, Fernando carved out a five-league ranch on the west bank of Garcitas Creek above grants to his brother and father.

Courtesy Map #4115, Texas General Land Office, Austin.

FERNANDO DE LEÓN

LEADERSHIP LOST

Carolina Castillo Crimm

ON 21 APRIL 1836 FERNANDO DE LEÓN, son of the founder of the empresario colony of Victoria, lost his position as land commissioner. With the end of Mexican rule in Texas, the thirty-eight-year-old no longer held in his hands the fates of hundreds of new Anglo-American settlers. He could no longer determine who would receive land or where it would be located. His leadership in the new Republic of Texas and control over land, the single most important source of power, prestige, and wealth in Texas, was gone almost overnight.[1]

Leadership can take many forms, but in Fernando's case the loss of the position as land commissioner had left him with no leadership at all. Fernando De León had not become the leader or patriarch of the De León family, which he should have been as the eldest son. His mother, Doña Patricia de la Garza De León, retained the power within the family and saw to it that everyone was cared for, something Fernando may have failed to do. Unlike his brother-in-law Plácido Benavides, Fernando had never been a military leader, although he did support Texian ideals and, had he not been jailed, might have fought with Benavides and the Texians. Unlike his brother-in-law José María Jesús Carvajal, Fernando had not been involved in state politics, although he provided Carvajal with his support while Carvajal was serving in the state congress in Monclova. Unlike his wife, Luz Escalera, Fernando appears to have paid little attention to serving as a religious leader by providing godparenthood protection to the Tejano community. Unlike José Antonio Navarro, who joined the new Texian settlers in their congress and provided a voice for the Tejanos in the Anglo political world, Fernando left Texas and did not return until after statehood. When he returned, however, he used the land he had retained to pay for lawyers to fight lengthy court battles for the one thing he knew and understood—the land. Over the years he regained over 50,000 acres, more land than anyone in the Victoria area.

What had happened to Fernando? Perhaps his years in New Orleans had changed him, or perhaps it was his desire to be accepted within the Anglo community. Had he adopted the Anglo view of the land as a source of private wealth and prestige rather than a family heritage? The English laws of primogeniture demanded that the land be handed down to the eldest son intact, even if the rest of the family was left without any inheritance. For the Tejanos, the land was to be shared with others, or passed on to heirs, or used to help the Tejano community. Where did Fernando's leadership lie?

The Spanish and Anglo cultures that came into contact in Texas had radically different views of land ownership. To the Spanish, land had always belonged to the king and was granted to his subjects that they might bring prosperity to themselves and to their monarch. On the frontier one's social standing determined the amount of land one received, but everyone received land. Once Mexico had achieved its independence from Spain, the idea of owning land merely to *señorear* (show off) without producing taxable goods had disappeared. Gone also was the king's fifth, a 20 percent tax on the goods produced. Land was given to those who would settle on it and provide goods that could be traded throughout the new country. The only cost was the survey and the paperwork, a concept foreign to the Anglo-Americans.

For the Anglo-Americans land was the source of wealth, power, influence, and social standing. Land ownership brought with it greed, violent land wars, and exclusion of those who desired to share the sources of water. In the United States all land belonged to the government and was sold for revenue. In 1819, in order to offset the effects of the recession then gripping the country, the federal government lowered the price of western lands to $1.25 an acre and sold the land in 640-acre tracts. Land speculators quickly bought up the land, divided it, and sold it to small farmers at a huge profit for as much as $10 an acre. Few could afford more than ten or twenty acres, and only the land speculators or the very wealthy, such as the southern plantation owners, could afford the hundreds of acres necessary to make a profit from cotton or other commodities.

It was into this world of conflicting views that Fernando De León was born in 1798 in northeastern New Spain. The Napoleonic Wars were transforming Europe and creating political and economic crises in the Americas. The weak and vulnerable Charles IV of Spain had abdicated his crown to Napoleon, who was bent on reestablishing the greatness of France's worldwide power. Part of the new empire planned by Napoleon included regaining the great landmass of Louisiana, which he did in 1800. His crack troops, sent to Haiti to reestablish French dominion, however, died by the thousands from yellow fever prevalent on the island. Without his troops and short of cash to fund his European wars, Napoleon sold Louisiana to the United States three years later. Texas, which the United States claimed as part of the Louisiana Purchase, became a critical pawn in the game of international politics. It was in Texas that Fernando grew to manhood.

Fernando's parents had been part of the settlements made by José de Escandón, the Spanish colonizer, in the expanding northeastern provinces of the Spanish empire where land became the physical evidence of one's wealth and power. His father, Martín De León, had been a muleteer and militia captain of Burgos, a town on the edge of the foothills of the Eastern Sierra Madre, and his mother, Patricia de la Garza, had come from a well-placed family in the port city of Soto la Marina. As a retired militia captain, De León received a grant of land to establish a ranch on the frontier. Thus, the couple became part of Spain's attempt to help settle the frontier and keep the French out of New Spain. Combining his land grant with Patricia's dowry of more than 9,000 pesos, Martín established the Santa Margarita ranch on the Nueces River in the growing province of Texas.[2]

In 1801 Martín and Patricia brought their small family to Texas, including three-year-old Fernando and his younger sister María Candelaria. While Patricia waited with the children at the small settlement of La Bahía del Espíritu Santo, Martín and his ranch hands began construction of the ranch. La Bahía, with its massive stone fort on the ridge overlooking the San Antonio River and the mission on the far side, had grown to include a small community of almost two thousand citizens whose homes of adobe, wattle and daub, and even a few of stone huddled close to the walls of the fort for protection from the occasional raids by Norteños. For the two years that the family waited at La Bahía, Fernando made friends with the children of the other soldiers and ranch owners who came and went from the distant ranches, friendships that would endure for the next fifty years. Patricia also added two more children to the family, José Silvestre (born in 1802) and a sister, María Guadalupe (born in 1804).[3]

Fernando learned the importance of land when the family moved to their ranch on the Nueces River, two days' ride south of La Bahía. On this land the family raised and sold cattle, mules, and horses at the markets in San Antonio or distant Saltillo. As a young boy, Fernando learned from the family *vaqueros* (cowboys) how to ride horses, work cattle, and raise mules. During the trips to San Antonio, the family traded the produce of their ranch—cattle hides, lard, soap, and mules and horses—for the many imported and expensive goods from Saltillo or Mexico City.

In addition to wealth from the land, the De León family made important religious and social connections within the Tejano community of South Texas through their growing number of children. When Patricia gave birth to two more sons, José Félix (1806) and Agapito (1808), and two more daughters, María de Jesús (later known as Chucha, 1810) and Refugia (1812), the family had to find godparents for the children from among the local ranch families. Godparenthood created a powerful bond with other families and established community leaders. These *comadres* and *compadres* became friends and benefactors who would be expected to offer support to their godchildren throughout their lives. Offering to become a godparent became a mark of prestige and leadership among the settlers of the ranches along the rivers in South Texas. Why Fernando did not take up this important mark of community leadership later in his own life is still a mystery.

The De León family had become wealthy enough to afford to educate their children. As the eldest son, Fernando was taught to read and write at a young age. According to the 1810 census, his parents maintained a teacher at the ranch to help the children learn to read and write and learn their Catholic catechism. According to family tradition, his mother insisted that her sons not carry guns to prevent them being perceived as low-class thugs. This admonition may well have led Fernando to refuse to participate in the later military encounters of the Texas Revolution.[4]

By the time Fernando was twelve years old in 1810, the world beyond the ranch and Texas had begun to intrude on his life and the lives of Texas settlers. Again, land had become the issue. Napoleon had taken the vast reaches of Louisiana from Spain and sold them to the United States. There was talk of possible war with the United States over the boundary of Texas. To try to hold the land, the Spanish crown sent settlers to establish ranches at San Marcos de Neve and soldiers to reinforce the province. Spanish settlers from Louisiana, meanwhile, made their way into Texas, fleeing from Anglo-American settlers who were flocking into their abandoned homes along the Mississippi River.

Even as conditions became more turbulent, Fernando learned to appreciate good land from his father's incessant search for better ranches. Martín De León never had received a proper title to the land at the Santa Margarita crossing, and when the lands of Mission

Nuestra Señora del Rosario were opened to settlers in 1807 he made a claim for some of it. It took several appeals, but the family finally moved to the Aransas River to establish a second ranch between the Aransas and Chiltipin Creek.[5]

The De León family soon suffered a reversal of fortune as a result of events in central Mexico. In September 1810, Miguel Hidalgo y Costilla launched a revolt in central Mexico against Spanish colonial authority. Although the rebellion was not successful, and independence did not come to Mexico for another eleven years, Fernando and his family learned of the failed revolution when anti-royalist revolts occurred in Texas from 1811 to 1813. Whether Martín De León and his family sided with the revolutionaries or the royalists is unknown, but the family stayed out of the political problems in San Antonio and La Bahía. When the republican revolutionaries took control in San Antonio in April 1813, the De León family moved back to the ranch on the Nueces River to avoid General Joaquín Arredondo, who arrived with a royalist army to reestablish royal power and execute the revolutionaries. With the terrors of revolution engulfing Texas, Martín De León moved the family to safety at Soto la Marina, his wife's hometown in northern Mexico.

Fernando was sixteen by the time royalist control was reestablished in Texas and the family returned from Soto la Marina to the Aransas River ranch, closer to the safety of the presidio at La Bahía and closer to their friends the Aldretes, to whom Patricia De León planned to betroth her eldest daughter. From 1815 to 1821, Fernando and the De León family faced the threat of Indian attacks, invasions by rebels, and filibusters and the uncertainties of political change in New Spain as royalists and insurgents battled over the country's future. In summer 1821 nationalists finally won the day, overthrowing the viceregal government and establishing an independent Mexico. Agustín de Iturbide, the leader of the nationalist forces, soon established himself as emperor, a position that was to last less than two years. Among the pressing issues facing the young nation were the status of public lands and the relationship between local and national governments.[6]

For the first year of its existence, the new government under Emperor Agustín I refused to grant land, since it was still unclear whether the public domain should be under the control of the individual states or the central government. That did not stop both conservatives and liberals from suggesting elaborate plans for colonization. The Mexican government feared that the Anglos would enter

Texas like the "Goths, Visigoths and other tribes assailed the Roman Empire."[7] But there was also the hope that settlers who were granted lands might become loyal citizens.

The new Mexican government, in keeping with the Spanish tradition, was offering thousands of acres in Mexican Texas to attract settlers. The concept was strange to the Anglos across the border, and when Stephen F. Austin, the first empresario, received his grant, he begged the Mexican government for the right to sell the land for at least a small profit. The government, more interested in encouraging settlers, ordered Austin to grant the land to the settlers, collecting only twelve cents an acre to pay for the cost of the paperwork.[8]

Martín De León and twenty-three-year-old Fernando, now a grown man, watched with growing concern as Austin arrived in Texas in 1821 to fulfill the contract his father had arranged with the royalist government the previous winter. The news of the tempting offer of thousands of acres for each settler at a cost of pennies an acre had spread like wildfire across the frontier towns in the United States, where land speculators were still profiting handsomely from the sale of land for far more than the government rate of $1.25 an acre. In Texas the requirements that one be a practicing Catholic and willing to pledge loyalty to Mexico seemed minor inconveniences to most would-be settlers. Austin was correct in guessing that he would have no trouble attracting colonists. By September 1821 he was inspecting the lands granted to him and beginning to bring in the first of a rapidly growing flood of colonists.

Finally, on 4 January 1823, Emperor Iturbide signed the Imperial Colonization Law. Austin received the first empresario contract in Texas. By 19 March 1823, however, Mexico's political elite had turned on Iturbide and removed him from office. The colonization process was once again in limbo. Representatives from throughout the country now met in Mexico City to begin work on a new constitution in which power would be parceled out among the individual states and the national government. Austin received a special dispensation to complete his contract, but Martín De León, the family patriarch, was concerned over the need to acquire land for his family, in particular Fernando. They had been planning to request a colonization contract of their own and asked San Antonio's provincial deputation for permission to establish a colony.

On 8 April 1824 Martín De León petitioned the provincial deputation at San Antonio, the seat of government in Texas, for permission to found a colony along the Guadalupe River with forty-one families. The town would be named Nuestra Señora de Guadalupe de Jesús. The provincial deputation added the name Victoria, perhaps in honor of Guadalupe Victoria, a hero of the War of Independence and one of the triumvirate ruling Mexico at the time. Martín also asked that taxes be abated for ten years, as had been done with Austin's colony. One of the supporters of De León's petition was Texas jefe político José Antonio Saucedo, who was already concerned with counterbalancing Anglo immigration with native-born colonists. Within seven days, Martín De León had received his contract to settle the new town, which would become known simply as Victoria. Only a month later, the national Mexican government joined Texas to Coahuila, creating the state of Coahuila y Texas, and disbanded the provincial deputation at San Antonio. The new government at Saltillo approved the Victoria colony, however, as did the national government in Mexico City.[9]

In spring 1825, perhaps inspired by the knowledge that he would soon possess land, Fernando had married María Antonia Galván. Martín De León with the newly married Fernando and the rest of the family and their retainers, as well as a few of the forty-one colonists he had listed in his petition, set out for the new settlement on the Guadalupe River. Fernando claimed a large tract of land for himself and his new bride. To his unbounded sorrow and to everyone's regret, María Antonia was the first death in the new colony.[10]

Don Martín's colony had been international from the start. By the time De León took possession, Irishman John Linn and his family may have already established a home within the boundaries of the colony, along with the families of John D. Wright and Joseph Ware. Don Martín welcomed the families and accepted their request for a legal grant of land since not all of his forty-one families had arrived. The local government at nearby La Bahía had objected to his allowing foreigners to receive land grants, but De León's assurances that the foreigners were proper Catholics and had sworn to be loyal Mexicans eased the concerns of local and state authorities. He also promised the government that the remainder of his forty-one families were on their way and would soon arrive—held up, so he claimed, by droughts in northern Mexico. In truth, the names of the new colonists were not those on the original list submitted in 1824, but the Victoria colony received more than the necessary number of settlers called for in the original contract, and Don Martín received his five leagues and five labors, as called for in his empresario contract.[11]

One of the most important activities at the new settlement of Victoria was the granting of land. The state government in distant Saltillo had been so concerned with the issue of colonization in Texas that its first law, even before the completion of the state constitution, had been a colonization law passed on 24 March 1825. Each grant of land had to be surveyed, titled, and registered with the state before a land commissioner was sent out to place the owners in possession of their lands. Although the first land commissioners were sent from Saltillo, Fernando De León would eventually be named the land commissioner for the De León colony, a position of tremendous power since anyone desiring land had to request it from him. Meanwhile, the capital at Saltillo had been inundated by Anglo-Americans hoping to acquire empresario contracts, and the De León family would soon find that the Saltillo government—with imprecise maps and little knowledge of their locations—had created potentially serious boundary conflicts with their neighbors.[12]

The first conflict over land between the Victoria colony and its neighbors began in October 1825. Green De Witt, one of those who had hastened to Saltillo to request an empresario grant, received a contract on 15 April 1825 to bring four hundred settlers within six years to land north and west of De León's Victoria colony, on the confluence of the Guadalupe and San Marcos rivers. Without accurate maps, however, it may have been inevitable that there would be problems over the boundaries. While Fernando was handing out land along the Guadalupe, his grants inevitably came into conflict with those of settlers whose lands had been surveyed by James Kerr for De Witt.[13]

Conflicts between Anglos and Tejanos continued to escalate. In December 1826 Fernando De León drove a cartload of corn to sell in Austin's colony along the Colorado River. Several months previously, Thomas Grey, one of Austin's settlers, had bought a donkey from Fernando's father but had left the animal to graze with De León's herds. When Grey came to claim the donkey, De León demanded payment of $25 or a cow and calf for having fed the donkey for the previous three months. Grey refused, and De León would not give up the donkey. When Fernando arrived in San Felipe de Austin, Grey pulled a gun on him and locked up the cart, corn, and oxen. Fernando, perhaps insulted over the affront, responded with violence, for which Austin jailed him. After Austin and Martín De León exchanged heated letters with the government, Fernando was finally allowed to leave with the cart and oxen. It was Fernando's first experience in jail, but not his last.[14]

Austin's was no longer the only empresario colony where Anglo-American settlers could request their league of land. The incoming Anglo-American settlers, however, had a hard time understanding the point of the empresario grants. The rough-and-tumble frontiersmen crossing the Sabine and Red rivers could not comprehend the idea of a paternalistic colonial leader whose duty was to grant them land, care for them, intercede for them with the distant government in Mexico City, and provide them protection from Indians or illegal traders. They vehemently objected to the requirement that they settle in a specific colony, or go to the colony's leader, in essence hat in hand, to request permission to settle there. Manuel de Mier y Terán, the inspector for the Mexican government in 1829, had found that few of the new arrivals were either Catholic or willing to be loyal to Mexico. On 6 April 1830 the Mexican government closed off the borders to any but German and Swiss Catholics or to those few, such as Austin and De León, who had successfully completed their contracts. The law did little to halt the influx of northerners who slipped across the Sabine illegally and settled wherever they could find vacant land. The law was rescinded two years later, but not before becoming a symbol of increasing Mexican hostility to Anglo-American settlement.

Under the circumstances, empresarios had to be both businessmen and government officials. Martín De León's sons split the chores between them. Whereas his younger brother Silvestre served as the alcalde of the colony, Fernando chose not to enter the political arena. He had already shown his preference for real estate and, as land commissioner he escorted potential settlers to locate home sites along the Guadalupe River or near the coast. He also became friends with John and Edward Linn, two of the early Irish Catholic setters. Fernando may have learned English from his association with the Linns or his constant contact with the Anglo settlers. He eventually became fluent enough to read in English, as is evidenced by his subscription to the New Orleans *Picayune*. He also had a chance to practice his English with one of the new arrivals to the Victoria colony.[15]

José María Jesús Carvajal, a native of San Antonio who had been educated in Kentucky under the patronage of Stephen F. Austin, arrived at the Victoria colony sometime around 1832, perhaps driven by the cholera epidemic then ravaging San Antonio. Carvajal had been trained as a surveyor, a job that proved to be one of the most beneficial and lucrative available in Texas at the time. He worked extensively among the Anglo-American colonists, establishing grants with land commissioner José Francisco Madero for the settlers of the Atascosito district, northeast of Austin's colony, a hotbed of illegal immigrant settlements. Juan Davis Bradburn, the commandant at Anahuac, jailed the two men for supplying titles to illegal immigrants but was finally forced to release them under orders from the governor of the state. Carvajal returned to Victoria, where he and Fernando became friends. Fernando hired Carvajal as the colony's surveyor, and the two men helped settlers locate homesites on the grassy plains along the rivers. Carvajal and Fernando became even better friends when Carvajal, even though a Protestant, married Fernando's sister Refugia. As brothers-in-law, the two men found they had much in common, including a belief in the liberal views of the Federalist Party.[16]

Plácido Benavides, with his three brothers, was also one of the new arrivals in Victoria, and he became closely involved with the De León family during 1832. Benavides hired on as the new teacher for the colony and served as the militia captain as well. Perhaps in his role as teacher, he met and fell in love with another De León daughter, Fernando's sister Agustina, whom he married in 1832, the same year Carvajal joined the family. Like Carvajal, Benavides also espoused the ideas of the liberal federalists.[17]

In August 1832 the De León colony leaders were invited to participate with Austin in a town meeting to redress their grievances against the Mexican government. Under both Mexican laws and the earlier Spanish laws on which they were based, the meeting was illegal since it was not the action of a duly constituted local government. Nevertheless, Martín De León sent José María Jesús Carvajal to represent the Victoria colony; Rafael Manchola, De León's son-in-law, represented nearby La Bahía. Fernando, uninterested in political action and busy in his position as land commissioner for the Victoria colony, did not attend. Little came of the petitions. In the following year, Stephen F. Austin was jailed for his seditious suggestion that Texas separate from Coahuila (not from Mexico) by force.[18]

By the end of 1833, the Law of April 6 had been rescinded and the flood of colonists had resumed. The new arrivals, however, brought a cholera epidemic with them, and during summer 1834, Martín De León, the founder of Victoria, passed away from the dreaded disease. Fernando, again choosing not to enter the political field, wrote to the ayuntamiento in San Antonio requesting that Plácido

Benavides, his brother-in-law, be placed in charge of directing the affairs of the colony. Fernando's brother Silvestre would remain the *regidor* (alderman). Fernando would continue in his position as land commissioner.[19]

With the rapid expansion of foreign immigration, government attitudes toward the land began to shift. The idea of selling public land instead of giving it away had become a necessity to pay for a militia to protect the state. In 1834 in Mexico City, President Santa Anna's government had moved to establish centralized control over the country by removing the liberal Constitution of 1824 and replacing it with a centralist constitution known as the Siete Partidas. Several of the Mexican states objected to losing power, and Santa Anna led troops into Zacatecas to put down revolts. The Coahuila y Texas state government, like Zacatecas, opposed the centralization of power, and the state congress had recently moved from Saltillo to Monclova.

José María Jesús Carvajal, serving as a Texas representative to the congress in Monclova, had helped pass laws that allowed the state government to sell eleven-league parcels on easy terms. The reason given by the government officials was to provide funding for a militia to combat Indian raids. In reality, the federalist government in Monclova feared the kind of devastation visited on Zacatecas and wanted to establish a militia to protect the state from Santa Anna's wrath. The main purchasers turned out to be Anglo-American land speculators, who offered promissory notes to buy up not just the eleven-league grants (56,655 acres) but, as Carvajal reported, four hundred leagues (1,771,200 acres) of land for little more than pennies an acre. The colonists in Texas, who were still restricted to one league, were furious and complained to Fernando, but there was little he could do. Fortunately for the Texian land owners, the would-be buyers never did produce the cash to pay for the land, and no one ever took control of the vast acreages.[20]

Fernando also became involved with Leonardo Manso, a newly arrived Mexican land speculator. The two men discovered another method of acquiring large amounts of land for very little money. Manso brought in fifteen Mexicans from Tamaulipas and Monterrey who could claim land as settlers in the De León colony. Fernando granted a league to each man, waterfront property along the edges of the La Vaca peninsula. Manso then paid each man between $300 and $500 for his land, or about $5,000, and transferred the titles to over 66,400 acres to his own name. He had gained far more than an eleven-league grant, which would have cost him over $21,000. Two years later, Manso sold the deeds in New Orleans to other speculators at a handsome profit.[21]

By 1835 the political situation in the center of Mexico had deteriorated and agitation was mounting in Coahuila y Texas. Carvajal fled from Monclova as Santa Anna sent his brother-in-law, General Martín Perfecto de Cos, to arrest the members of the Monclova congress. Carvajal went into hiding on the De León ranches in Victoria where Plácido Benavides, the town alcalde, protected him. Fernando De León and the family faced the difficult question of which side to support in the growing political controversy. The War Party, which contained a significant segment of young, single men who had arrived in Texas since 1832, and many of whose members were slaveholders or Southerners who had gained little from the Mexico government, pushed for separation, not just from Coahuila but from Mexico itself. The Peace Party, formed for the most part from Austin's settlers who feared losing their lands, opposed any altercations with the government that had given them their generous land grants.[22]

The De León family was also divided in its views, and Fernando was in a particularly difficult position. All of his adult life he had steered clear of politics and the military, but by 1834 he had to choose between the 1824 states' rights constitution or President Santa Anna's newly instituted centralist regime of 1834. It was in Fernando's best interest to oppose Santa Anna and the centralists, since under the new system the central government controlled the sale of lands and Fernando would lose his power to grant lands to settlers. He opposed the separation of Texas from Mexico, a view espoused by many of the radicals among the War Party, since his position of land commissioner would also disappear under an Anglo regime. His hope was to return Mexico to the Constitution of 1824, and Fernando joined his brother Silvestre and brothers-in-law Carbajal and Benavides in their support of the moderate wing of the War Party. The rest of the family voted to stay out of trouble and refused to join either party.

Fernando spent the remainder of 1835 completing titles to dozens of land grants for the Victoria colony. It is possible that during this time, as well as during the spring of the following year, Fernando offered to take possession of land grants for those who had decided to leave Texas. There is no record of his having purchased the land from his fellow Tejanos, but the land records indicate that Fernando held the titles to more than 100,000 acres of land, including land grants belonging to family members Valentín García, Fulgencio Bueno, Desiderio García, and others.[23]

By October 1835 Stephen F. Austin had returned from prison in Mexico City and joined the War Party. The first shots of the Texas Revolution were fired at the settlement of Gonzales when Colonel Ugartechea in San Antonio ordered his soldiers to collect the cannons at Victoria and Gonzales. These cannons had been given to the settlers to protect them from Indians. Benavides, in Victoria, turned over the useless cannon without complaint, but the settlers at Gonzales refused, draping their cannon in a sheet that read "Come and Take It."[24]

On 20 September 1835 General Cos and two shiploads of soldiers landed at Copano Bay in Texas and demanded that the citizens of Goliad, Victoria, Refugio, and San Patricio send representatives to pay their respects. Victoria sent no one. Fernando, still involved with land affairs, chose to remain in Victoria. He did not join Plácido Benavides, who had formed a militia unit of thirty men, including Silvestre De León and Manuel Carvajal, to resist General Cos. Although the federalist Tejanos captured the fort at La Bahía and opposed the centralist General Cos, they did not go so far as to join the Texians in their desire to separate from Mexico.[25]

In December, while Benavides joined Stephen F. Austin in the attack on San Antonio, Fernando moved his mother and the rest of the women out of Victoria to the ranches. With the defeat of General Cos on the ninth, Plácido and Silvestre returned to Victoria to celebrate their victory, certain that the war was over. Representatives of the War and Peace parties had met in November to form a state government and voted in support of the Constitution of 1824, much to the satisfaction of Fernando and many Tejanos.[26]

While Fernando and the citizens of Texas celebrated, President Santa Anna, hearing of his brother-in-law's defeat, gathered an army of six thousand men and with money extorted from the church and citizenry marched for Texas. Fernando and José María Jesús Carvajal did not plan to engage in military activities, but they knew the rebels needed support. The two men, joined by Peter Kerr, gathered a herd of horses to take to New Orleans to exchange for supplies for the Texians. On their return, Mexican forces captured their ship, the *Hannah Elizabeth*, and both Fernando and Carvajal were taken in chains as traitors to the Casamata fort in Matamoros. In February, Plácido Benavides, then stationed at Goliad under Major Robert Morris, slipped into Matamoros and successfully freed his two brothers-in-law, although twenty of his own men were captured. Fernando and Carvajal had nothing to show for their attempts to assist the Texas cause.[27]

By the time the two men returned to Victoria, General José de Urrea had been ordered by General Santa Anna to march up the east coast of Texas to capture San Patricio, Goliad, and Victoria. Fernando remained in Victoria while both Texians and Tejanos made a mass exodus from the town. John Linn headed for Gonzales to join General Sam Houston, begging Fernando to protect his wife and fifteen-day-old child and the other women of his household who had left to find passage at the port of Linnville. When the women failed to find a boat, Fernando moved them to the De León ranch, where Patricia de la Garza De León hid them from Mexican soldiers.[28]

Fernando, well known to his fellow citizens in Victoria as an opponent of Santa Anna's centralist views, chose not to leave town as General Urrea arrived. Perhaps Fernando was counting on the support of those to whom he had given land. Whether he realized it or not, he had also acquired numerous enemies who hated him for not granting them better lands. Several of the Texian settlers, perhaps to ingratiate themselves with the Mexican general, turned Fernando in as a federalist sympathizer. They assured the general that he was hiding supplies for the Texians and later claimed Fernando had taken their supplies for his own personal use. Although no supplies were ever discovered, Fernando was thrown in jail, where he spent the remaining two months of the war.[29]

Santa Anna's defeat at San Jacinto on 21 April 1836 changed the fortunes of the Tejanos who had hoped to remain part of Mexico. The victorious Texians had already voted for independence at Washington-on-the-Brazos on 2 March 1836, and the victory at San Jacinto assured them of a chance at an independent republic. Santa Anna, captured by Sam Houston, had ordered his generals to return to Mexico. Fernando was freed, and the centralists in Victoria were scrambling to join General Urrea as he withdrew to Mexico.

Much to his chagrin, Fernando De León soon learned that his enemies were not through with him. When General Thomas Rusk, in charge of the Texian forces, arrived in Victoria, he was informed that Fernando had disclosed the location of supplies to the Mexican forces. Rusk promptly jailed Fernando until he could determine the truth of the allegations. Evidently Rusk did not worry about losing his prisoner and allowed Fernando to bathe daily in the river. It was an ideal opportunity for those who hated the Tejanos to take a potshot at the unarmed man. A volunteer named Brantley and his friends succeeded in wounding Fernando. Rusk, embarrassed by the episode and unable to control the unruly volunteers, freed Fernando and allowed him to return to the family ranch.[30]

The volunteers from the United States, who had arrived in Texas too late to take part in the fighting, had become a riotous mob over whom General Rusk had little control. In the absence of provisions from the new government, the volunteers felt free to pillage homes and ranches throughout Texas. The De León homes and ranches became a specific target of those who believed that Fernando and his family had supported the Mexican government. Doña Patricia De León and Fernando complained to Rusk, but there was little the general could do.

In June word arrived from the border that the Mexican government planned another attack to retake Texas. Rusk, who suspected the loyalties of the Tejano population, ordered all of the Tejano families to move to the east so they could not afford help to any invading soldiers. Uninterested in the military problems of Texas, Doña Patricia determined to move her whole family to safety, planning a "summer sojourn in New Orleans."[31] The family loaded what goods they could onto fifteen mules rented from Phillip Dimmitt, while Texian volunteers jeered and stole what they could of the family's possessions and appropriated the horses from the corral.[32]

In New Orleans, Fernando and the family settled into a town with which Fernando had long been familiar. John Linn, their Texas friend, later reported that the De León family lived in poverty in New Orleans. Compared to their lifestyle as the leading family of Victoria, they may indeed have felt pinched, but several factors suggest that they were not suffering. Fernando's December 1836 trip to exchange horses for supplies indicates that he was well known to the New Orleans merchants and bankers, some of whom may have provided him credit. It is possible that Fernando maintained accounts with several merchants who already held his funds. Neither Fernando nor his brothers or brothers-in-law sold any of their lands in Texas, something they could easily have done had they needed money. Several of the De León women, who evidently did need funds, sold some of their Texas lands for $1.00 or more an acre, better than the going price for Texas lands, and invested the money in mortgages to ensure their future safety. Perhaps the family's letters to John Linn in Texas bemoaned their financial straits and exaggerated their condition. For the first time in their lives the De León family had to concern

themselves with paying bills and worrying about money, but it is unlikely that they lived in poverty.[33]

Meanwhile, in Texas, the newly arrived volunteers still clamored
for large land grants. The Texian government, unlike the Mexican
government, had no intention of giving land away and created the
General Land Office to control land sales. Those who had fought at
San Jacinto could claim payment in land for their service, but the
amount of land had dwindled from a league of over 4,428 acres to
the standard American measurement of a section, only 640 acres. Incoming settlers, hoping for the leagues of land, were furious to find
that the earlier settlers held the best land and offered it at exorbi-
tant prices. Without local land commissioners such as Fernando to
supervise land grants, fraud became rampant. Spanish land grants
were easily forged and witnesses could be paid to testify. Both Texian
and Tejano settlers found themselves dispossessed of their lands. To
prevent further abuse, the government closed the General Land Office, which had been open for little more than a year.[34]

In Victoria, Edward Linn, the local surveyor and Fernando's
friend, did his best to protect the thousands of acres controlled by
the De León family. Part of the difficulty lay in the immense size of
the Spanish and Mexican land grants. Newcomers crossing the wide-
open prairies had no idea that the land belonged to anyone and felt
free to settle wherever they saw a likely spot. Landowners often had
no idea that squatters had taken up residence on the land until they
were called into court to prove their boundaries. As Linn reported,
the *Houston Morning Star* had compounded the problem by inaccurately stating that the De León family had sided with Santa Anna and
therefore forfeited their lands. Many of the new arrivals had squat-
ted on the family land or bought the property at tax sales, and they
swore to fight the attempts by the De León family to reclaim their
land through lawsuits. There was little Fernando could do from Louisiana, but his Benavides kin, aided by Edward Linn, paid as much as
they could of the taxes and ran off squatters when they found them.

The long nine-year sojourn in Louisiana had been hard on the De
León family. By 1845, Patricia had lost three of her daughters and
sons-in-law to yellow fever in Louisiana and in Soto la Marina. The
family decided to return to Texas, which had joined the United States.
They believed the U.S. government would be able to extend protection to the citizens that the pitiable Republic of Texas had not been
able to provide. The family returned to find that almost all of their
land had been sold for taxes or to satisfy debts. Doña Patricia, still

owner of the large home on Victoria's town square, sold it for $7,000 to Robert Carlisle and Bridge Quinn, who had been living in it. She held the mortgage and received $700 a year, more than enough to keep her comfortably in a small house in town. When they later failed to pay the mortgage, she sued them and won.[35]

On the family's return, Fernando went back to the one thing he knew—the land. He may not have been willing to fight in the military or join in the melee of the political world, but when it came to land he was determined to regain as much of his property as he could. In 1845 he hired A. H. Phillips, who agreed to take the cases in exchange for a league of land. The partnership between the two men lasted successfully for the next ten years. During the 1847 spring term of the district court, Fernando and his lawyer attacked the squatters. He sued Andrew Neill, S. A. White, M. I. Hardy, and Murphree and Van Bibber for ejectment, to remove them from his property. The trials dragged on for four years before Fernando finally won the cases and regained his original 5,000 acres plus an additional 22,000 acres. He also initiated the case of *F. De León v. James Robinson*, against the judge who had ruled to take his land ten years earlier. Even after the death of Robinson and the completion of the probate hearings, De León continued the case, and in 1851 he succeeded in regaining the land Robinson had taken from him. Although Fernando did not regain the full 100,000 acres, by the end of 1851 he still owned more than 50,000 acres of land scattered in Victoria and surrounding counties.[36]

Fernando, in spite of his wealth and position, had remained a widower from 1825 until 1848. At age fifty his land holdings, especially after the court victories, made him the most eligible bachelor in Victoria. That year he met Luz Escalera, the daughter of family friends from Victoria. The forty-year-old spinster had a good head for business, and the two seemed well suited. The couple married later in the year at the church in Victoria, and the De León family happily welcomed the new addition. Luz and Fernando also adopted young Francisco Santiago, the youngest son of Fernando's brother Silvestre, who had been killed in 1842 by cattle rustlers. Francisco Santiago, soon better known as Frank, had more than 20,000 acres in his own right from his father's property, and with the 50,000 acres still owned by Fernando the small family was very comfortable.

Regrettably, the relationship between Fernando and his mother had become strained, in spite of the marriage to Luz Escalera. In 1847 Doña Patricia sued her son in court. Plácido Benavides had died in Opelousas, Louisiana, of yellow fever, and Fernando's sister had passed away shortly afterward when the family returned to Soto la Marina, leaving their three daughters in the care of Fernando's mother. In 1847 Pilar was thirteen, Librada twelve, and Matiana ten. Their uncle Ysidro Benavides had taken good care of the estate, protecting their inheritance during the nine years they had been in Louisiana and Mexico. He had paid the taxes on Plácido's league of land and rented out the Benavides "Round House" in Victoria plus two town lots in order to provide funds for the girls. On Ysidro's death in 1845, however, Fernando had become guardian for his nieces. Evidently he was not the caretaker Ysidro had been, and the money for the girls stopped.

In May 1847 Patricia de la Garza petitioned the Court of Victoria County through her attorney, W. H. Delano. Claiming she was destitute, Doña Patricia asked that the court permit the liquidation of some of the property. She argued the need for the sale of the land because her son Fernando, acting as guardian, had claimed he had no funds in his possession.[37]

Neither Patricia nor Fernando were destitute or without funds. The Benavides estate was still providing $381.20 in rents and income every year, and Doña Patricia was still receiving the $700 yearly income from the mortgage of the house on the town square in Victoria, as well as money from mortgages in Louisiana. Fernando, for his part, had just leased four leagues of land to William Dally and sold 640 acres to Alva Fitzpatrick for $640. He had also sold several lots in town. The petition to the court may have just been a legal necessity in order to sell some of the estate property, but it is interesting that Fernando gave up the guardianship of the three girls and passed it to Edward Linn when the case was settled.[38]

By October 1850 it was evident that there was some problem between Fernando and his mother. In her final will and testament Doña Patricia called on Edward Linn rather than her eldest son to be the executor of her will. After listing her children and how much each had borrowed from her over the years, she forgave the debts owed with the exception of Fernando's. To her eldest son she left nothing, and she left the $1,000 that he owed her to be collected by his brothers and sisters.[39] Doña Patricia de la Garza De León passed away in 1850 and Fernando died just three years later, never assuming the mantle of leadership of the family, the colony, or his fellow Tejanos.

What had happened? Fernando had lived the majority of his youth as the eldest son of a large family that had grown in wealth and prestige. As the eldest son he should have become the patriarch and led the family, the colony, and the community. When Martín De León established the colony of Victoria in 1824, Fernando had his choice of the positions of responsibility in the colony. The job of land commissioner, out of the many jobs available, carried the most visible authority. Newly arrived settlers had to come to Fernando to petition for land, and it was up to him to decide where or if he would show them land. Inevitably people fawned over him, hoping to remain in his good graces. He worked hard for the colony, spending much of his time in the saddle squiring colonists around the colony, but he may have been more interested in the trappings of power than in carrying out the onerous and extensive daily duties of correspondence. His signature never appears on any of the land surveys or on the thousands of pages of communication with the government—the first handled by his brother-in-law Carvajal, the second by Plácido Benavides, the one-time teacher.

At the time of his father's death in 1834, Fernando had chosen not to become the colonial leader but remained land commissioner. Had he become greedy for the land? He had become involved with Leonardo Manso but he did not keep any of those lands for himself. He also did not sell lands to New Orleans speculators. He did, however, acquire more than 100,000 acres of land as colonists began to flee Texas in 1836. Much of the land was not in his own name.

During the years of the Texas Revolution and Republic, Fernando suffered as none of the rest of the family had to do. Jailed by the Mexicans at the Casamata, again by General Urrea, and again by General Rusk, then losing everything as the family moved to New Orleans, Fernando spent the next nine years in New Orleans and Opelousas, gossiping and gambling, one of a thousand other refugees. It is possible that, by the time the family returned to Texas in 1845, Fernando had become greedy, bitter, and self-centered, no longer interested in helping anyone but himself.

Fernando should have been the patriarch of the family, supported by his mother. Upper-class nineteenth-century Latin American families such as the De León clan were ruled by dominant males who were prominent public figures and cared for their relatives, both male and female. When Fernando failed to care for his nieces, however, he incurred his mother's wrath and may well have lost his position of prominence within the family. He also refused to serve as godfather to other families within the Tejano society. Only once, and this after he had married Luz Escalera, did he serve as godfather to anyone in the Tejano community. This too indicated an unwillingness to become a guardian of the community. It is unknown if his failure to provide godparenthood occurred because he had given up his Catholic heritage and joined his Carvajal brother-in-law in the Protestant church. If so, it may have been this final blow that created the rift between Fernando and his devoutly Catholic mother. At a time when the incoming Anglos threatened the stability and permanence of the Tejano world, Fernando focused only on regaining his land. He failed to be a leader to both his family and his community.

Self-centered greed, however, was the hallmark of the Anglo world, and Fernando's success in regaining 50,000 acres and the potential wealth from the sale and rental of this land made him powerful in the eyes of the Victoria Anglos. His fellow Tejanos might not accord him the prestige to which he had long been accustomed, but the new Texians, racist though they might be, could not help but respect Fernando's success as a landholder. As he lost prominence in the Tejano world, he tried to become part of the Anglo community. He contributed land to bring the railroad into Victoria, and his subscription to the *New Orleans Picayune* indicates his attempt to maintain ties to the Anglo business world.

Redemption for Fernando as a Tejano may have come at the end. By marrying Luz Escalera and leaving her almost 20,000 acres of land, he provided a powerful and wealthy new matriarch for the Tejano community and for the De León family. By adopting Francisco Santiago, his brother's son, Fernando gave his nephew a successful start in both the Anglo and Tejano worlds. For the first time in his life, he served as godfather to a Tejano family, and the land sales he made during the last three years of his life, perhaps influenced by his new wife, were to his fellow Tejanos at reasonable prices. He had returned to leadership in the Tejano world.

After his death in 1853, his wife Luz used the land to provide her Tejano relatives and friends with dowries, gifts, and land grants. She gave loans and helped the Tejano community survive in the Anglo world. When she passed away, all of the land she had received from Fernando had been shared among the Tejano community. Fernando's legacy, therefore, may reflect not his loss of leadership of the family or the Tejano community but his success in adapting to the Anglo ways. In the end, with power derived from regaining the land in the Anglo courts, he won the admiration of the Texian land owners.

Notes

1. Although much of the information for this essay is drawn from my book *De León: A Tejano Family History* (Austin: University of Texas Press, 2004), this story of Fernando De León is based on additional research and new information.

2. Inventory of Goods of Patricia de la Garza, Index to Deed Records, 2:591, Victoria County Clerk's Office, Victoria, Tex. [VCCO].

3. Gloria Candelaria Genealogy Records, De León family, Victoria, Tex., prepared from Victoria County census records by Gloria Candelaria, Victoria Hispanic Genealogical and Historical Society of Texas, Victoria, Tex. .

4. Martín De León Papers, O'Connor Room, Victoria County Public Library, Victoria, Tex.; Census of Santa Margarita Ranch, Sergeant José de Jesús Aldrete, 10 November 1811, Bexar Archives at the Center for American History, University of Texas at Austin [BA]; Interview with Estella Zermeño, December 2006, Goliad, Tex. .

5. De León Colony Papers, Texas General Land Office, Archives and Records Division, Austin [DLC].

6. Harris Gaylord Warren, *The Sword Was Their Passport: A History of American Filibustering in the Mexican Revolution* (Baton Rouge: Louisiana State University Press, 1943), 33–35, 71–73; Kathryn Garrett, *Green Flag over Texas: A Story of the Last Years of Spain in Texas,* reprint (New York: Pemberton Press, 1969), 150–62; Josefina Zoraida Vázquez, "Los Primeros Tropiezos," in *Historia General de México* (Mexico City: El Colegio de México, 1976), 3:5; William Edward Syers, *Texas, the Beginning, 1519–1839* (Waco, Tex.: Texian Press, 1978), 136–37; Oakah Jones Jr., *Los Paisanos: Spanish Settlers on the Northern Frontier of New Spain* (Norman: University of Oklahoma Press, 1979), 21; Nettie Lee Benson, "Texas as Viewed from Mexico," *Southwestern Historical Quarterly* 90 (January 1987): 219; Donald E. Chipman, *Spanish Texas, 1519–1821* (Austin: University of Texas Press, 1992), 236-39; Nettie Lee Benson, "The Provincial Deputation," in *Mexico: Harbinger of Provincial Autonomy, Independence, and Federalism* (Austin: University of Texas Press, 1992), xi, 19, 23, 24–25; Jaime E. Rodríguez O., *The Emergence of Spanish America: Vicente Rocafuerte and Spanish Americanism, 1808–1832* (Berkeley: University of California Press, 1975), 1–2, 40–48.

7. Quoted from the *Archivo histórico diplomático mexicano,* in Walter H. Timmons, *Tadeo Ortíz: Mexican Colonizer and Reformer,* Southern Studies, Monograph 43 (El Paso: Texas Western Press, 1994), 15.

8. Benson, "Texas as Viewed from Mexico," 219; Chipman, *Spanish*

Texas, 236–39; Eugene C. Barker, *Life of Stephen F. Austin, Founder of Texas, 1793–1836* (Austin: University of Texas Press, 1985), 112; Gregg Cantrell, *Stephen F. Austin: Empresario of Texas* (New Haven, Conn.: Yale University Press, 1999), 177.

9.   Michael P. Costeloe, *La primera república federal de México, 1824–1835: un studio de los partidos politicos en el México independeinte*, trans. Manuel Fernández Gasalla (Mexico City: Fondo de Cultura Económica, 1975), 24; Contract with State of Coahuila y Texas, DLC; Resolution of the Provincial Deputation, San Fernando de Béxar, 13 April 1824, Bexar County Courthouse, Spanish Archives, San Antonio, Tex. .

10.   Arthur B. J. Hammett, *The Empresario: Don Martín de León (The Richest Man in Texas)*, (Kerrville, Tex.: Braswell Printing, 1971), 10; Manuel Barrera, *And Then the Gringos Came: The Story of Martín de León and the Texas Revolution* (Laredo, Tex.: Barrera Publications, 1992), 60–61; L. Randall Rogers, *Two Particular Friends of Stephen F. Austin* (Waco, Tex.: Texian Press, 1990), 61; Candelaria Family Group Records for Fernando De León, and María Antonia Galván.

11.   Alcalde of Goliad Juan José Hernández to the Governor of the State, 26 March 1825, DLC; Record of Translations, no. 55, Archives and Records Division, Texas General Land Office, Austin [GLO]; Original letter in Catálogo del Fondo Presidencia Municipal, 26 March 1825, Saltillo Municipal Archives [SMA]; José Antonio Saucedo to Excelentísimo Señor Governador del Estado de Coahuila y Texas, D. Rafael González, 14 July 1825, SMA; Saucedo to Gonzales, 10 June 1825, DLC; Record of Translations, 56, GLO; González to José Antonio Saucedo, 17 May 1825, Catálogo del Fondo Presidencia Municipal, SMA; José Antonio Saucedo to Juan Martín de Veramendi, 11 April 1825, BA; De León to Saucedo, n.d., photocopy in Martín De León Papers, O'Connor Room of Victoria County Library, Victoria, Texas [MDL-O'CVL]; Padilla to Jefe, 6 October 1825, DLC, original in BA, same date.

12.   Benson, "Texas as Viewed from Mexico," 244; H. P. N. Gammel, *The Laws of Texas, 1822–1897* (Austin: Gammel Book, 1898), 1:99; Gifford White, *1830 Citizens of Texas* (Austin: Eakin Press, 1983), 3.

13.   Martín De León to Governor González, n.d., photocopy in MDL-O'CVL; Martín De León to Saucedo, 12 November 1826, BA.

14.   Barker, *Life of Stephen F. Austin*, 112; Cantrell, *Stephen F. Austin*, 177.

15.   Although there are no legal records indicating Fernando's position in the colony, there are references to his run-ins with Indians along the coast while locating ranch sites for settlers. He was also later

named the land commissioner for the colony. Hammett, *Empresario,* 10–11; Barrera, *Then the Gringos Came,* 70–71; Subscription to New Orleans *Picayune,* n.d., in MDL-O'CVL.

16. Nodé Quintellen McMillen, "Surveyor General: The Life and Times of José Maria Jesús Carbajal," manuscript, Rosanky, Tex., 1990, 16–20; Joseph E. Chance, *José María de Jesús Carvajal: The Life and Times of a Mexican Revolutionary* (San Antonio, Tex.: Trinity University Press, 2006), 13–37; Margaret Swett Henson, *Juan Davis Bradburn: A Reappraisal of the Mexican Commander of Anáhuac* (College Station: Texas A&M University Press, 1982), 42–45.

17. Hammett, *Empresario,* 10; Barrera, *Then the Gringos Came,* 60–61; Candelaria, Family Group Records, Benavides, and Carbajal.

18. Cantrell, *Stephen F. Austin,* 255–62; David J. Weber, ed., *Troubles in Texas, 1832: A Tejano Viewpoint from San Antonio,* trans. Conchita Hassell Winn and David J. Weber (Austin: Wind River Press, 1983), 2–3; Minutes of the Ayuntamiento, 14 October 1832, "Libro formado por el Capitán de Milicias," Archivo General de la Nación [AGN]; *Gaceta del Gobierno Supremo del Estado de Coahuila y Tejas, 1933,* Eberstadt Collection, box 3N177, no. 2, CAH.

19. Fernando De León to J. Saucedo, 19 August 1834, BA.

20. Decree of 19 April 1834, in Malcolm McLean, *Papers Concerning Robertson's Colony in Texas* (Arlington: University of Texas at Arlington, 1983), 10:54–55; Cantrell, *Stephen F. Austin,* 306–7.

21. Leonardo Manso purchases, Index to Deed Records, vols. 2–3, VCCO.

22. Cantrell, *Stephen F. Austin,* 298, 299. There are no written records of the sides chosen by the De León family, but their actions during the next few years indicate their adherence to the two sides.

23. Fernando De León, Luz Escalera De León, Index to Deed Records, VCCO.

24. John J. Linn, *Reminiscences of Fifty Years in Texas* (New York: D. and J. Sadlier, 1883; reprint, Austin: State House Press, 1986), 105, 107.

25. Hobart Huson, *Refugio, a Comprehensive History of Refugio County: From Aboriginal Times to 1953* (Woodsboro, Tex.: Rooke Foundation, 1953), 212–13; Stephen L. Hardin, *Texian Iliad: A Military History of the Texas Revolution, 1835–1836* (Austin: University of Texas Press, 1994), 15–16; Hobart Huson, *Captain Phillip Dimmitt's Commandancy of Goliad, 1835–1836* (Austin: Von Boeckmann-Jones, 1974), 32–33; Carlos E. Castañeda, *Our Catholic Heritage in Texas, 1519–1936* (Austin: Von Boeckmann-Jones, 1950), 6:277, 284.

26. Hardin, *Texian Iliad,* 67–68.

27. Linn, *Reminiscences*, 259; McLean, *Papers Concerning the Robertson Colony*, 11:240–42; Hardin, *Texian Iliad*, 109–11, 158–60.

28. Linn, *Reminiscences*, 248–49.

29. Roy Grimes, *300 Years in Victoria County* (Victoria, Tex.: Victoria Advocate, 1968; reprint, Austin: Nortex Press, 1985), 88.

30. Linn, *Reminiscences*, 248; Grimes, *300 Years*, 86; Paul D. Lack, *The Texas Revolutionary Experience: A Political and Social History, 1835–1836* (College Station: Texas A&M University Press, 1992), 152–54.

31. Fairfax Catelet to Editor, Velasco, 20 July 1836, in *The Papers of the Texas Revolution: 1835–1836*, ed. John H. Jenkins (Austin: Presidial Press, 1973), 495–96.

32. Noah Smithwick, *Evolution of a State or Recollections of Old Texas Days*, comp. Nanna Smithwick Donaldson (Austin: University of Texas, 1983), 102; Demand for payment of rental of 15 mules to Patricia De León, Phillip Dimmitt to Thomas Rusk, from Corpus Christi, June 1836, Thomas Jefferson Rusk Papers, CAH; Fernando De León petition to the Legislature, December 1849, Records of the Legislature, Archives Division, Texas State Library, Austin.

33. Patricia de la Garza to Martín De León, 1801, Presas del Rey, in Patricia de la Garza to P. B. Cocke, Deed, 1:34, 24 January 1837, Deed Records, VCCO; María Antonia de la Garza, Tutorship of León De León, 1:94, 23 January 1837, Index to Deed Records, VCCO; María Antonia de la Garza, Executrix for Minor, León De León, to P. B. Cocke, Deed, 1:94, 23 January 1837; VCCO; María de Jesús De León Manchola to P. B. Cocke, 23 January 1837, Deed Records, VCCO.

34. Smithwick, *Evolution of a State*, 200–202.

35. *Patricia de la Garza v. Robert Carlisle and Bridget Quinn*, Case no. 24, Fall Term 1849, settled Fall Term 1851, 25-A District Clerk's Miscellaneous Records, Civil Court Docket, Victoria College/University of Houston Library, Victoria, Tex. [VC-UH].

36. *Fernando de León v. A. Neill*, Ejectment, Case no. 30, Spring Term 1847; *Fernando de León v. S. A. White*, Ejectment, Case no. 59, Spring Term, 1847; *Murphree and Van Bibber v. Fernando de León*, Ejectment, Case no. 82, Spring Term, 1847; *Fernando de León v. M. I. Hardy*, Case no. 18, Spring Term 1847, in Civil Court docket, 1847–1859, District Court Records, VC-UH; *Fernando de León v. James Robinson*, Spring Term 1847, Case no. 29, Ejectment; and *Fernando de León v. T. W. Robinson, Adm. Of James Robinson, dec'd*, Bar Docket, Spring Term 1851, Civil Court Docket, 1847–1859, District Court, VC-UH.

37. Estate of Plácido Benavides, 8 June 1838, 2:43–46, probate Records,

VCCO; Petition of Patricia de la Garza, May term, 1847, filed for record 29 December 1848, 1:527, VCCO.

38.   Fernando De León to William Dally, Lease, 1:131, 16 February 1847, and Fernando De León to Alva Fitzpatrick, 13 January 1847, 3:105, Deed Records, VCCO.

39.   Probate Records, Will of Patricio [sic] Garza De León, 17 October 1850, 2:591, VCCO.

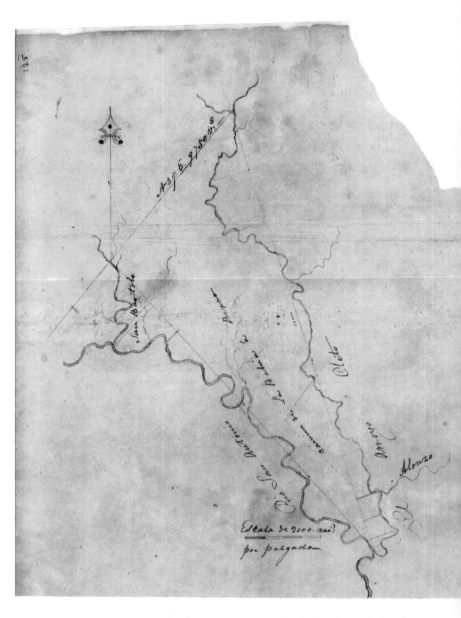

As jefe político, Ramón Múzquiz participated in the land speculation that thrived in Texas during the 1820s and 1830s. As a Mexican national, he obtained an eleven-league grant that he divided into multiple surveys. This plat represents a survey made of a tract previously on Mission Espíritu Santo ranchland that was returned to the public domain when the government secularized the mission.

Courtesy Spanish Collection 130/3, p. 12, Texas General Land Office, Austin.

RAMÓN MÚZQUIZ
THE ULTIMATE INSIDER
Andrés Reséndez

IT IS EASY TO FEEL SYMPATHETIC toward those hardy Mexican Texans whose only guilt was to live through a tumultuous era of revolutions and wars. Life was heavy-handed to them. But at least we can learn from their difficult existence. Ramón Múzquiz was one such tortured soul.[1] Like his contemporaries, Múzquiz possessed the ability to survive and even thrive in a difficult frontier environment. But, unlike most of his peers, Don Ramón retained a sense of fairness and proportion even as Texas descended into bitter partisan politics, ethnic strife, and ultimately all-out war. He was equally accepted by political allies and rivals, by business partners and competitors, by Mexicans and foreigners. In fact, he remained in good stead with most everyone he had occasion to meet and thus became the ultimate insider in an exceedingly fractious world. For this reason alone Ramón Múzquiz's biography remains as relevant today as it did nearly two centuries ago.

Múzquiz belonged to one of the most prominent families of explorers and settlers in the entire northeast of New Spain. He could trace his lineage back to Joseph Antonio de Ecay Múzquiz, one of the founders of the town of Santiago de la Monclova, Coahuila. More than a century later the family still thrived in the area. Ramón was born in 1797 in the town and presidio of Santa Rosa in the municipality of Monclova. To get a sense of his early circumstances, suffice it to say that his birthplace, which also functioned as the clan's ancestral home, would be later renamed Múzquiz to honor the memory of another family member, Melchor Múzquiz, who briefly occupied the presidency of Mexico during 1832.[2] Within this sprawling family Ramón belonged not to a dying twig but to a promising branch. He was the son of Catarina González de Paredes and Lieutenant Miguel Francisco de Ecay y Múzquiz.[3] By the end of the eighteenth century, Lieutenant Múzquiz was the presidial commander of Santa Rosa. This was a position of authority and privilege that nonetheless required considerable sacrifice.[4]

In 1800, when Ramón was still a toddler, Lieutenant Múzquiz was dispatched to Nacogdoches to take command of the military post there. At that time Nacogdoches was the remotest Mexican town in

Texas and easily the most exposed to the advancing wave of foreign settlers. It also lay along a crucial corridor employed by various indigenous and nonindigenous groups engaged in the horse trade between Texas and Louisiana. In short, Nacogdoches showcased all the perils but also all the opportunities that Texas had to offer. And Ramón's father found himself at the center of it all. Lieutenant Múzquiz regularly visited Indian camps and confronted peripatetic individuals harboring all kinds of schemes. His most memorable achievement was the capture of Philip Nolan and his band of adventurers in 1801 (he also prevented Nolan's subsequent escape by discovering that a certain Don Pablo Lafita had smuggled a metal file into Nolan's cell).[5]

The Múzquiz family must have possessed a distinct sense of noblesse oblige and patriotism. Yet the unruly frontier also offered some avenues of advancement that Lieutenant Múzquiz did not overlook. His responsibilities as military commander did not prevent him from becoming involved in some commercial ventures. He was even accused of contraband trade at La Bahía del Espíritu Santo (and also of having an illicit relationship with the wife of Juan de la Cruz).[6] Although it is impossible to ascertain the veracity of the accusation, smuggling was common among military commanders posted in border areas. It simply came with the territory. The rewards that could be reaped were enormous, and the regulations coming out of Mexico City must have seemed outright silly in a place like Nacogdoches.

In 1804 Lieutenant Múzquiz was ordered to go back to Coahuila along with his hundred-man detachment.[7] But by then his ties to Texas were impossible to sever. From his base in central and northern Coahuila the able lieutenant would continue his activities to the north. In fact, he served as presidial commander of San Antonio in 1806 and as late as 1820 he still organized an expedition against some Indians in the vicinity of Rio Grande along the Texas-Coahuila border.[8] For the younger Múzquiz those years must have constituted an invaluable apprenticeship in everything that would be important in his life—from the character of Indians and Anglo-Americans, to the intricacies of the imperial bureaucracy, to the astonishing profits that could be made by the sheer buying and selling of goods.[9]

In his tender youth Ramón must have decided that the military life that had brought so much recognition to his forebears was not well suited to him. But he did follow in his father's footsteps in one crucial regard: they both built their lives around the linkages between Coahuila and Texas. And thus, in the twilight years of Spanish rule, Ramón launched his career in the civilian world as postmaster of the city of Monclova, overseeing regular mail deliveries to San Antonio.[10]

Mexico's independence from Spain brought several novelties to the frontier, chief among them the easing of trading restrictions with the United States. Foreign merchants—long accustomed to being turned away or imprisoned or having their wares confiscated—were now welcomed. Conversely, Mexican traders were able to make their way to the United States, open lines of credit in various stores, and head back home loaded with merchandise. During the colonial period Mexican customers could only dream of buying calicoes, whisky, shoes, felt hats, or shaving kits at affordable prices. Now they could not get enough of these goods.[11]

The opportunities for young, entrepreneurial, and well-placed individuals like Múzquiz must have been endless. Múzquiz had started out, like his colonial predecessors, by taking goods from Coahuila into Texas. Already in 1823 he was importing fifty-eight mule loads, including such profitable articles as wine and *aguardiente*, a strong alcoholic beverage.[12] But soon enough Múzquiz made the transition into the new commerce with the United States; he began making regular business trips to Louisiana and established an impressive network of suppliers in New Orleans, ship captains plying the routes to the Texas coast, customs officials in Goliad and San Antonio, and a growing list of customers in Coahuila and Texas. All told, he became one of the most successful Mexican merchants to be found anywhere in Texas.[13]

However, just as Múzquiz busied himself consolidating his business network and opening a grocery store in San Antonio, duty called. In May 1825 he was named secretary to the ailing jefe político of Texas, Don José Antonio Saucedo.[14] Why choose a relative newcomer like Múzquiz for the key post of secretary? It is difficult to know for certain, but Saucedo was already well acquainted with Ramón's father when they both coincided in San Antonio back in 1806, Saucedo as alcalde and Lieutenant Múzquiz as commander of the presidial troops.[15] Saucedo must have become persuaded that the connections of the Múzquiz family in Coahuila would serve him well in an era when Coahuila and Texas had become a single state. It also helped that Ramón was a prospering businessman and came across as responsible and efficient.

For Ramón himself the appointment was a mixed bag. On the one hand, it confirmed his acceptance into Texas politics and represented an obvious recognition of his social and political standing. His extended family could only feel proud of this young Múzquiz who was beginning to climb the administrative hierarchy of Texas. But on the other hand, his secretarial duties constituted a serious distraction from his booming business. He would have to devote considerable time to writing letters instead of overseeing business transactions. Above all, he would lack mobility. Every time he had to leave Texas to go to New Orleans or elsewhere in Louisiana or to Coahuila, he would have to ask for permission, a process that could take weeks if not months—a deadly prospect in an occupation in which expediency and timeliness were everything. His newfound duties would undoubtedly result in a financial setback. So from the start Don Ramón insisted on being paid fairly and regularly.[16] Unfortunately, the reality did not live up to his conditions. Far from receiving a fair compensation, his salary was reduced in 1827. And thus Múzquiz found himself in the unenviable position of having to resign because of "the frequent setbacks to my interests and the lack of monies available to this office."[17]

Yet the transplanted Coahuilan was not allowed to walk away so easily. Instead, he was entrusted with even greater responsibility. In spring 1827 a new state constitution was been promulgated, a constitution that in many ways enshrined in law the subordination of the less developed and more distant Texas to the more heavily populated Coahuila, and Ramón Múzquiz was poised to become a key player in this system. Before the year was out the governor appointed Múzquiz to succeed Saucedo as jefe político of Texas.[18] He took office on 1 January 1828. Múzquiz allowed himself a rare moment of vulnerability: "Owing to my lack of talent and knowledge, I will not be able to carry out my duties with utmost perfection," he admitted. "But I vow to make every sacrifice and avail myself of every means, no matter how costly, to bring happiness to these people which is the ultimate object of my high office."[19]

Múzquiz found his tenure as jefe político as much of a mixed blessing as his previous employment. Of course his base salary was higher, and this time it was not cut. He also learned to juggle public office and private business in advantageous ways (it would be called conflict of interest today, but the notion did not exist in the 1820s). For instance, Múzquiz had military escorts accompany his wagons full of merchandise as they moved from Goliad to San Antonio.[20] He also petitioned for eleven *sitios* of land by the Trinity River.[21] Although the land-granting process was largely beyond his hands, Múzquiz must have been aware that his investiture tilted the odds decidedly in his favor.[22] Without a doubt his high office furthered his economic interests; it was an accepted facet of political life. But not all were advantages. In times of necessity Mexico's government called on its most favored children for support. At the end of 1829, Múzquiz was asked to make a loan of 3,482 pesos (a very sizable sum of money) for the upkeep of the Texas military.[23] As he was finding out, the Mexican administration was a vast patronage network in which resources moved in both directions. Moreover, his official duties continued to detract from his commercial ventures. Barely seven months into his appointment, Múzquiz asked for a leave of absence to look after his economic interests.

Don Ramón's first term as jefe político was exceedingly successful. When the time came to choose a successor in 1830, the Tejano political elite—perennial ayuntamiento members such as the Navarros, the Seguíns, the Veramendis, and the Casianos—did not hesitate to nominate him again. An electoral commission had to propose a list of three candidates, and Múzquiz's name topped the list. The commission's endorsement even hinted that Múzquiz could stay on indefinitely: "Is it not a constitutional mania to change one political chief by another just to satisfy a certain longing for novelty?" the electoral commissioners asked with obvious intention.[24] He held the position until July 1834.

Why did the Tejano elite throw its lot so solidly behind Múzquiz? Once again it is difficult to say for certain. But there are some clues. Virtually all influential Tejanos who had a say in the reappointment of Múzquiz were active participants in the Louisiana-Texas trade. As one of the most successful San Antonio merchants, Múzquiz emerged as an inspiring example, a valuable partner, and a leader willing to keep the door between Mexico and the United States wide open. For example, when the federal government decided to close off the port of Matagorda to international trade in 1828, Múzquiz and his Tejano allies protested vigorously and pressured the national government into reopening the port.[25] The commercial interests of all of these individuals were closely aligned. Múzquiz also appears to have been able to please his Tejano allies in matters of land distribution. He worked effectively with ayuntamiento members and state authorities to make available enormous tracts of land around the San Antonio-Goliad area. The lands from the recently secularized missions were especially appealing because, as Múzquiz himself would later explain, "The fathers had vast knowledge of the advantages offered by the land on which they chose to build their missions."[26] All told, members of the Tejano elite were able to accumulate land under Múzquiz's administrations.[27]

Beyond the decided support of fellow Tejanos, Múzquiz also enjoyed considerable favor among Anglo-Texan settlers. Throughout his life Múzquiz had brushed shoulders with the *americanos del norte,* starting in the early 1800s during his father's tour of duty in Nacogdoches. But the full implications of their presence in Texas became clear only after Mexico enacted a series of liberal colonization and trading policies in the 1820s. As a young merchant from Coahuila operating in the San Antonio-Goliad area, Múzquiz must have found himself directly in competition with foreign-born traders. In 1828 a visitor observed that, in San Antonio, "what little trade exists is conducted by foreigners and two or three Mexicans, and their monopoly is blatant."[28] By then foreign traders were introducing merchandise worth 60,000 pesos while Tejano merchants accounted for only about 15,700 pesos.[29] But the intense competition did not prevent Múzquiz from supporting the activities of foreign-born entrepreneurs and establishing close alliances, and almost certainly friendships, with some of them—like Philip (Felipe) Dimmitt, a Kentuckian who had arrived in Texas in 1822 and become a supplier of the Texas military garrisons. Twenty years later Múzquiz and Dimmitt were still carrying on a lively correspondence and discussing joint investments.[30]

Múzquiz's support for Anglo-American colonization is most poignant and evident in the controversial role he played with regard to slavery. On 15 September 1829, on the anniversary of Mexico's independence, President Vicente Guerrero decreed the abolition of slavery.[31] The decree was laconic and unambiguous:

Article 1. Slavery is hereby abolished.
Article 2. Everyone who thus far has been considered a slave is now free.
Article 3. Former slave owners will be compensated according to the corresponding laws and as circumstances permit.

Guerrero was the second president elected under the Constitution of 1824, an ardent liberal, and a mulatto veteran of the wars of independence. His unexpected decree caused commotion throughout Coahuila and Texas.

Múzquiz had long been acquainted with the peculiar institution. In fact, he had grown up in a household with slaves. In 1799 his father purchased María del Carmen Ramírez, a thirty-three-year-old mulatto woman, and a twelve-year-old boy named José María del Refugio Guajardo, most likely for domestic service. These two slaves remained in the Múzquiz household until 1806, when Ramón was already nine years of age.[32] Prominent Mexican Texans would occasionally purchase slaves. José Casiano, a fellow Bexareño and one of Múzquiz's closest trading partners, bought a black slave and a mulatto boy as late as 1841.[33] Clearly, Múzquiz had direct, personal knowledge of the peculiar institution. Moreover, as a well-informed jefe político, he must have been keenly aware of the vital role played by slave labor in the Anglo-American colonies. The cotton plantations and cattle ranches stood to suffer a devastating blow with the emancipation decree.

Múzquiz learned about President Guerrero's decree in a letter from the governor of Coahuila y Texas on 16 October 1829. He had a difficult choice to make. After consulting with some of his allies and friends in San Antonio, the jefe político resolved to suspend the publication of the emancipation decree. In the meantime he would urge President Guerrero to grant Texas an exemption. The case Múzquiz made was meticulous and persuasive. He noted that Stephen F. Austin's first colonists had been specifically granted the right to hold slaves. The emancipation decree would therefore break solemn promises made earlier. After dwelling on the importance of slave labor for the economy of Texas, the embattled jefe político also pointed out that these unfortunate men and women—more than a thousand of them in all of Texas according to his estimate—had already been enslaved before arriving in Mexico. And thus, "while philanthropy and the natural sympathies of humanity cry out in favor of liberty, the positive laws which regulate society take the side of property and declare it a sacred and inviolable right."[34] Múzquiz concluded that the publication of the emancipation decree would result in general unrest, disturbance of public order, and even a serious insurrection, and for these reasons he urged the state governor and the president of the republic to reconsider. Múzquiz put his career on the line to protect the livelihood of the Anglo-American colonies of Texas and succeeded. By December 1829, Texas had been exempted from the abolitionist decree.

None of this means that the jefe político was a mindless supporter of Tejano and Anglo-American interests; nor does it mean that his administrations were devoid of conflict. Especially during his second term, the jefe político was forced into steering an all-too-elusive middle course between promoting the economic interests of his Tejano and Anglo-American constituents and consolidating the Mexican nation in Texas.

Above all Múzquiz was a Mexican nationalist. This is hardly surprising given his family's lengthy involvement in the colonization of the northeastern reaches of New Spain. His chief aim as jefe político was to develop Texas *as part of the Mexican nation.* Keeping a liberal trading policy with the United States and inviting foreign-born settlers into Texas were means (perhaps necessary and personally profitable, but nonetheless mere means) toward a greater national end. And yet by the early 1830s the profound Anglo-Americanization of Texas had put this vision into question. Don Ramón seemed especially concerned about the lack of respect for Mexican law prevalent in the colonies. The signs were plain to see. Starting in 1830 many Anglo-American merchants chose to defy Mexico's tariff regulations. Vessels bound for the colonies simply refused to clear customs, ran the blockades, and even traded fire with Mexican soldiers garrisoned at Anahuac and Velasco.

Foreign-born colonists also seemed oblivious to any restrictions on slavery. Even though the jefe político had been a conspicuous proponent of slavery, he became incensed in May 1832 when he learned that a posse of seven Anglo-Americans from Austin's and De Witt's colonies had entered San Antonio to apprehend four adult slaves and a boy: "The crime committed by [Henry] Brown and his accomplices is of such a nature and scope," wrote an irate Múzquiz, "that it tramples over the laws of a hospitable country that has received them in her bosom regarding them as adoptive sons, and they return the favor by making a mockery out of the authorities charged with preserving the security of this town and of the entire Department."[35] The case is especially interesting because the Anglo-Americans were in some sense acting on their property rights, the very argument invoked by Múzquiz less than three years earlier to defend the preservation of the peculiar institution in Texas.[36] And yet during that time San Antonio had also emerged as a safe haven for runaway slaves. Interestingly, two of the five slaves, one named Peter and his son Tom, had reached San Antonio a month earlier and appeared before the alcalde "demanding the protection of the laws in their favor and claiming that they had been illegally introduced by Alejandro Thompson at the end of 1830." Boldly, Peter and Tom asked not only that they be declared free but "that the same status be made extensive to the rest of their family that had remained with the owner." Múzquiz appears to have been sympathetic to these runaways. He initiated legal proceedings against Brown and his posse because, "even though the kidnapping was not perpetrated on five completely free men, at the very least these unfortunate beings had put themselves under the protection of the laws of Mexico."[37]

A flashpoint of Anglo-American disregard for Mexican law occurred during the conventionist movement of 1832–33 spearheaded by the ayuntamiento of San Felipe. In summer 1832 the local authorities there called on all other municipalities to send representatives to a convention that was to meet on 1 October 1832. They would discuss such thorny matters as Mexico's tariff regulations, the issuance of land titles in East Texas, and the repeal of an anti-immigration clause contained in the so-called Law of 6 April 1830. None of the Mexican ayuntamientos chose to attend. Conventions were simply not part of Mexico's political repertoire. Traditionally, such requests had to come out of the ayuntamientos and channeled through the jefe político to higher authority. And besides, the agenda was obviously geared toward the Anglo-American colonies. To add insult to injury, the convention decided to request the separation of Texas from Coahuila without any formal representation from the Mexican towns.

Múzquiz was caught in the middle. He could not endorse a procedure that so patently disregarded his authority. The jefe político declared the proceedings illegal and ordered the convention dissolved. "But you are not to understand from this," Don Ramón wrote to Stephen F. Austin in a more conciliatory tone, "that I am opposed to the objects which that ayuntamiento has in mind. Altogether to the contrary, I should have wished to further them to the limit of my legal power."[38] For the conventionist leaders, however, this was not enough. Undaunted, a more radical wing of the movement called for a second convention that was to start on 1 April 1833. In Múzquiz's mind a Rubicon had been crossed. He wrote to the governor of Coahuila y Texas stating his fear that the Anglo-American colonists were aiming at independence. At the same time he tried to find some common ground with the colonists, urging the ayuntamiento of San Felipe to ask permission to hold this second convention and thereby legalize the meeting and "restore confidence in the good faith of the colonists."[39]

As the political situation deteriorated, Don Ramón withdrew from politics during much of 1833 and 1834. There were several reasons for this. He must have been unsettled by the assertiveness of the colonists in the wake of the conventionist movement. Had his policies in favor of Anglo-American immigration, freedom of trade, and slavery been misguided? Was he abetting the dismemberment of Mexico's territory? Beyond these political ruminations there were personal matters. Since summer 1832, Múzquiz had suffered from an illness (characterized by "calenturas intermitentes") that had sidelined him from administrative duties for months.[40] He kept complaining of his health for much of this period. He also became anxious about his commercial ventures. In March 1833 he requested a leave of absence that would last for almost a year. Judging by the number of commercial invoices in his name, he must have used his time wisely. Finally, 1833 was a tragic year. A cholera epidemic ravaged much of Mexico. Múzquiz's longtime partner and confidant, Juan Martín Veramendi, lost his life at that time. Don Ramón returned to his post on 1 March 1834 only to resign four months later because of another bout with illness.[41]

For a time it must have seemed as if Múzquiz's political life was drawing to a close. But he staged a return in March 1835 when he was appointed vice-governor of Coahuila y Texas on the same ticket that elected the staunchly federalist Agustín Viesca as governor. His election could not have occurred at a more dramatic time. The entire country was engulfed in a political showdown. As centralism gained momentum in central Mexico and became endorsed by President Santa Anna, Coahuila y Texas became one of the last and most radical federalist bastions. As one historian has rightfully observed, the very election of Viesca "constituted a direct challenge to Santa Anna's administration."[42] Governor Viesca made a dazzling entrance into Monclova, the seat of the embattled federalist state legislature and the very epicenter of the federalist movement within the state, and immediately took steps to obtain arms and men to resist a possible military intervention by the central government.[43]

Interestingly, even though Don Ramón was originally from the district of Monclova and his election as vice-governor must have required his presence there, he remained eerily aloof, preferring to devote his time to commercial matters. In March 1835, when he was elected vice-governor, he initiated a leisurely overland trip to New Orleans by way of Natchitoches from which he would not return until late April or early May.[44] And even afterward, the only records we have of him pertain to negotiations with customs officials in Goliad and San Antonio. He was reluctant to become involved in politics. But when Governor Viesca was imprisoned in June 1835 during his bold attempt to move the seat of the state government from Monclova to

San Antonio, the political initiative landed once again at Múzquiz's doorstep. Could he assume the governorship?

Múzquiz was an attractive choice. For the centralists he was far more palatable than the radical Viesca. Indeed, throughout the revolutionary period Don Ramón enjoyed "a frank and warm relationship" with Colonel Domingo de Ugartechea, military commander of Coahuila y Texas, and with General Martín Perfecto de Cos, commander of the eastern interior provinces and the most visible leader of centralism in the region.[45] At the same time, the former jefe político did not hide his political sympathies for the federalist movement. In fact, he regarded Santa Anna's government as nothing more than a "military and ecclesiastical theocracy."[46] The people of Texas were naturally drawn to Múzquiz after having worked with him for the better part of a decade. A Committee of the Jurisdiction of Columbia, for example, recommended in early July 1835 to "write officially to don Ramón Múzquiz, declaring, if he will proceed to administer the Government, the people of the Department [of Brazos] will rally around sustain and support him."[47] R. M. Williamson, while addressing the people of San Felipe in late June 1835 and urging them to seize San Antonio militarily, noted that "don Ramón Múzquiz the Vice Governor, who by the constitution is now your Governor, has expressed his willingness to act provided the Colonists will sustain him, but he dares not attempt it so long as St. Antonio is in possession of the enemy. What can you or will you do, unless you bring him into the colonies and re-establish the Government."[48]

It was a moment of truth. One wonders what would have happened had Don Ramón accepted the leadership of Texas in those critical times. But, as it turned out, events on the ground took their own course. In August 1835 President Santa Anna named another Múzquiz, Rafael Ecay Múzquiz, to the governorship of Coahuila y Texas.[49] General Cos briefly considered the idea of reappointing Don Ramón as jefe político of Texas, but nothing came of that.[50] Ramón Múzquiz remained in his adopted San Antonio through these perilous times. He was elected president of the committee for the commemoration of Mexico's independence in San Antonio to be celebrated on 16 September 1835.[51] When General Cos's troops occupied the town, Múzquiz was asked to provide quarters for the Mexican commander.[52] And when the largely Anglo-Texan forces laid siege to San Antonio in December, the former jefe político was named a commissioner in the negotiations leading to the withdrawal of General Cos's troops.[53]

Clearly, Múzquiz was on speaking terms with both sides. By April 1836 he was discussing the possibility of reestablishing regular mail deliveries between Coahuila and Texas, which had been interrupted by the political upheavals. He was also present when the Alamo fell and assisted in the identification of the bodies of Travis, Crockett, Bowie, and some of the other defenders.[54] At last the former jefe político decided to leave San Antonio for good in May 1836. His losses stemming from the Texas Revolution were formidable. All of the merchandise that he had purchased during his 1835 trip to New Orleans, estimated at more than 30,000 pesos, was seized by the Mexican warship *Moctezuma*. He also lost his comfortable house on the northeast corner of the main square of San Antonio when President Houston signed an act of congress in November 1836 enabling Erastus "Deaf" Smith to select any house and lot of his choosing for the services he had rendered to the cause of Texas. He chose the home of the former jefe político.[55] By the late 1830s all Múzquiz had left in Texas were a few scattered pieces of land.

The former jefe político of Texas went back to Monclova, where he lived out the rest of his life. His family's prominence and close alliance with the influential Blanco family enabled Don Ramón to regain a position of leadership quickly.[56] In 1837 he was named prefect of the district of Monclova.[57] In 1849 he assumed the position of vice-governor of the state of Coahuila, and in 1853 he served again as prefect of the district of Monclova.[58]

Múzquiz died in the city of Monclova on 27 November 1867.[59] Ramón Múzquiz's star had crossed the Texas sky briefly but brightly. His rise to prominence had been meteoric, and so had been his demise. Noblesse oblige. He became entangled in Mexico's endless revolutions, as he put it, "fighting against the oligarchs who support the Constitution of 1836 and in favor of those wish to reestablish that of 1824."[60] It was a struggle that would not end within his lifetime.

Notes

1. *Múzquiz* is sometimes spelled *Músquiz* just as *Ecay y Múzquiz* is sometimes rendered as *Eca y Múzquiz* or *Eca y Músquiz*. In spite of the spelling variants, all belong to the same family. I have chosen *Múzquiz* simply because it is the spelling commonly used by most of the descendants who still thrive around Coahuila and Texas. It was my good fortune to meet some of them at the Tejano Leadership symposium conducted at Texas State University in San Marcos on 14 October 2006.

2. The history of the Múzquiz family has to be pieced together from a variety of sources. On the colonial antecedents one needs to turn to the Múzquiz (Coahuila, Mexico) Collection WA MSS S-1482 at the Beinecke Rare Book and Manuscript Library, Yale University, New Haven, CT. A copy of this last source can also be found at the Archivo General del Estado de Coahuila (AGEC) in Ramos Arizpe, Coahuila, right outside Saltillo. While conducting research at the AGEC, it was my good fortune to strike up a conversation with Lucas Martínez Sánchez, the director of the archive. He graciously gave me several essays and a book that he wrote, all of which contain valuable information about the Múzquiz family based on direct archival sources in both Monclova and Saltillo. See especially Lucas Martínez Sánchez, *La familia Blanco Múzquiz: Patriotas de Monclova* (Ramos Arizpe: Archivo General del Estado de Coahuila, 2006), 2–41; and Lucas Martínez Sánchez, *Jesús Carranza Neira-Santiago Vidaurri Valdés: Correspondencia 1856–1864* (Saltillo: Gobierno de Coahuila/Colegio Coahuilense de Investigaciones Históricas, 2006), 109.

3. Catarina González de Paredes was born in March 1760 in Santa Rosa. She died in 1855 at the advanced age of ninety-five. Lieutenant Miguel Múzquiz was baptized in Santa Rosa in 1745. He was the son of Joseph de Ecay y Múzquiz and María de la Garza. He was known as the *capitán Chiquito* ("small captain"). Martínez Sánchez, *La familia Blanco Múzquiz*, 8.

4. In various receipts for purchases of slaves at the real de minas de San Pedro Boca de Leones between 1799 and 1806, Miguel Múzquiz claims to be a citizen of the royal town and presidio of Santa Rosa, Coahuila. See microfilmed edition of the Bexar Archives at the University of Texas Archives [BA], reel 29, frames 131–33 and real 29, frames 187–91; Commandant General Pedro de Nava to Governor Juan Bautista Elguezabal, 4 August 1800, BA, authorizing the transfer of Lieutenant Múzquiz to Nacogdoches. Lieutenant Múzquiz was already in Nacogdoches by January 1801, when he protested having to share the commission with his predecessor, Lieutenant Miguel del Moral. Lieutenant Miguel Francisco Múzquiz to Juan de Elguezabal, 30 January 1801, BA.

5. Commandant General Pedro de Nava to Governor Juan Bautista Elguezabal, 7 July 1801, BA.

6. Commandant General Nava to Governor Elguezabal, 21 July 1801, BA.

7. Nava to Elguezabal, 10 April 1804, BA.

8. Bill of sale of a slave by Lieutenant Múzquiz, 22 January 1806, BA.

As late as 1820, Lieutenant Múzquiz was involved in an expedition against the "barbarous Indians," 12 December 1820, in AGEC, Fondo Colonial, C45, E54, 3F.

9.   It is quite possible that little Ramón, his mother, and the rest of the family only got to Nacogdoches to rejoin Lieutenant Múzquiz in 1802. See Commandant General Nava to Governor Elguezabal, 25 May 1802, BA.

10.   The Bexar Archives contains several certificates of mail going to San Antonio bearing his signature in 1818 and 1819, e.g. BA 60:550, 640.

11.   For a more thorough discussion of the impact of economic liberalization on Mexico's northern frontier, see Andrés Reséndez, *Changing National Identities at the Frontier: Texas and New Mexico, 1800–1850* (New York: Cambridge University Press, 2005), chapter 3.

12.   Import receipt issued by customs officer Gaspar Flores, San Antonio, 29 March 1823, BA. Unfortunately the receipt does not say where the goods were coming from. But a letter written a few days later, and also referring to Múzquiz's imports, sheds additional light. Francisco Joseph Bernal to Juan Martín de Veramendi, 19 April 1823, BA. In this letter Múzquiz and his partner Don Francisco Madero are both identified as being "del comercio de Monclova." The letter also refers to wine and *aguardiente* and the import duties that should be paid. These are articles that merchants from Coahuila typically sold in places like Texas and New Mexico. Though I cannot rule out the possibility that Múzquiz was already procuring these goods from Louisiana, what little evidence we have indicates that he started out as a more traditional merchant plying the route between Coahuila and Texas and only subsequently became involved in the Louisiana-Texas trade.

13.   For instance, in 1827 George Maya, captain of the New Orleans ship *Minerva*, brought a full load belonging to Ramón Múzquiz and Manuel Iturri. See José Bonifacio Galán, Comisario Particular de la Bahía del Espíritu Santo, to the Comisario Particular de la ciudad de Béxar, 7 December 1827, BA.

14.   Múzquiz to Saucedo, San Antonio, 28 July 1825, BA. Saucedo had already requested the appointment of Múzquiz in May. See Saucedo to the ayuntamiento of Béxar, 28 July 1825, BA.

15.   Saucedo actually oversaw the sale of two of Lieutenant Múzquiz's slaves in 1806. Bill of sale of María del Carmen Ramírez and José María del Refugio Guajardo, 10 May 1806, BA.

16.   Numerous letters concerning Don Ramón's salary as secretary of the jefe político of Texas are extant in the Bexar Archives, beginning

with Múzquiz to Saucedo, 28 July 1825, BA. See also BA 84:891–97 and 97:444–47, among others.

17. Múzquiz to Saucedo, 27 August 1827, BA.

18. According to Article 147 of the 1827 constitution of Coahuila and Texas, the governor, "on the proposition of the electoral council and supported by the recommendations of the ayuntamientos of the respective Departments, shall appoint the jefes políticos of each Department except in the state capital." On the appointment of Múzquiz as jefe político, see Saucedo to the ayuntamiento of 27 December 1828, BA; and Múzquiz to Viesca, 1 January 1828, BA.

19. Ramón Múzquiz to the ayuntamiento of Béxar, 1 January 1828, BA.

20. Francisco González de la Lama to Colonel Antonio Elozúa, Military Commander of Texas, 6 January 1828, BA.

21. *Sitio* was the correct term for the measure of area that came to be known as the "league" in Mexican Texas because it measured one square league, or 4,428.4 acres. Eleven league grants totaled almost 49,000 acres, although grantees could break up the acreage in different parcels.

22. Report of Antonio Padilla, 21 October 1828, BA.

23. Lucas de Palomino, 11 January 1830, BA.

24. José Antonio Navarro, on behalf of the ayuntamiento and comisión electoral to the governor of Coahuila y Texas, 22 September 1830, BA.

25. Múzquiz to comandante general Antonio Elozúa, 1 July 1828, BA; and Commander Elozúa to Múzquiz, 4 July 1828, BA.

26. Ramón Múzquiz to Philip Dimmitt, 8 June 1835, Dimmitt Papers, Center for American History, University of Texas at Austin.

27. The final decree of secularization of 1824 required the San Antonio municipal authorities to distribute former mission lands among the descendants of neophyte Indians or citizens who did not own property. But poorer residents still ended up selling to more affluent ones, thus resulting in land concentration. Some of the largest Tejano landholders include Miguel Arciniega, José Casiano, Manuel Castillo, Francisco de la Garza, José Antonio de la Garza, Ramón Múzquiz, José Antonio Navarro, Luciano Navarro, Francisco Ruiz, Erasmo Seguín, and Juan Nepomuceno Seguín. Individual holdings can be found in Gifford White, ed., *The 1840 Census of the Republic of Texas* (Austin: Pemberton Press, 1966). Unfortunately, the 1830 census did not include property records.

28. José María Sánchez, " A Trip to Texas in 1828," in Carlos E. Castañeda, trans., *Southwestern Historical Quarterly* 29 (April 1926): 260–61.

29. San Antonio Census, 31 December 1828, Eugene C. Barker Texas

History Collection 2Q300, 206:218–25, Center for American History, University of Texas at Austin [CAH]. The profit made by both groups was estimated at 50 percent.

30. The Dimmitt Papers contain several letters to and from Múzquiz from the early 1820s through the late 1830s.

31. This was not the first time the federal government had attempted to abolish slavery. As early as 14 July 1824 the authorities of Texas had received a decree abolishing slavery throughout Mexico, granting freedom to any slaves entering Mexico, and urging port authorities to confiscate the cargo of any slaving ship. See decree in BA 77:485. For the background of the abolition decree of 1829, see Alessio Robles, *Coahuila y Texas desde la consumación de la independencia hasta el tratado de paz de Guadalupe Hidalgo*, 2d ed. (Mexico: Editorial Porrúa, 1979): 1:227–42; Eugene C. Barker, *The Life of Stephen F. Austin, Founder of Texas, 1793–1836* (Nashville, TN: Cokesbury Press, 1925), 203–44; Barker, "The Influence of Slavery in the Colonization of Texas," *Mississippi Valley Historical Review* 11 (June 1924): 3–36; and Randolph B. Campbell, *An Empire for Slavery: The Peculiar Institution in Texas, 1821–1865* (Baton Rouge: Louisiana State University Press, 1991), chapter 1.

32. Receipt for purchase of María del Carmen Ramírez, San Pedro de Boca de Leones, 23 October 1799, BA; and receipt of purchase of José María del Refugio Guajardo, San Pedro de Boca de Leones, 16 November 1799, BA. San Pedro de Boca de Leones was an important mining center and evidently a hub for the buying and selling of slaves.

33. Cassiano-Pérez Collection, box 2, folder 112, CAH.

34. Barker, *Life of Stephen F. Austin*, 244.

35. Múzquiz to Green De Witt, 27 May 1832, BA.

36. The case is rather complicated. Three of the adult black slaves appeared to have come from Arkansas, where they had been enslaved by Cherokees. The other two had been recently introduced into Texas, as explained below.

37. Múzquiz to governor of Coahuila and Texas, 3 June 1832, John W. Smith Collection, box 2, Daughters of the Republic of Texas Research Library at the Alamo, San Antonio.

38. Múzquiz to Austin, 11 October 1832, cited in Barker, *Life of Stephen F. Austin*, 408.

39. Múzquiz to governor of Coahuila and Texas, 11 January 1833, and Múzquiz to ayuntamiento of San Felipe, 27 February 1833, both cited in Barker, *Life of Stephen F. Austin*, 417 and 418, respectively.

40. Múzquiz to Governor, 30 July 1832, BA.

41. Múzquiz's request for leave of absence, 26 March 1833, BA; invoices of goods belonging to him, 9 April 1833, BA. Resumption of duties as jefe político, 27 February 1834, BA.

42. Alessio Robles, *Coahuila y Texas*, 1:532.

43. Reséndez, *Changing National Identities*, 154–60.

44. Múzquiz to Dimmitt, 10 March 1835, and Múzquiz to Dimmitt, New Orleans, 27 April 1835, both in the Dimmitt Papers.

45. Múzquiz to Dimmitt, 6 June 1835, Dimmitt Papers.

46. Ibid.

47. The Committee of the Jurisdiction of Columbia to the Political Chief of the Brazos Department, James B. Miller, Columbia, 3 July 1835, in *Papers Concerning Robertson's Colony in Texas*, 10:484.

48. Address of R. M. Williamson, Chairman of the meeting at San Felipe, 22 June 1835, *Papers of the Texas Revolution 1835–1836*, no. 329.

49. The tortuous road leading to this appointment is best recounted by Alessio Robles, *Coahuila y Texas*, 2:32–37.

50. General Martín Perfecto de Cos to General Ugartechea, 7 July 1835, BA.

51. Minutes of the committee, 16 August 1835, BA.

52. Letter to Governor Eca y Múzquiz, 21 September 1835, BA.

53. Article 18 of the capitulations, 11 December 1835, in *Papers of the Texas Revolution*, no. 1447.

54. Carlos Castañeda, *Our Catholic Heritage in Texas, 1519–1936* (Austin: Von Boeckmann-Jones, 1950), 6:292.

55. McLean, *Papers Concerning Robertson's Colony*, 14:251.

56. See especially Martínez Sánchez, *La familia Blanco Múzquiz*.

57. Appointment of Ramón Múzquiz as prefect of the district of Monclava, Monclava, 11 November 1837, in AGEC, F.S. XIX, C3.

58. Appointment of Múzquiz as vice-governor, Saltillo, 31 August 1849, in AGEC, F.S. XIX, C5, F9, E1, 3F. He would step down on 19 June 1850. See AGEC, F.S. XIX, C4, F3, E11, 2F. Second appointment of Múzquiz as prefect of the district of Monclova, 9 December 1853, AGEC, F.S. XIX, C8, F7, E9, 2F.

59. Lucas Martínez Sánchez, *Jesús Carranza Neira-Santiago Vidaurri Valdés*, 109.

60. Múzquiz to Dimmitt, 5 March 1839, Dimmitt Papers.

The son of a Corsican merchant, José Antonio Navarro lived to become the most prominent and respected member of the Tejano generation that brought about Texas independence. A signer of both the Texas Declaration of Independence and the state constitution of 1845, he was honored with the naming of Navarro County.

Courtesy #1979/181-24, Texas State Library and Archives Commission.

JOSÉ ANTONIO NAVARRO

THE PROBLEM OF
TEJANO POWERLESSNESS

James E. Crisp

JOSÉ ANTONIO NAVARRO was one of the most important and most celebrated Tejanos of the nineteenth century. His list of political offices and appointments is long and impressive. He was the first alcalde of San Antonio de Béxar elected after Mexico declared its independence in 1821.[1] Later in that decade he served as a Texan representative in the legislature of the combined state of Coahuila y Texas, and in the early 1830s he was appointed by that state's government to be the land commissioner for the Anglo-American colony of Stephen F. Austin's fellow empresario, Green Dewitt.[2] In 1835, Navarro was chosen by the federalist legislators of Coahuila y Texas to represent the state as a senator in the national Mexican congress—an honor he pointedly declined to accept.[3] Within a few months he was instead a signer of the Texas Declaration of Independence of 1836, and in 1845 he became one of the handful of men and the only native Texan to frame both the constitution of the Texas Republic and that of the new State of Texas. He represented Bexar County in the Congress of the Republic of Texas and after American annexation in the Texas State Legislature—where he was honored by his peers with the naming of Navarro County in 1846.[4]

His less formal accomplishments are no less significant, but they also hint at some of the controversy surrounding Navarro's career. He was one of the closest friends and confidants of Stephen F. Austin throughout Austin's life in Texas, and he was a key player in passing legislation (including the protection of slavery) that guaranteed the growth of Anglo settlement in Texas.[5] His most memorable service to the Texas Republic was as a reluctant representative of President Mirabeau Buonaparte Lamar in the ill-conceived Texan expedition to Santa Fe in 1841—a role that brought Navarro immense suffering in the dungeons of Mexico. Yet Navarro's perceived faithfulness to Texas during his long imprisonment—especially when contrasted at the time to the alleged treason and apostasy of his fellow Tejano Juan Seguín—gave to Navarro a moral grandeur in Texas that lasted until the end of a political career that spanned a half-century.[6]

Navarro used that exalted position to advocate the rights (and to urge the responsibilities) of his fellow Tejanos in the years after his escape from Mexican custody in 1845. During the 1850s, at the height of his fame and influence, Navarro became the first Tejano, and the first native-born, historian of Texas. His historical writings were no mere academic exercise. As he looked back across four long decades to trace the earliest struggles of the Tejanos for liberty in the doomed revolts of 1811 and 1813 against Spain, Navarro was simultaneously urging Tejanos to fight again for their liberties, but this time under the new flag of the United States of America.[7]

In his political and historical writings of the 1850s, Navarro gave a great deal of thought to the problem of powerlessness—a condition faced repeatedly by both him and his Tejano compatriots at many times and in many forms, individually and collectively. There is a Navarro family tradition that José Antonio maintained a symbolic representation of powerlessness as a part of his most personal emblem: his cattle brand. The small "o" ring at the top of the "N" in the conjoined letters "JAN" that constituted his brand was said by a descendant in 1936 to represent "the huge ring in the prison floor to which he was chained for three and one-half years in Mexico on the orders of Santa Anna."[8]

Though the story is probably apocryphal, there is no doubt that concerns about the problem of powerlessness, his own and his people's, were seldom far from Navarro's mind throughout his life. His first experience with abject powerlessness came suddenly and with a vengeance in his eighteenth year, when in 1813 his community of San Antonio de Béxar suffered severe retribution for its citizens' complicity in a bid to win independence from Spanish rule.

Navarro's life in San Antonio had begun calmly enough in 1795, as one of twelve children of the successful merchant Angel Navarro, a native of Corsica who had arrived in Texas in 1777. In 1783 Angel married Josefa Ruiz y Peña, whose brother José Francisco Ruiz would come to exert a profound influence on his nephew José Antonio. More than once, Navarro and Ruiz would have to flee Texas together for their lives, largely because of revolutionary activity in which Francisco was unquestionably the dominant influence.[9]

The young José Antonio seemed destined at an early age to lead the quiet life, however. A childhood injury fractured his leg, which never healed properly and left him permanently disabled.[10] He was sent as a ten-year-old in 1805 to Saltillo to receive a formal education, but his studies seem to have been cut short not long before the death of his father Angel in 1808.[11] José returned to San Antonio to take up the mercantile trade, but he never lost his love of books and learning.

He eventually read enough law on his own to become an intermittently practicing attorney, and his later writings show a command of European history and political thought that was unusual on the isolated Texas frontier.[12]

The rumblings of revolution had first come to San Antonio in January 1811, when the retired military officer Juan Bautista de las Casas, inspired by Father Hidalgo's *grito de Dolores,* engineered a short-lived coup with the aid of some of the city's leading citizens against Governor Manuel Salcedo. Writing about this revolt from the perspective of the 1850s, Navarro called it "the first occasion in which the Mexicans of San Antonio de Béxar announced their desire to break forever the chains of their ancient colonial slavery."[13]

The restrictive rule of New Spain on this far northern frontier—stifling to both trade and ideas, and experienced by most of the inhabitants as a debilitating cycle of neglect and abuse—may have made the Tejanos feel as powerless as slaves, but in retrospect Navarro saw no great ideological cause behind the first revolt in Texas.[14] With few exceptions, he said, the Bexareños of 1811 still showed the "sweet conformity of a simple people,"[15] satisfied to entrust their happiness to the wisdom of their two sovereigns: one celestial, the other terrestrial. They might even have remained happy in this state of "blind obedience" to God and king, except that even then new ideas and aspirations were coming from "across the seas and through the narrow trails . . . [to] Texas," as he put it, "transmitted from the neighbor republic to the north."[16]

Some of these ideas came to San Antonio with the motley crew of Hispanic and Anglo revolutionaries who besieged the city in 1813 in the name of independence. The ragtag army under the nominal command of Bernardo Gutiérrez de Lara (which included many Anglo-Americans who seemed to think that Texas would make a fine addition to the United States) had captured both Nacogdoches and Goliad in 1812. By spring 1813, Gutiérrez received Governor Salcedo's surrender of San Antonio.[17]

The rebel cause was undermined by factional bickering, however, exacerbated by the complicity of Gutiérrez in the murder of Salcedo and his chief officers, whose throats were slit on the banks of the Salado River by their captors. Navarro, an eyewitness to the return of the guilty "assassins" into San Antonio, attempted to explain what kind of "revolutionaries" could commit such a deed. They were, he said, men of "extreme . . . ignorance and ferocious passions. . . . Among the Mexicans of that time, with some exceptions, there was no clear political sentiment. They did not know the importance of the words 'independence and liberty' and they did not understand the reasons for the rebellion of the priest Hidalgo as [anything] other than a shout for death and war without quarter on the *gachupines,* as the Spaniards were called."[18]

Nevertheless, José's uncle Francisco Ruiz had joined the rebel army, only to experience utter defeat when Spanish troops under General Joaquín de Arredondo struck back at the battle of Medina on 18 August 1813—the bloodiest battle ever fought on Texan soil.[19] With his fugitive uncle and a brother-in-law, Navarro fled east to Louisiana, where he spent a miserable three years wandering from one Mexican exile community to another. He considered these years a waste—he neither furthered his formal education nor learned English—but at least he escaped the fate of the powerless Bexareños who remained behind to face the wrath of General Arredondo.[20]

More than three hundred citizens were condemned to be shot, many of them dragged directly from the confessional to the firing squad. Many of the women of the town were crowded together in a public building, where they had to grind corn for the Spanish soldiers (and were forced to satisfy the soldiers' carnal appetites, as well).[21] It was a shattered city and a shunned family to which Navarro returned in 1816, when his mother obtained for him a royal pardon.[22]

The unrepentant uncle Francisco Ruiz remained an exile until the declaration of Mexican independence by Agustín de Iturbide in 1821 reunited the Navarro and Ruiz families in San Antonio and brought them back into the good graces of the government. Coincidentally, in August 1821, just a month after Navarro's older brother Angel had the pleasure of administering the oath of independence to the former Spanish governor, Stephen F. Austin arrived in the city, ready to begin his life's work.[23]

Austin found willing partners for his colonization plans in José Antonio Navarro and Francisco Ruiz, who (whether because of or de-spite their time in Louisiana) were quite unafraid of Americans. Austin and Navarro, similar in age and temperament, became especially close. They shared a vision of a Texas made populous and prosperous by Anglo immigration; they also shared an understanding that the men of capital and enterprise who would develop Texas would need laborers on a large scale—and this meant slaves.

When a new constitution for Coahuila y Texas promised to ban the further introduction of slaves into the state in 1827, Navarro was in a key position in the legislature's Committee on Colonization to introduce and push through a contract labor law that allowed colonists the subterfuge of bringing in their "servants or hirelings" under supposedly voluntary indenture agreements signed outside of Mexico—even when those contracts carried ninety-nine-year indentures.[24]

Navarro and the entire Tejano political establishment worked diligently to smooth the entry of the thousands of Anglo-Americans flocking into Texas to join Austin's colonists, even as the national government in Mexico City was having serious second thoughts about this immigration. The Tejanos and Austin managed to have Texas exempted from the abolition of slavery that was decreed by President Vicente Guerrero in 1829, and when further American settlement in Texas was prohibited outright by the Mexican Law of 6 April 1830, Tejano leaders not only protested but also connived with Austin to circumvent the law until it was repealed in 1834.[25]

In the meantime, the Tejanos had become outnumbered in Texas by the new arrivals. As the land commissioner for the Green DeWitt colony (headquartered at Gonzales) in 1831–32, Navarro saw firsthand some of the problems associated with the surge of Anglo-American immigrants.[26] In April 1832 he wrote to Samuel May Williams, chief assistant to Stephen F. Austin, complaining that a Mr. W. Moreland, one of the DeWitt colonists, had attempted, right under Navarro's whiskers ("casi en mis varvas") and despite Navarro's warning, to transfer illegally a large land grant to another Anglo-American after Moreland had decided to leave Texas for good.[27] Navarro was livid—he said that he was hardly able to control himself—and angry at both Moreland and the Texas surveyor general, Thomas J. Chambers (himself something of a shady land dealer), who seemed to countenance Moreland's "clandestine contract."[28] Yet Navarro nevertheless seemed to accept the new demographic realities and their consequences as inevitable: "We cannot deceive ourselves," he told Williams in the same letter, observing that "we all know the sad theater of speculation into which Texas has been converted with respect to lands. It may be well that we recognize this and accommodate, yielding to the irresistible imperative of circumstances."

Historian David Weber has argued that a fear of being politically overwhelmed by the Anglo settlers lay behind the refusal of the San Antonio ayuntamiento to request the separation of Texas from Coahuila in the formal *representación* sent from Béxar in December 1832 to the state capital.[29] Yet this document (a list of complaints and requests drafted at the instigation of Stephen F. Austin by a committee of six Bexareños including José Antonio Navarro) urged the government to allow the northerners, whether "capitalists" or merely industrious citizens, to be once again allowed to emigrate to Texas.[30] Moreover, in contrast to Weber, Jesús de la Teja and John Wheat have interpreted this key Tejano political document as actually showing a consonance of opinion between Tejanos and Anglo-Texans, and as implying if not stating outright the goal of eventual separate statehood for Texas.[31]

The Béxar *representación* laid the blame for most of Texas' troubles on the neglect with which the frontier district was treated by Coahuila. The Anglo-Texans agreed, and a convention of them sent Stephen F. Austin to Mexico City in 1833 to present their own explicit demand for separate statehood for Texas. Where the Bexareños did differ from their blunt neighbors was in their realization that one did not achieve political goals in Mexico by making demands on the government; one certainly did not (as Austin so imprudently did in his letter of 2 October from Mexico City to the Béxar ayuntamiento) urge the organization of Texas as a separate state without the blessing of the national government.[32]

The imprisonment this risky letter earned Austin seemed not to surprise Navarro. He told Austin's secretary, Samuel Williams, that although he hoped Austin would be completely cleared in Mexico City, Navarro had previously warned him as a friend about how to avoid such sorrows—but Austin had behaved instead like a child when he did not get his way.[33]

This does not mean, however, that Navarro saw the Mexican national government under Santa Anna as blameless. On the contrary, he wrote to Williams on 8 October 1834, as Austin sat in a Mexico City jail, that he expected nothing from the rise of centralism under Santa Anna but "militarism and the civil death of sacrosanct liberty." Navarro swore that he had rather see all of Texas "reduced to ashes than to live as a slave [powerless, in other words] under a despotic government." The time was fast approaching, he told Williams cryptically, when "the stakes would become both precious and necessary."[34]

Navarro's decisive moment came early in the following year, when he declined the appointment to the national senate from Coahuila y Texas on the advice of his uncle Francisco Ruiz, who felt even more certain that a moment of truth was approaching for Texas.[35] By the restless summer of that year, rather than taking his seat in congress, Navarro was helping Samuel Williams escape from military custody in San Antonio by distracting the guards and providing Williams his own fast horse.[36] And by fall 1835, Stephen F. Austin was back in

Texas, leading an "army of the people" to besiege the Mexican garrison at San Antonio. The Texas Revolution was in full swing.[37]

Navarro may have been surprised at how quickly the revolution radicalized Texas politics. The rebel army that took Béxar in December flew the Mexican tricolor in defense of the federal Constitution of 1824 that Santa Anna was ravaging.[38] But by February 1836, when Ruiz and Navarro were sent by the Bexareños as delegates to the Texan convention at Washington-on-the-Brazos, they were being warned by some of the Anglo soldiers in San Antonio not to come back if they did not vote for independence from Mexico.[39]

Navarro was hesitant, but again Tío Francisco took the lead, taking his trembling nephew by the arm as he rose to sign the Texas Declaration of Independence on the second of March.[40] When Navarro found himself a captive in Mexico and facing death for treason to that country a few years later, his Mexican military lawyer told the judges that Navarro had had no choice but to submit to the dominant political forces in Texas in 1836.[41] Later, as Navarro pleaded for his release from prison in 1843, he suggested that he was among those delegates to the 1836 convention "who were dragged along by the torrent which carried all before it in this tumultuous assembly."[42]

Even after his escape and return to Texas, Navarro admitted to his closest Anglo friends that he had been extremely reluctant to see the separation from Mexico, and that he had never dreamed that he would take part in such a movement.[43] But once he had committed himself, the die was cast. Even when he thought he would never see his family again—even when he had been officially condemned to death and his life was on the line—he bent but never broke. He told his jailers that he was a man "forever Mexican" who wished to God that the revolution had not forced him and his fellow Tejanos to make such a wrenching choice.[44] But after swearing loyalty to Texas, he never did forswear.[45]

Yet he had to have had second thoughts. The surge of Anglo-Americans and the land grabs that swallowed up the patrimony of many Tejanos led him to speak out in the Texas Congress in 1839 against such practices, but to no great effect.[46] It is telling that Navarro confided to his friend Reuben Potter that he had accepted—with great misgivings—the appointment by President Lamar to be a commissioner on the 1841 Santa Fe expedition with the rationalization that if the Texans were successful "he might prove a useful protector to a Mexican population brought suddenly under the military control of another race."[47]

It is interesting to compare Navarro's defense of vulnerable Tejano landholders in the Texan Congress in 1839 with another plea for Tejano rights made on the floor of the Texan Senate in 1840 by Juan Seguín. Navarro appealed to the Anglo-Texans' sense of fairness and to their sympathy for a "poor, ignorant people, destitute of all ideas of legal forms," who had enjoyed a long-undisturbed possession of their lands, but who now faced the consequences of a legal paper trail gone cold through the vagaries of revolution, war, and secession, not to mention the likely apathy of the Mexican government in following the "train of formalities" necessary to perfect a title to land. Now these "unfortunate people," said the lawyer and statesman Navarro,

> cannot come forward with their titles. They know nothing of the forms necessary to their defence; nor even any thing of the very language in which they are called on to defend themselves. Encouraged by such circumstances, there are not wanting men, who, hungry for land, and calculating on their skill in the chican[e]ry of the existing laws, as well as on the helpless ignorance of the innocent settlers, have surveyed the property of these simple people; and in some instances, have even effected a forcible intrusion upon the disputed land.[48]

The Congress, said Navarro, should pass special legislation guaranteeing the land titles of the citizens of Bexar County who found themselves in such dire straits.

Seguín, the warrior and statesman, also drew attention to the language barrier that put Tejanos at a disadvantage, but he chose not to dwell on their weakness but rather on the rights due to those who had helped to create the Texas Republic:

> The dearest rights of my constituents as Mexico-Texans are guaranteed by the Constitution and the Laws of the Republic of Texas; and at the formation of the social compact between the Mexicans and the Texians, they had rights guaranteed to them; they also contracted certain legal obligations—of all of which they are ignorant, and in consequence of their ignorance of the language in which the Laws and Constitution of the land are written. The Mexico-Texians were among the first who sacrificed their all in our glorious Revolution, and the disasters of war weighed heavy upon them, to achieve those blessings which, it appears, [they] are to be the last to enjoy.[49]

No one experienced more poignantly than Juan Seguín the rapid deterioration of the position of Tejanos in the Texas Republic that followed the incursions of the Mexican army in 1842. Twice the Mexicans captured San Antonio—the first time spreading false stories of Seguín's treasonous collaboration with them, and the second time bringing the "turncoat" Seguín to fight alongside them after he had been forced into exile from Texas by hostile mobs of Anglo soldiers during the intervening summer.

What Seguín had demanded in his 1840 speech was that the Tejanos, while retaining their ethnic identity as "Mexico-Texians," be recognized as equal members of the civic community. A similar plea, made against the backdrop of severe ethnic strife in Texas, was made even more pointedly by another group of "Mexico-Texians" in 1843. Twelve former prisoners of war—captured soldiers from Santa Anna's army who had elected to claim Texas citizenship after the revolution—published a statement in the Houston *Morning Star* which said in part:

> We are aware that during a season of past excitement, we were looked upon with suspicion and distrust, our motives, actions, and movements watched, but we say, ungenerously and unjustly so, and we . . . hereby declare, that we consider ourselves as Freemen and *Texians,* by adoption—willing ready at any moment to defend this soil. . . . We no not deny being Mexicans, far from it—but we *deny* and *defy* the Despot of Mexico, . . . Our motto is: "where Liberty dwells—there is our country."[50]

To put the matter bluntly but analytically, using the terminology employed by Tejano historian David Montejano, both Seguín and the ex-prisoners were trying to avoid the treatment of Mexicans in Texas as a "race," subject to "policies of discrimination or control." In other words, says Montejano, "The notion of race does not just consist of ideas and sentiments; it comes into being when these ideas and sentiments are publically articulated and institutionalized. Stated more concisely, 'race situations' exist when so defined by public policy."[51]

This was the potential situation into which José Antonio Navarro returned after his dramatic escape from the Mexican fortress prison of San Juan de Ulúa in January 1845.[52] After boarding a British vessel that took him to Cuba, he returned to Texas by way of New Orleans, landing in Galveston in the first week of February. He was greeted at the docks by admiring crowds who had already heard of his escape.

The military companies of the island city turned out to escort him to his hotel, and he was praised as a "long oppressed but unyielding patriot."[53] The Ninth Congress, meeting at Washington-on-the-Brazos, passed a joint resolution granting Navarro indemnification for the losses he had suffered in support of the republic.[54] He proceeded from Galveston to Houston, where he received more honors, and then across the breadth of the Republic of Texas to his ranch near San Antonio.[55]

It is hardly surprising to find that the Anglo-Texans praised the faithful patriot Navarro, who had refused to betray Texas even when reportedly offered a bribe and his freedom by Santa Anna,[56] while they reviled the "traitor" Seguín, notwithstanding the persecutions that had caused his defection.[57] But even some of the celebrations of Navarro's patriotism carried a threat to Tejanos in general. This remarkable statement by a Galveston editor was echoed elsewhere in the republic: "Although born and reared in the desert surrounded city of San Antonio de Béxar, Col. *Navarro is not of the abject race of Mexicans.* His father was a Corsican of good birth, and, what is worthy of remark, was born under the same roof with that [prodigy] of the human race, Napoleon Bonaparte."[58]

Navarro found his chance to stand up to the challenge of racist policies almost immediately after his return, when he was elected to represent Bexar County in the 1845 convention that wrote a constitution for the new American state of Texas. The delegates came together on the Fourth of July in Austin, where the first regular order of business was the granting of permission to José Antonio Navarro to engage the services of an interpreter. The second order of business was the favorable response to the invitation to join "the federal Union."[59]

Though Navarro was the only Tejano (and only native Texan) delegate to the convention, he was extraordinarily effective in protecting his fellow Mexican Texans from explicitly racist policies. He was successful in preventing the use of the term "white" in defining the rights of citizenship and the franchise in the new state of Texas, though he was a pragmatist who went along with the constitutional exclusion from these rights of "Indians not taxed, Africans and the descendants of Africans."[60]

Navarro also had to deal in the convention with "men, hungry for land" who might use the "chicanery of the laws" to attack the property rights of the Tejanos.[61] In the final days of deliberation, Lemuel D. Evans, a delegate from East Texas, demanded the constitutional nullification of all claims originating under Spanish or Mexican rule within twenty leagues (about sixty miles) of the existing Texas border with the United States; a cancellation of all land claims emanating from Mexican authority after 1 January 1832; and the prohibition of landholding in Texas by "foreigners."[62] This was too much for Oliver Jones, one of Stephen F. Austin's "Old Three Hundred" original colonists who, like Navarro, had once served in the legislature of the Mexican state of Coahuila y Texas.[63] Jones offered a hostile (and successful) amendment to Evans's motion that would have nullified every single land grant ever made in Texas prior to its entry into the American union (thus assuring the motion's defeat).[64] Navarro then added insult to injury toward Evans's cause when he suggested, perhaps bitterly but certainly with tongue in cheek, that in order to eliminate any difficulties with titles and land grants,

> every settler who may have located his claim upon any grants heretofore made by the former governments of Spain and Mexico, shall be bound within the term of two years from the date of the adoption of this Constitution, to enclose the same with a stone wall on all sides, of eight yards height at least. The obligation shall devolve upon his heirs and assigns, on pain, in case of not complying with it, or in case of neglect to keep said wall in constant repair, so that there never shall be a breach in it to the extent of one yard, then, and in those cases, he shall forfeit all his claim to said land.[65]

Before the delegates had time to reflect that some of Navarro's fellow Tejanos would have had less difficulty in keeping their lands even under these ludicrous provisions than they did under the conditions that prevailed in the southwestern borderlands, a parliamentary maneuver quashed Evans's already fatally amended motion.[66] Navarro was a feisty debater and never afraid to use satire, irony, or dry wit to confound those who would denigrate the character and abilities of "Mexicans." He also showed himself to be a shrewd advocate, well versed in the constitutional provisions of three republics. He was the oratorical star of the Texas constitutional convention of 1845, even though he had to speak through a translator.[67]

In the aftermath of the American annexation of Texas and the war with Mexico that followed, not only did more immigrants pour into the state, but also the boundary of Texas was effectively extended to the Rio Grande, encompassing many more Hispanic property holders. With even more pressure coming from "men, hungry for land,"

Navarro sought to employ the same alliance of "old settlers"—Hispanic and Anglo—against those using the "chicanery of the laws" that had been so effective in the 1845 constitutional convention. The front page of the Houston *Democratic Telegraph and Texas Register* of 30 November 1848 featured a lengthy essay penned by Navarro at his San Jeronimo ranch the previous summer. The shrewd Tejano warned that his "predictions [were] beginning to be verified," and that sharp operators were swarming into Texas, putting down claims to old titles that were said to be "defective."[68]

Not just Tejanos were vulnerable, wrote Navarro, but also all old settlers who had claimed land under Mexican laws—laws that among other things required that the grantees be Roman Catholic and of good moral character, and that permanent landmarks of stone masonry be erected. These and many other technicalities could obviously be used to undermine the property rights of many of the leading citizens of the state. As a direct result of Navarro's publication, a meeting in Houston of "Old Settlers" was called for Texas Independence Day 1849 by men who were determined that land titles awarded by Mexico should not be subjected to debilitating lawsuits.[69]

In the 1850s José Antonio Navarro came to the defense of the Mexicans of Texas with his most stirring prose, in essays published in English-language San Antonio newspapers for the edification of the Anglo-Texans who now made up the majority of the city's population. These essays were eventually collected and published in Spanish in 1869 under the title *Apuntes Historicos Interesantes*. In this work Navarro praised the valor of the Tejanos who sacrificed their lives in the revolutions of 1811, 1813, and 1836 and stiffly corrected Anglo would-be historians whose accounts of Texan heroism began only with the coming of the North Americans.[70]

Navarro defended Tejanos against both American and Mexican detractors. The Mexican nation, he charged, had rewarded the heroes of San Antonio who had stood up against the Spanish with nothing but indifference and ingratitude, sowing a germ of bitterness and discontent among the Tejanos. He urged the Americans not to make the same mistake, but to "treat with more respect this race of men who, as the legitimate proprietors of the land, lost it together with their lives and their hopes, to follow in the footsteps of those very ones who now enjoy the land in the midst of peace and plenty."[71] The Tejanos, in other words, were sacrificing their lives and fortunes for liberty long before the coming to Texas of the Americans, who should now appreciate their fellow revolutionaries rather than dismiss them as the passive pawns of despots.

Most important, Navarro in the 1850s presented the same message of Tejano pride to the Tejanos themselves. As he joined with the "repatriated" Juan Seguín to urge Bexareños to resist the nativist Know Nothing movement during the 1855 election campaign, Navarro called on them to lift themselves up from "the dust of indifference" and to remember that they were the "descendants of those 'zapadores Hispano-Mejicanos' who conquered" San Antonio.[72]

Like Seguín, whose own wrenching dilemma of national loyalty and identity had played out so differently in the 1840s, Navarro appears to have found more comfort under the Stars and Stripes than the Lone Star of the Republic. The spreading of the United States over San Antonio was, he said, the work of a "Divine Providence," and it was no disgrace to be "invited to become adoptive sons of a grand and free nation." Merging Tejano pride with American patriotism, Navarro proclaimed:

> The American flag covers us, to it we belong, and for it we ought to sacrifice our lives if it is necessary; its brilliant constellations give us plenty of light with which to see and defend our rights. Why should we appear to be strangers in our own land where we were born? Why should we not be pure Americans in order to earn the benefits of her institutions?—then they will not frighten us with that bugbear ["ese coco"] that we are of another origin; then our American convictions will blot out the apathetic images and will elevate us to think, feel, and participate in all of the transactions of our adopted country.[73]

Navarro was no fool. He knew, as he wrote in a letter to the "border bandit" Juan Cortina in 1860 when Cortina was up in arms against the legal establishment and the armies of two nations, that "into our country appear from time to time some evil genius speculators, rogues, whose thirst for the acquisition of land, which they are incapable of gaining through industry or good deeds to the country, impels them to be infamous persecutors of an honorable [but] weak citizen, or someone who appears to them illiterate, in order to claim their rights." But Navarro maintained to Cortina that "that class of infamous men has nothing in common with the law-abiding and honorable nature of the American people in general," and he urged the outlaw to throw himself on the mercy of the courts.[74]

Navarro and his family supported the Confederacy during the Civil War, but it should be clear to anyone viewing his life as a whole that his ultimate loyalty until he died in 1871 was to the Tejano people among whom he was born, and to whom he gave a half-century of service. His methods were persuasion, the law, and political action. His goal was to empower his people, whatever flag flew over San Antonio.

Notes

1. Anastacio Bueno Jr., "In Storms of Fortune: José Antonio Navarro of Texas, 1821–1846" (M.A. thesis, University of Texas at San Antonio, 1978), 30.

2. Ibid., 35, 59.

3. Navarro claimed illness in declining election to the national congress in 1835. See the letter to Navarro from Diego Grant and José M. J. Carvajal, 29 April 1835, José Antonio Navarro Papers, Center for American History, University of Texas at Austin [CAH].

4. *New Handbook of Texas*, s.v. "Navarro, José Antonio."

5. Gregg Cantrell, *Stephen F. Austin, Empresario of Texas* (New Haven, Conn.: Yale University Press, 1999), 204–5, 344.

6. For a direct comparison of the Anglo-Texan views of Seguín and Navarro, see James E. Crisp, "Anglo-Texan Attitudes toward the Mexican, 1821–1846" (Ph.D. diss., Yale University, 1976), 368–403.

7. David R. McDonald and Timothy M. Matovina, eds., *Defending Mexican Valor in Texas: José Antonio Navarro's Historical Writings, 1853–1857* (Austin: State House Press, 1995).

8. Gus L. Ford, ed., *Texas Cattle Brands: A Catalog of the Texas Centennial Exposition Exhibit 1936* (Dallas, Tex.: Clyde C. Cockrell, 1936), 3, quoting A. N. Langston. My thanks to David R. McDonald of San Antonio for sharing his research from his forthcoming biography of José Antonio Navarro and for identifying the source of this quotation as the Arthur Navarro Langston cited in an inaccurate and misleading footnote found in Joseph Martin Dawson, *Jose Antonio Navarro: Co-Creator of Texas* (Waco, Tex.: Baylor University Press, 1969), 91. Dawson claimed, apparently based on the statement by Langston, that Navarro altered his brand on returning to Texas from his Mexican imprisonment in 1845, though this seems not to have been explicitly stated by Langston. Adding to the confusion, Langston is also quoted in *Texas Cattle Brands* as saying that Navarro "did not register his brand," though editor Gus L. Ford, citing "a M[anu] S[cript] in the Bexar Archives" as his source, says that the brand was

"granted November 7, 1833, at Atascosa to José Antonio Navarro." That manuscript with Navarro's original brand has not been found.

9. *New Handbook of Texas*, s.v. "Navarro, José Angel." See also Jacob De Cordova, *Texas: Her Resources and Her Public Men*, 2d ed. (Philadelphia: J. B. Lippincott, 1858; reprint, Waco, Tex.: Texian Press, 1969), 145–53.

10. Although there are conflicting historical accounts of the timing and cause of Navarro's injury to his leg, the most forthright version from Navarro himself is to be found in his letter from prison to the president of the Republic of Mexico, written 26 September 1843; see "Jose Antonio Navarro and Santa Fe Expedition, 1841–1845," [E. C.] Barker transcripts from the Archivo General de México, [Dept. of] Guerra y Marina, 338:51–52, CAH.

11. De Cordova, *Texas*, 145; *New Handbook of Texas*, s.v. "Navarro, José Antonio."

12. A good example of Navarro's breadth of knowledge is to be found in his *Apuntes Historicos Interesantes* (Privately published, San Antonio, Tex., 1869), a facsimile of which appears in McDonald and Matovina, *Defending Mexican Valor*. In an essay originally written in 1857, Navarro compared the growing appeal of republican institutions over monarchist ideology in early nineteenth-century Texas. Navarro refers to this monarchist ideology as "las ideas y costumbres ultramontanas" (*Apuntes*, 12). The English translation of this passage in *Defending Mexican Valor* reads: "The appeal of ideas and customs from beyond the mountains faded before the incomparable satisfaction of a people-king in the Americas; the tottering Spanish rulers would very soon be broken apart by the moral strength of republican institutions." This literal translation of "ultramontanas" obscures Navarro's meaning. What he was actually referring to were "ultramontane" ideas. Ultramontanism was the policy of a faction in the Roman Catholic Church that favored increasing and enhancing the power and authority of the pope. Navarro is using the word to describe the ideas and customs of those whom he accused of giving blind obedience ("ciega obediencia") to an earthly king as well as to a heavenly sovereign. See *Apuntes*, 11–12; *Defending Mexican Valor*, 61, 74–75.

13. McDonald and Matovina, *Defending Mexican Valor*, 68.

14. See David J. Weber, *The Mexican Frontier, 1821–1846: The American Southwest under Mexico* (Albuquerque: University of New Mexico Press, 1982), 9–10.

15. This is my admittedly literal translation of Navarro's "dulce conformidad de un sencillo Pueblo" (*Apuntes*, 11). McDonald and Matovina

render the phrase as the "complacent conformity of an untutored community" (*Defending Mexican Valor*, 74).

16. McDonald and Matovina, *Defending Mexican Valor*, 75.

17. *New Handbook of Texas*, s.v. "Gutiérrez-Magee Expedition."

18. McDonald and Matovina, *Defending Mexican Valor*, 50.

19. *New Handbook of Texas*, s.v. "Medina, Battle of."

20. "José Antonio Navarro[,] San Antonio de Bexar . . . Autobiographical Notes," in Charles Adams Gulick Jr. and Katherine Elliott, eds., *The Papers of Mirabeau Buonaparte Lamar*, 3:597–598 [*Lamar Papers*].

21. Notes given by José Antonio Navarro to M. B. Lamar, 18 May 1841, *Lamar Papers* 3:525–27.

22. De Cordova, *Texas*, 146.

23. Ibid.; Cantrell, *Stephen F. Austin*, 93–94.

24. Eugene C. Barker, *The Life of Stephen F. Austin, Founder of Texas, 1793–1836* (Austin: University of Texas Press, 1969), 210; Randolph B. Campbell, *An Empire for Slavery: The Peculiar Institution in Texas* (Baton Rouge: Louisiana State University Press, 1989), 23–24.

25. Barker, *Life of Stephen F. Austin*, 207–18; Cantrell, *Stephen F. Austin*, 267–73.

26. Bueno, "In Storms of Fortune," 59–63.

27. José Antonio Navarro to Samuel M. Williams, 12 April 1832, Samuel M. Williams Papers, Rosenberg Library, Galveston, Tex., item no. 23–0923. (All translations from this letter are my own.)

28. Ibid.; *New Handbook of Texas*, s.v. "Chambers, Thomas Jefferson."

29. Weber, *Mexican Frontier*, 253–54; David J. Weber, ed., *Troubles in Texas, 1832: A Tejano Viewpoint from San Antonio with a Translation and Facsimile*, trans. Conchita Hassell Winn and David J. Weber, DeGolyer Library Publication Series, vol. 1 (Dallas, Tex.: DeGolyer Library and Southern Methodist University Press, 1983), 11.

30. Weber, *Troubles in Texas*, 4, 30; Barker, *Life of Stephen F. Austin*, 354–56; Cantrell, *Stephen F. Austin*, 262.

31. Jesús F. de la Teja and John Wheat, "Béxar: Profile of a Tejano Community, 1820–32," *Southwestern Historical Quarterly* 89 (July 1985): 33–34.

32. Gregg Cantrell argues persuasively that Austin's letter of 2 October 1833, which was followed up by a second letter to San Antonio on 16 October urging the same action toward separate statehood, was more calculated than rash, however imprudent it ultimately proved to be. Austin, says Cantrell, had heard that the Anglo-Americans in Texas were planning to take the drastic action of declaring separate statehood in yet another (illegal) convention, and he hoped to deflect any retaliation by the national government toward the Anglo-

Texans by persuading the Bexareños to take the lead. See Cantrell, *Stephen F. Austin*, 267–73.

33. José Antonio Navarro to Samuel M. Williams, 26 February 1834, Samuel M. Williams Papers, Rosenberg Library, Galveston, Tex., item no. 23–1274 (my translation).

34. José Antonio Navarro to Samuel M. Williams, 8 October 1834, Samuel M. Williams Papers, Rosenberg Library, Galveston, Tex., item no. 23–1363 (my translation—assisted where the original letter is too faded to read by an earlier handwritten partial English translation, which is also a part of item no. 23–1363).

35. De Cordova, *Texas*, 149.

36. Margaret Swett Henson, *Samuel May Williams: Early Texas Entrepreneur* (College Station: Texas A&M University Press, 1976), 73–74.

37. Stephen L. Hardin, *Texian Iliad: A Military History of the Texas Revolution* (Austin: University of Texas Press, 1994), 25–27.

38. Herman Ehrenberg, "The Fight for Freedom in Texas in the Year 1836," trans. Peter Mollenhauer, ed. Natalie Ornish, in Natalie Ornish, *Ehrenberg: Goliad Survivor, Old West Explorer* (Dallas, Tex.: Texas Heritage Press, 1997), 159. Ehrenberg claims that the Mexican General Cos, whom the rebels defeated at San Antonio in December 1835, flew first a blood-red standard and then raised "the black standard of death." This paragraph (and many other paragraphs) were omitted from the Ehrenberg memoir in Herman Ehrenberg, *With Milam and Fannin: Adventures of a German Boy in Texas' Revolution*, trans. Charlotte Churchill, ed. Henry [Nash] Smith (Dallas, Tex.: Tardy Publishing, 1935), 91. See James E. Crisp, "Sam Houston's Speechwriters: The Grad Student, the Teenager, the Editors, and the Historians," *Southwestern Historical Quarterly* 97 (October 1993): 202–37.

39. Amos Pollard to Gov. Henry Smith, 13 February 1836, in *The Papers of the Texas Revolution, 1835–1836*, ed. John H. Jenkins (Austin: Presidial Press, 1973), 4:324–25.

40. R[euben] M[armaduke] Potter, "The Texas Revolution: Distinguished Mexicans Who Took Part in the Revolution of Texas, with Glances at Its Early Events," *Magazine of American History* 2 (October 1878): 585. Potter was a close associate of Navarro and was his interpreter when he served in the first legislature of the State of Texas (602).

41. Andrés Reséndez, trans. and ed., *A Texas Patriot on Trial in Mexico: José Antonio Navarro and the Texan Santa Fe Expedition*, Library of Texas no. 9 (Dallas, Tex.: DeGolyer Library and William P. Clements Center for Southwest Studies, 2005), 92–93.

42. José Antonio Navarro to Don Antonio López de Santa Anna, 19 September 1843, in "Jose Antonio Navarro and Santa Fe Expedition, 1841–1845," [E. C.] Barker transcripts from the Archivo General de México, [Dept. of] Guerra y Marina, 338:14–17 (quotation, 16), CAH. (my translation).

43. De Cordova, *Texas*, 148, 150.

44. José Antonio Navarro to Don Antonio López de Santa Anna, 19 September 1843, in "Jose Antonio Navarro and Santa Fe Expedition, 1841–1845," [E. C.] Barker transcripts from the Archivo General de México, [Dept. of] Guerra y Marina, 338:14–17 (quotation, 16), CAH (my translation).

45. Navarro's most famous quotation is the classic line, "I have sworn to be a free Texan. I shall never foreswear" (De Cordova, *Texas*, 152). The source is not Navarro's own writings but a biographical sketch written in 1858 by early Texas historian Jacob de Cordova, a bilingual acquaintance of Navarro who had come to Texas in 1837. Many subsequent accounts are based on the sketch published by De Cordova in 1858, when Navarro was very much alive and one of the best-known men in Texas. See the "Introduction" by Dayton Kelley in De Cordova, *Texas*, iii–vii. The following variation on the quotation attributed by De Cordova to Navarro is today carved into a massive limestone panel in the Grand Lobby of the Bob Bullock Texas State History Museum in Austin: "I will never forsake Texas and her cause. I am her son." Although the inscription dates the statement to 1842 and implies that it is a translation of Navarro's words, the two sentences are actually taken from a longer quotation attributed to Navarro without documentation in Daniel James Kubiak's book for young readers, *Ten Tall Texans* (San Antonio, Naylor, 1967), 53. The bogus quotation apparently entered scholarly discourse, and ultimately found its way to the museum's planners, by way of Joseph Martin Dawson's biography *Jose Antonio Navarro*, 73.

46. "Remarks of Mr. Navarro on a bill to issue titles to certain lands in the county of Bexar," *Telegraph and Texas Register* (Houston), 30 January 1839.

47. Potter, "Texas Revolution," 597. There is a rather bombastic and chauvinistic anonymous manuscript attributed to José Antonio Navarro in the Papers of José A. Navarro III in the Library of the Daughters of the Republic of Texas at the Alamo in San Antonio. The original bears no date, but "June, 1841" has been added to the manuscript in typescript. The "supposed" attribution to Navarro is in the heading to a translation of the document done by his grandson, also

named José Antonio Navarro, on 30 June 1936. The document bears
the following heading: "A los habitantes de Santa Fe y los demas
pueblos de Nuevo Mexico al Oriente del Rio Grande." Another copy
of this address may be found in the José Antonio Navarro Papers at
the Center for American History, University of Texas at Austin. The
tone of the address "To the Inhabitants of Santa Fe and the rest of
the People of New Mexico East of the Rio Grande" may be sensed in
an excerpt from a professional translation done by Dora E. Guerra
for the DRT Library in November 1977: "You have observed how this
[Texan] Government, with the innate vigor of Hercules, rose from
its very birth, invincible, and you see now how well established it is,
secure and impervious to the vacuous, boastful, threats hurled from
afar by an enemy who was impotent from the beginning in subjugat-
ing an infant nation. The day is not far when you will see it become
the richest, most powerful nation in America." This document was
in fact written not by Navarro but by his friend Reuben M. Potter at
the explicit request of President M. B. Lamar. This may be seen not
only by the correspondence between Potter and Lamar but also by
a comparison of Potter's handwriting (from originals in the Lamar
Papers in the Texas State Library and Archives) to the text of the
document, which is clearly in Potter's hand. Potter wrote to Lamar
on 29 May 1841 that he was sending "the proposed form of a proclamation to the people of Santa Fe which I have drawn up in Spanish
and English according to your request. I submitted the Spanish copy
to D[o]n Antonio Navarro with a request that he should not only
correct it but make any changes in the matter it contained which he
might deem advisable; but he assured me that he thought it needed
only a slight retouching of the style which he gave it by altering a
few words." See Potter's letters to Lamar of 29 May 1841 (*Lamar
Papers*, 3:531 and 5:474) and 5 June 1841 (*Lamar Papers*, 3:532). The
document in the DRT Library is almost certainly a draft given by
Potter to Navarro. The final copy appears never to have made it to
Santa Fe; likely it was burned along with other papers carried by the
Texans when the Santa Fe expedition was captured by the Mexican
army in September 1841 at Laguna Colorada near present Tucumcari,
New Mexico.

48. "Remarks of Mr. Navarro on a bill to issue titles to certain lands in
the county of Bexar," *Telegraph and Texas Register* (Houston), 30 January 1839, 3 col. 4. Navarro, of course, gave his address in Spanish. He
closed by saying that he "should apologize to the house for detaining
them with observations, made in a language foreign to most of its

members." Seguín also used "the Castilian tongue" when he spoke in Congress. See the *Telegraph and Texas Register* (Houston), 19 May 1838.

49. *City Gazette* (Austin), 5 February 1840.

50. Statement of Bernardo Arze et al., *Morning Star* (Houston), 10 October 1843. The editor of the *Morning Star* estimated in this issue that between fifty and one hundred of the former Mexican prisoners of war desired "to remain in Texas, and claim the privileges of citizens."

51. David Montejano, *Anglos and Mexicans in the Making of Texas, 1836–1986* (Austin: University of Texas Press, 1987), 4–5.

52. Reséndez, *A Texas Patriot,* xv. The most reliable account of Navarro's almost miraculous escape is to be found in George Wilkins Kendall, *Narrative of the Texan Santa Fé Expedition,* Library of Texas No. 7, Gerald D. Saxon and William B. Taylor, eds. (Dallas, Tex.: DeGolyer Library and William P. Clements Center for Southwest Studies, 2004), 237–38.

53. *Telegraph and Texas Register* (Houston), 29 January and 5 February 1845; *Morning Star* (Houston), 6 February 1845.

54. H[ans] P[eter] N[ielsen] Gammel, comp., *The Laws of Texas, 1822–1904* (Austin: Gammel-Statesman, 1904), 2:1142. The resolution was approved on 3 February 1845.

55. *Telegraph and Texas Register* (Houston), 12 February 1845.

56. Romanticized (and probably exaggerated) accounts of Navarro's resistance to temptations to commit treason were written by his friends Jacob de Cordova and Reuben M. Potter. See de Cordova, *Texas,* 151–52, and Potter, *Texas Revolution,* 598–601.

57. For the use of the term "traitor" for Seguín, see James Morgan to J. W. Webb, 31 October 1842, James Morgan Papers, Rosenberg Library, Galveston, Tex. . Reports of Seguín's depredations on the Southwestern frontier appeared in the same issue of the Houston *Telegraph* that reported Navarro's triumphant arrival in Galveston. See the *Telegraph and Texas Register* (Houston), 5 February 1845. The best accounts of Juan Seguín's life are by Jesús F. de la Teja, whose chapter on Seguín is found elsewhere in this volume, and the late, great historian and cartoonist Jack Jackson. See Jesús F. de la Teja, ed., *A Revolution Remembered: The Memoirs and Selected Correspondence of Juan N. Seguín,* 2d ed. (Austin: Texas State Historical Association, 2002); Jack Jackson, *Los Tejanos* (Stamford, CT: Fantagraphics Books, 1982). See also James E. Crisp, "Race, Revolution, and the Texas Republic: Toward a Reinterpretation," in *The Texas Military Experience: From the Texas Revolution through World War II,* ed. Joseph G. Dawson

III (College Station: Texas A&M University Press, 1995), 32–48, 200–210.

58. From the *Civ[ilian]* (Galveston), quoted in the *Northern Standard* (Clarksville), 6 March 1845 (my emphasis).

59. *Journals of the Convention, Assembled at the City of Austin on the Fourth of July, 1845, for the Purpose of Framing a Constitution for the State of Texas* (Austin: Miner and Cruger, Printers to the Convention, 1845), 6–11.

60. *Journals of the Convention* [1845], 54, 341; *Debates of the Texas Convention*, Wm. F. Weeks, reporter (Houston: J. W. Cruger, 1846), 157–59. For a discussion of the debate over this issue and Navarro's role in it, see Crisp, "Anglo-Texan Attitudes," 413–18. The eight Californianos who sat in their prospective state's convention in 1849 failed in their attempt to keep the same fateful word "white" out of California's constitution, and they soon paid for their failure with forfeited legal rights. See Leonard Pitt, *The Decline of the Californios: A Social History of the Spanish-Speaking Californians, 1846–1890* (Berkeley: University of California Press, 1970), 42–47.

61. See note 48.

62. *Journals of the Convention* [1845], 317. Evans had settled in the Texas Republic in 1843. See the *Biographical Directory of Texan Conventions and Congresses, 1832–1845* (Austin: [House of Representatives], 1941), 81.

63. *Biographical Directory of Texan Conventions*, 117.

64. *Journals of the Convention* [1845], 318.

65. Ibid.

66. Ibid., 318–19.

67. Said Reuben Potter of Navarro: "He was the most eloquent Spanish orator whom I have heard; but this gift was mainly thrown away upon an assemblage whom he had to address through an interpreter. Had early education made the English language as available to him as his sonorous native tongue, he would not only have been a star in the Congress of Texas, but have passed from it to that of the United States." Potter, *Texas Revolution*, 602–3.

68. *Democratic Telegraph and Texas Register* (Houston), 30 November 1848, 1 cols. 1–2. The essay had been translated, at Navarro's request, by George Fisher in Houston.

69. Ibid.; George Fisher to Samuel M. Williams, 2 December 1848, Williams Papers, item no. 23–2119. The subject of Tejano land loss after the Texas Revolution and Mexican war is an immense, complicated, and controversial one and cannot be adequately covered in

this essay. Interested readers should start with Armando C. Alonzo, *Tejano Legacy: Rancheros and Settlers in South Texas, 1734–1900* (Albuquerque: University of New Mexico Press, 1998); and Andres Tijerina, *Tejano Empire: Life on the South Texas Ranchos* (College Station: Texas A&M University Press, 1998). See also Montejano, *Anglos and Mexicans in the Making of Texas.*

70. See note 12.

71. McDonald and Matovina, *Defending Mexican Valor,* 58, 76.

72. "Segunda Junta Democratica, De los Ciudadonas Mejico-Tejanos del Condado de Bejar," *El Bejareño* (San Antonio), 21 July 1855 (my translation). Navarro's letter "To the Mexican Citizens of San Antonio" was read aloud to this meeting. Its reading, reported the group's president, Narciso Leal, was interrupted several times with "thunderous applause" ("truenos de aplausos").

73. Ibid. (my translation).

74. José Antonio Navarro to Juan N. Cortina, 4 January 1860, Records of the Term of Samuel Houston, Texas Office of the Governor, Archives and Information Services Division, Texas State Library and Archives Commission, Austin (my translation). Navarro wrote the letter to Cortina at Houston's request. Navarro's son, José Angel Navarro, was sent by Houston to the border along with fellow commissioner Robert H. Taylor to investigate Cortina's uprising. See *New Handbook of Texas,* s.v. "Navarro, José Ángel (1828–1876)."

Antonio Manchaca

José Antonio Menchaca, who rose to the rank of captain in the service of Texas, wrote one of the handful of Tejano accounts of the Texas revolutionary period that have survived. Less historically prominent than José Antonio Navarro, he was an honored Texas War of Independence veteran who had the distinction of having the community of Manchaca in southern Travis County named for him.

Courtesy McArdle Companion Notebook, Texas State Library and Archives Commission.

JOSÉ ANTONIO MENCHACA

NARRATING A TEJANO LIFE

Timothy Matovina

A BOISTEROUS CROWD paraded through the streets of San Antonio to the city's Alamo Plaza on the morning of 2 March 1859. Led by a band of musicians and members of the Alamo Rifles volunteer militia, the entourage included about twenty persons with badges identifying them as the "veterans of '36," military officers, the San Antonio Fire Association, the mayor and other local officials, teachers and school children, and the general populace, all gathered to celebrate the twenty-third anniversary of Texas independence. Prominent on the speaker's platform erected for the occasion were two San Antonio Tejanos: José Antonio Navarro, one of three Mexican-descent signers of the Texas Declaration of Independence, and Antonio Menchaca, a veteran of the Texas Revolution renowned for his valor at the decisive battle of San Jacinto. According to the local newspaper report of this event, the speaker for the occasion, I. L. Hewitt, "was repeatedly applauded in a very enthusiastic manner, and especially in his allusions to the two venerable patriots on the platform, Col. Navarro and Capt. Manchaca [sic]."[1]

Hewitt extolled Navarro as a signer of the Declaration of Independence, a participant in the ill-fated 1841 Texan Santa Fe expedition, and subsequently a prisoner in Mexico who refused President Antonio López de Santa Anna's offer of clemency if he would renounce his loyalty to Texas. Then the orator went on to exalt "Capt. Antonio Manchaca [sic], he who today bears the Lone Star flag,—Mexican born—'Twas he who fought shoulder to shoulder with the Texans at the battle of San Jacinto—True and faithful to our country then, may he long live to enjoy the fruition of his patriotism."

Yet amazingly, in this same speech, with both Menchaca and Navarro seated behind him on the dais, Hewitt claimed Texas' winning of independence from Mexico demonstrated that "no enemy however countless in their numbers can force the bold Anglo Saxon to yield to a tyrant's decrees—independent in thought and action, his political freedom he claims as his birthright." This seeming contradiction reflected a common contention in ceremonial rhetoric around the Alamo and celebrations of Texas independence: the act of joining those who fought for independence created a free Texas and transformed people from various nations and backgrounds into true Texans and true Americans.

Depictions of Menchaca that focus primarily on his military exploits and his "American" loyalties continued beyond his own lifetime. In the introduction to the partial publication of Menchaca's memoirs, his longtime acquaintance James Newcomb avowed that the Tejano's "sympathies carried him into the ranks of the Americans." He even went so far as to describe Menchaca's physical characteristics as bearing "the marks of a long line of Castilian ancestors," rhetorically severing Menchaca from both his Tejano loyalties and his Mexican heritage. Similarly, the obituary of Menchaca published in the *San Antonio Express* avowed that he was "born a Mexican" but that "when the Texas war for independence came on, Don Antonio was found upon the side of our people, a contestant for that liberty and those privileges of citizenship which are bequeathed to the American." Claims such as these reveal a larger pattern regarding some Tejanos and others deemed loyal to the Texas or U.S. causes. James Crisp has noted similar rhetorical commentaries regarding nineteenth-century Tejanos like José Antonio Navarro, whose patriotism led Anglo-Americans to claim he was "not of the abject race of Mexicans" but rather "a Corsican [European] of good birth." In more contemporary times, Edward Linenthal shows that public ceremonies at the Alamo continue to mediate a message of "patriotic conversion" whereby through courage in battle those of diverse backgrounds leave behind their ancestral heritage to become Texans and Americans.[2]

Though Menchaca's memoir itself encompasses a section on the Texas Revolution that is disproportionate in length to other subjects treated, the focus on his status as a veteran of that revolution was further amplified in Frederick Chabot's 1937 publication of a portion of the memoir, which ends the narrative at the battle of San Jacinto because apparently Chabot had less than half the memoir at his disposal. A critical edition of the memoir has yet to be published and, of the four leading nineteenth-century San Antonio Tejano figures known to have left behind their recollections—Juan Seguín, José Antonio Navarro, José María Rodríguez, and Menchaca—the latter's memoir is the only one that remains unpublished in its entirety.[3] Indeed, many researchers are unaware of the unpublished portion of Menchaca's memoir and its recollections and musings on the events, social life, people, physical structures, and legends that shaped San Antonio's history.

Menchaca's memoir reveals some essential considerations about nineteenth-century Tejano biography: how Tejanos like Menchaca perceived themselves and wanted to be remembered, their views of Tejano character, and their understanding of the Tejano legacy during the tumultuous century of change, which in Menchaca's own lifetime had seen them pass from being part of Spain, Mexico, the Republic of Texas, the United States, the Confederate States of America, and then the United States again. A critical reading of the memoir shows that, unlike contemporaries such as Newcomb or the orator Hewitt, Menchaca saw neither his military service nor the Texas victory over Mexico as an eradication of the Tejano past and a transmogrification of Tejano patriots into Anglo-Texans or Anglo-Americans. The memoir contains its share of hyperbolic statements and inaccurate details and as a historical record must be read with a hermeneutic of suspicion, as David McDonald clearly demonstrates in his judicious assessment of Menchaca's erroneous treatment of Juan Martín de Veramendi's actions as governor of Coahuila y Texas. Nonetheless, a biography of Menchaca cannot be complete without careful attention to how he narrated his own life and times during his twilight years. Coupled with other available primary documents on Menchaca's life, his memoir is not just another source for the events they narrate but, more important, a firsthand account of the perceptions, biases, and mindset of nineteenth-century Tejanos like Menchaca as they looked back over the span of their lives.

Native San Antonian José Antonio Menchaca was the son of Juan Mariano and María Luz (Guerra) Menchaca. According to the local parish baptismal register, Father Gavino Valdez baptized the eight-day old José Antonio on 17 January 1800, his godmother being Concepción Flores. Inexplicably, no name for a godfather is given. Menchaca's grandfather, Marcos Menchaca, served in the Spanish military and first brought the family to San Antonio when he received a land grant along San Pedro Creek in 1762. Marcos married Josefa Cadena and they had two sons, José Manuel and Menchaca's father, Juan Mariano.[4]

Little is known about Menchaca's early years, save for his recollections of the battles for Mexican independence from Spain fought in or near San Antonio during his early teens (see below). In 1826 he married Teresa Ramón, a descendant of a military leader stationed at San Antonio during the early eighteenth century. Apparently the Menchacas' social circle was not limited to their fellow Tejanos.

One of their daughters, Antonia Manuela, married French émigré Jean Batiste Ducuron La Coste, and another, María Antonia, married P. E. Neuendorff. Their sister Joaquina married Texas Revolution veteran John Glanton, though by at least one account Glanton gained the hand of his reportedly beautiful bride at gunpoint. Shortly after their marriage, Glanton headed west, leaving Joaquina and their infant daughter behind. A few years later Yuma Indians in Sonora killed Glanton in retribution for atrocities he committed as a "soldier of fortune, outlaw, and notorious bounty-hunter and murderer."[5]

The most often remembered—and one could add controversial—aspect of Menchaca's life is his military service during the Texas Revolution, particularly his exploits at the battle of San Jacinto. Historian Stephen L. Hardin has avowed that "Menchaca had no intention of enlisting in the rebel [Texas] army." He cites the recollections of Enrique Esparza, who at the time of the Alamo battle was the eight-year-old son of Alamo defender Gregorio Esparza and survived the battle inside the fortress walls with his mother and siblings. Some seven decades later the aging Esparza attested that General Santa Anna offered the Alamo defenders a period of amnesty and that "among the surnames of those I remember to have left during the time of this armistice were Menchaca, Flores, Rodriguez, Ramirez, Arocha, Silvero."[6] Although Esparza is the only known source who mentions the armistice and departure of these Tejanos, Hardin correctly notes that the most convincing evidence comes from the testimony of Menchaca himself; in his memoirs he states that he left San Antonio just before the Alamo battle and only entered the Texan army when forced to do so. One key passage appears to be an apologetic about why he did not join his friend Jim Bowie and others in defending the Alamo; Menchaca states that Bowie and Tejano military leader Juan Seguín "made a motion to have A[ntonio] M[enchaca] and his family sent away from here, knowing that should Santa Anna come, A. and his family would receive no good at his hands" (23).[7] But it is not clear why Menchaca and his family would have been in greater danger at Santa Anna's hands than anyone else who chose to join the Alamo defenders. After he headed east with his family, Menchaca states that General Edward Burleson conscripted him into the Texas army.

Though long esteemed for his courage in the battle of San Jacinto, in his memoirs Menchaca mentions nothing about these exploits, only that he fought in the battle and that the Texan commanders "made me take my men who were Mexicans and put large pieces of

white paste board on their hats and breasts lest they should be mis-
taken for Santa Annas men and killed" (80). José María Rodríguez, a
native San Antonian whose father Ambrosio was Menchaca's com-
rade in the battle, avers in his memoir that an unspecified "Mexican
history of the battle" relates "an officer of tremendous size, speaking
Spanish, urged his men forward in a voice of thunder to give no quarter and that they slaughtered the Mexicans like sheep. . . . The man
he referred to, is supposed to have been Don Antonio." Hardin cites
Henry Stuart Foote's 1841 account based on eyewitness interviews of
the battle. Foote states that Texas soldier and statesman Thomas Jefferson Rusk claimed Menchaca refused to help a Mexican officer who
begged him for mercy. Surrounded by Anglo-Americans apparently
eager to hear how he would respond, Menchaca reportedly retorted,
"I'm no Mexican—I'm an American," and told his fellow Texan soldiers to shoot him. Hardin concludes that "such incidents indicate
that Tejanos killed [Mexican] centralists with every bit as much rel-
ish as did vengeful Texians."[8]

Yet Hardin's latter conclusion and the single incident and primary
source on which it is based are not corroborated in other primary documentation. Menchaca's alleged claim that he was no longer Mexican
but American sounds more like the rhetoric of the aforementioned
Newcomb or Hewitt than any known Tejano source; given that the
battle of San Jacinto won Texas independence and was nine years
before U.S. annexation, it seems particularly odd that a native Tejano
like Menchaca would have identified himself as an "American." It is
unlikely that, if such a dramatic incident occurred, Menchaca forgot
it or thought it was too unimportant to record in his memoirs. He
might possibly have been too embarrassed or ashamed of such a brutal episode to recount it. But in the 1870s would Menchaca have been
concerned that associating himself with retribution on the Mexican
army at San Jacinto could soil his reputation? Indeed, far from claiming he sought vengeance on the Mexican forces, Menchaca's memoirs recount a subsequent event that seems even more likely to have
drawn his name into ill repute among his contemporaries: his narration that he offered the detested prisoner Santa Anna every form
of assistance at his disposal. The strongest conclusion one can draw
from extant sources is that Menchaca's reputation as a formidable
adversary at San Jacinto is evident in Anglo-American, Tejano, and,
according to Rodríguez, Mexican reports of the battle.

Menchaca continued to serve in the Texas army until the Mexican forces withdrew from Texas, at which point he went with

several other Tejanos to escort their families back to San Antonio from Nacogdoches, where they had fled during the wartime hostilities. According to Juan Seguín nearly everyone on this return expedition became ill "and for several days, Captain Menchaca, who was the only person able to stand up, had to drive the whole train, as well as attend to the sick." After reestablishing his family at San Antonio he engaged in further military service; the following March an order from Commander Seguín instructed Captain Thomas Pratt that "Capt. Manchaca [sic] accompanies you and is subject to your order although as he is acquainted with the Country and Language you may find it eligeable to consult with him on such points as may be necessary."[9]

Subsequently Menchaca provided intermittent service in military engagements with Indians and in patrol duty to watch out for Mexican troops, although apparently he did not fulfill an 1842 mandate to raise a military company, inasmuch as official correspondence ten months later indicates that Texas Congress appropriations included funds for troops only under the command of renowned Texas Ranger Jack Hays. In September 1842 Menchaca was part of a group that sought to defend San Antonio from Mexican troops under the command of General Adrián Woll, but these defenders quickly abandoned their effort when they discovered that the force aligned against them was a formidable contingent of the regular Mexican army. Menchaca's leg was reportedly injured in this skirmish when a cannon ball dislodged a stone that struck him. The Mexican army took him prisoner but quickly released him. An Anglo-American prisoner wrote in his diary that "Antonio Menchaca's release is likewise effected by the intercession of his family and that of his Mexican friends"; General Woll's official reports of his expedition state that he freed five prisoners "on account of being Mexicans whose families and themselves have offered to be hereafter faithful to the Supreme Government."[10]

Menchaca's memoirs are consistent with Woll's official report, attesting that Woll freed him "on one condition & that is that you will give me your word of honor never again to take up arms against Mexico" (116). Menchaca went on to state that he faithfully fulfilled his "parole of honor never more to take up arms against Mexico" (123). Though in 1844 Texas president Sam Houston appointed him to serve as an Indian escort, his steadily advancing age and injured leg may have contributed to his decisions about further military duty. Like many other Tejanos, he did not enlist for the war between the United States and Mexico that erupted in 1846; at least 140 Tejanos applied for land grants as veterans of the Texas Revolution, but in the Mexican War only twenty soldiers with Spanish surnames were among the six thousand Texas volunteers in the U.S. forces.[11] In any event, whether his motive was one or a combination of these factors, his participation in the 1842 defense of San Antonio during the Woll expedition was Menchaca's last engagement in military conflict mentioned in extant sources.

Menchaca's military record earned him the acclaim of many contemporaries. Besides receiving public recognition at events like Texas Independence Day celebrations, during the last years of his life he was a member of the Texas Veterans Association, a group of Texas Republic veterans founded in 1873. His renown also frequently drew him into the more elite Tejano circles of San Antonio. But his prominent status did not translate into economic luxury. He was listed, perhaps incorrectly, as a laborer on 1830 census rolls. An 1838 joint resolution of the Texas Senate and House of Representatives granted him "one of the houses and lots in the city of San Antonio, which may be confiscated to the public use." The 1840 census of the Republic of Texas listed him as holding one town lot in San Antonio, presumably the location of his private residence, as well as two horses above the four head not counted because of the taxation purpose of the census rolls. He was also the agent of record for his widowed mother, who owned one town lot. After U.S. annexation his level of prosperity remained relatively constant. In 1850 on the first U.S. census conducted in San Antonio, he was listed as a "merchant" who owned real estate valued at $2,000; a newspaper report from seven years later mentions Menchaca as one owner of transport carts loaded with goods that left San Antonio for the coast under armed guard during the infamous Cart War.[12]

Still, in comparison to other San Antonio Tejanos, Menchaca's retention of his homestead and mercantile interests placed him ahead of many contemporaries. Although incomplete, the census of 1840 showed that Tejanos owned 85.1 percent of the town lots in San Antonio, along with 63.8 percent of all land acreage titled to local residents. On the 1850 census, they owned only 9.1 percent of real estate values claimed. Similarly, in 1830 when Tejanos constituted nearly all the population of San Antonio, the census showed that most residents were farmers and only 14.8 percent were laborers. No employment listings were given in the 1840 census, but 61.4 percent of the Tejano population were in labor positions according to the 1850 census. Menchaca was comparatively prosperous, but only in relation to a San Antonio Tejano population undergoing a significant downward trend in economic status from landowners to a working underclass.[13]

Menchaca did not complacently accept the woes of his fellow Tejanos. He was a frequent witness for Tejano parties in court cases, particularly for veterans seeking the compensation due them by law for military service in the Texas Revolution. Convinced that the just claims of many Tejano veterans had been denied or unduly delayed as compared to the more prompt approvals their Anglo-American counterparts received, in 1875 Menchaca was one of nineteen Tejano signers of a letter to the Texas comptroller of public accounts that sought to "disabuse [the comptroller's] mind of any prejudice" against Tejano veterans and demand for themselves and their comrades "simply justice and nothing more." His support of fellow Tejanos was so strong that apparently he did not even hold grudges against those who supported the Mexican side in the Texas Revolution. For example, he provided a deposition to support the legal claims of Francisco Esparza, a San Antonio native who, unlike his Alamo defender brother Gregorio, had opted to fight in the Mexican army during the December 1835 Texan siege of San Antonio and was on reserve with the Mexican forces during Santa Anna's Texas campaign. James Newcomb summed up Menchaca's leading role as a legal advocate when he quipped that "in later years, when the titles to almost every foot of ground in the old city and county of Bexar were litigated in the courts, Captain Menchaca became a standing witness to prove up the genealogy of the old families."[14]

In his laudatory, and perhaps hyperbolic, recollections of his friend several decades after his death, Newcomb also recalled Menchaca's role as a leader in Tejano social activities. Newcomb remembered "Captain Menchaca as the umpire at the Sunday cock fight. Amusements and entertainments in those days [the antebellum period] were limited to the Sunday cock fight—the fandango [dance]—the Saint's [sic] days." In sharp contrast to his claim that Menchaca had been received into the presumed superior inner circle of Anglo-Americans, Newcomb went on wistfully to describe the era of more prominent Tejano festivities and feasts as simpler and more serene than the bustling times of the early twentieth century in which he wrote, adding that Menchaca's umpire duties "required a man of stern character and unbending dignity to decide the fine points of these tournaments."[15]

Menchaca's political career and activism were another means through which he promoted Tejano interests. In the years after Texas independence he served several terms on the San Antonio city council and as mayor pro tem from July 1838 to January 1839, completing the term of resigned mayor William Dangerfield. Like other Tejano elected officials, he sought with limited success to stem the tide of Anglo-American encroachment on local real estate, as in 1838 when as mayor pro tem he wrote the General Land Office commissioner to alert him of Anglo-American attempts to take unlawful possession of San Antonio city land. He joined other San Antonio Tejano as well as Anglo-American leaders to press the national government of Texas for services like local postal delivery and funding for military protection. A similar San Antonio coalition also offered financial and moral support for federalist rebellion in the northern states of Mexico; this conflict potentially could have combined the population of that region with Texas to form a new nation in which the proportion of Mexican-descent to Anglo-American residents would have increased significantly.[16]

After a two-year disruption of local elections after the Woll expedition, Menchaca was once again elected to the city council in 1844, but subsequently his career as an elected official subsided along with that of his Tejano contemporaries. During the period of the Texas Republic (1836–45), Tejano electees to the city council accounted for 73.2 percent of the total, but they were just 24.2 percent during the first fifteen years after U.S. annexation; in 1860 not a single Tejano served on the council. Menchaca was elected to the council one final time in 1849, but for unknown reasons he resigned a month before completing his term. The year after the anti-foreigner, anti-Catholic Know Nothing Party swept the 1854 San Antonio municipal elections, he ran for the city council again but lost. He remained active in political events and causes, as in 1860 when he helped organize a San Antonio visit of Governor Sam Houston to promote pro-Union views. Earlier that year Houston had warmly endorsed Menchaca for a federal government appointment, which apparently never materialized; Menchaca's only subsequent elected positions were terms he served as ditch commissioner just before the American Civil War and once again during Reconstruction.[17]

In the years leading up to the Civil War, Tejanos like Menchaca split with their Democratic allies from the mid-1850s Know Nothing political controversies because the party supported secession and bitterly opposed Menchaca's friend and ally Governor Houston. But in the tumultuous decade following the war, some Tejanos, particularly members of the older and more influential families like Menchaca, realigned with the Democrats and resisted Reconstruction efforts that granted African Americans greater equality. Other Tejanos joined the Radicals, who advocated for African American voting and citizenship rights. Each group of activists formed its own political club and had its own Spanish-language newspaper. Menchaca's active involvement in the Democratic Party and platform was evident in his campaign efforts for Horace Greeley's unsuccessful presidential bid against Ulysses S. Grant in the 1872 national elections, as well as his selection in 1875 as a delegate to the Democratic state convention. At a local celebration of Mexican Independence Day in 1871, Menchaca even publicly compared the heroic efforts of Father Miguel Hidalgo, who led the struggle for Mexican independence from Spain, to contemporary initiatives to elect Democratic candidates and overthrow Radical rule. Yet Tejanos from both political parties, including Menchaca, were able to unite in support of an 1876 municipal effort that attracted the first railroad lines to the city. Apparently though the rights of African Americans in an Anglo-American-dominated society did not elicit a unilateral response among Menchaca and his fellow Tejanos, advocacy of their own rights and self-interest remained a powerful force for inciting their collective action.[18]

Menchaca died peacefully on 1 November 1879 after enduring a short illness. Besides lauding his Texas patriotism and military service, his obituary noted that one of his "most remarkable characteristics . . . was his retentiveness of memory. His stories of the war with Mexico, and of the thrilling scenes that marked the history of this city in her virginity, have ever won the listener." Employing a frequent misspelling of his name during his lifetime, the town of Manchaca in Travis County, about ten miles southwest of Austin, is named for him; the genesis of this honor is that Menchaca had reportedly once camped at the nearby springs that also bear his name. After two previous post offices founded on the site had closed, two years after Menchaca's death the arrival of the railroad in the area led to the establishment of the town on a more permanent footing and its formal naming as Manchaca.[19]

Menchaca's long-standing activism on behalf of his fellow Tejanos continued into the last decade of his life through issues like pension discrimination against Tejano veterans and the advisability of expending municipal funds to attract railroads to the city. In this context, then, his mid-1870s memoir is part of a wider effort of the aging Menchaca to promote what he perceived to be Tejanos' interests as well as their legacy. The memoir opens with the observation that "I was born in 1800. Was baptized in the church of San Fernando de Austria [San Fernando de Béxar] on the 12 [17] Jan. same year" (13). It then proceeds to narrate his life and key events in San Antonio history during the first half of the nineteenth century. The manuscript itself is presented in eighteen chapters, though the original draft of the first nine chapters is lost and the delineation of these chapters is not labeled on the extant copy. But from a chronological standpoint Menchaca's memoirs of San Antonio from 1800 to the 1845 U.S. annexation of Texas and subsequent war with Mexico can be roughly divided into three major sections: the period of struggle for Mexican independence from Spain, the fight for Texas independence and its aftermath, and local events during the period of the Texas Republic. A final section adds some remarks on the history of San Antonio before 1800. Three of the four sections are roughly equal in length, with the exception being the section on the Texas Revolution, which is three times longer than the others and constitutes nearly half the memoir.

Menchaca dictated the memoir to newspaper reporter Charles Merritt Barnes shortly after the Louisiana native moved to San Antonio in 1874. Menchaca's native language was Spanish and at one point in the memoir he states that he gave a public speech through an interpreter because "I did not like to Speak English for fear of making them laugh at my pronunciation" (126). The text of the manuscript is not polished and contains an occasional Spanish loan word. Does the mode of expression reflect Barnes's attempt to transcribe Menchaca's statements literally, his own shorthand rendering of them, or, most probably, some combination of both? Moreover, did Barnes record Menchaca's words with little prompting, or are some of the major topics treated in the memoir a response to Barnes's queries and interests? There is no evidence that leads to indisputable answers to these questions. Suffice it to say the critical reader must bear in mind, not only that the manuscript records the recollections of a nearly octogenarian Tejano looking back over a life in times of rapid political and social change, but also that they were recorded through the pen of a young Anglo-American reporter who in his career displayed a marked interest in colorful stories of local interest. With this in mind, in what follows I focus primarily on the broad themes of the memoir, especially two major concerns most likely to reflect Menchaca's own perspectives: his portrayal of the Tejano legacy and Tejano character.

Though the bulk of the memoir consists of personal recollections from the first half-century of Menchaca's life, the final section implicitly reveals a prideful conviction that Menchaca's ancestors and other Spanish-speaking residents founded and developed San Antonio. Titled "A History of the Settlement and Inhabitants of San Antonio," this section begins with the observation that "Mexican & Canary [Island] Settlers" (132) established the original developments around San Antonio's Military and Main Plazas and, despite the obstacle of Native Americans who "were very troublesome and continually harassed them" (131), built homes and established what came to be the city of San Antonio.

As in other sections of the memoir, Menchaca presents some dates and details incorrectly, such as his claim that "my Great Grand Father Don Pedro Acon y Frillo and Old Captain Manchaca and his wife" (130) were among the original Canary Islander settlers. In light of the attempts to "Americanize" Tejano patriots like Menchaca in print and in public speech, his self-identification with the Canary Islander elite is no mere passing reference. Three other passages in the memoir mention the Canary Islanders, all in a positive light. Other Tejanos, such as José María Rodríguez, went so far as to make the highly exaggerated claim that into the nineteenth century Canary Islanders were "people of pure Spanish descent" who lived in segregated isolation on the west side of the San Antonio River and "took great pride in preventing any inter-marriage with mixed races and when one did mix he lost his caste with the rest."[20] In a racially conscious and stratified society like nineteenth-century Texas, the claim of a European bloodline must be seen in part as a claim for legitimacy. At the same time, in connecting his family and community to the founders of San Antonio—note his statement that "Mexican & Canary [Island] Settlers" (132) established the city around its two main plazas—Menchaca showed his pride that San Antonio's origins are rooted not in Anglo-American or U.S. initiatives but in the eighteenth-century efforts of Spanish-speaking pioneers.

Evidence of San Antonio's origins were noteworthy in the "prominent historical land marks" (144) that Menchaca's memoir then proceeds to highlight: the parish church of San Fernando, the Spanish missions including the Alamo in its initial foundation as Mission San Antonio de Valero, and Alameda Street, which Spanish subjects had cleared through cottonwood trees as a promenade leading to a park area used for dances and other festivities. Expanding his treatment of the accomplishments in San Antonio during the Spanish colonial era enshrined in these historical sites, Menchaca adds a claim that a Canary Islander sent as a gift to the king of Spain the first buffalo ever transported to Europe. Though the name of the donor is not given, Menchaca's recollection reveals his esteem for the exploits and the formative role of Hispanics in San Antonio.[21]

Menchaca's memoir ends rather abruptly with two legends that accentuate the legacy of the early Spanish Franciscans in Texas. In the first a band of Franciscans is beset with a large and hostile group of Indians, until the renowned missionary Antonio Margil de Jesús lifted up his eyes and "in the twinkling of a bed post the Savages were transmogrified into deer" (154). The second recounts a traveling group of friars who, thirsty after passing several days without water, came upon a grape vine, prayed over it, pulled it out, and to their delight saw water come bursting forth. According to Menchaca's recounting of the legend, this incident marked the origins of the San Marcos River, though other versions claim it was the San Antonio River.[22] These legends of miraculous assistance for Spanish friars, which Menchaca suggests were established tales among his Tejano contemporaries, further enhance his laudatory account of Spanish-speaking residents' efforts in San Antonio's early history with the implication that divine providence accompanied them in their endeavors.

Consciously or not, Menchaca's eclectic rendering of San Antonio's early history contested Anglo-Americans' tendency to perceive their presence in Texas as initiating an era of progress for benighted Mexican-descent residents. Even Anglo-American defenders of Tejanos ascribed to a view of Tejano inferiority. One 1852 San Antonio editorialist who objected to a fellow journalist's attack on the Tejano character noted:

> It is lamentably true that our Mexican population, generally, do not occupy as high a position in the scale of morality and intelligence as is desirable; yet every one who knows their former condition, and will take into consideration their former mode of life, as well as the demoralizing effect of the Government under which they lived previous to the establishment of the Texas Republic, must admit that they are reforming as rapidly as could have been expected.[23]

Consistent with other nineteenth-century San Antonio Tejano memoirs like those of José Antonio Navarro and Juan Seguín, Menchaca's emphasis on the Tejano contribution to San Antonio and Texas history before Anglo-Americans ever arrived serves as a corrective to demeaning views of the Tejano past and integrity.

Menchaca's personal recollections are also consistent with his accentuation of Tejano struggle and heroism beginning with their initiatives to win Mexican independence from Spain when he was a young boy. He recounts the turbulent years of insurgency and counterinsurgency between 1811 and 1813, a violent period that significantly shaped the lives of various other Tejanos treated in this volume: José Antonio Navarro, José Francisco Ruiz, José Antonio Saucedo, and Juan Seguín. In the latter year insurgents wrested control of San Antonio, brutally killing Governor Manuel Salcedo and other crown officials, only to lose the town again and endure similarly harsh reprisals from the Spanish royalist forces under the command of General Joaquín de Arredondo. Menchaca's version of these events reflects the native San Antonian perspective of being caught in the violence and bloodshed, as he chronicles the names and fate of various local families and individuals. Arredondo ordered that several women accused of insurgent loyalties be crowded into cramped quarters and coerced to prepare food for his troops. Many of their male counterparts suffocated to death in prison, were led before firing squads, or were forced into hard labor.[24]

Menchaca suggests his sympathies and those of his fellow established San Antonio residents were with the cause of independence, even making the exaggerated claim that local officials appointed to run the town after insurgents under José Bernardo Gutiérrez took it were "all gentlemen of the City of San Antonio, descendants of the first families who emigrated from the Canary Islands" (15).[25] He describes the period between the Spanish commander Arredondo's reconquest of the city and the winning of Mexican independence eight years later as a time of economic distress, weak leadership, and frequent Indian depredations. Conversely, he states that San Antonio "underwent a great change for the better" in the years immediately after Mexican independence (20).

One of the most striking features of Menchaca's personal anecdotes is his narration of his honorable and charitable interactions with friend and foe alike, people of varied backgrounds and political persuasions. In this first section he relates that, during the Arredondo occupation of San Antonio, a fellow San Antonian accused

Menchaca's father of a minor infraction. When the authorities arrested Menchaca's parents and ordered his father to be publicly flogged and his mother placed in confinement and servitude of the royalist army, the fourteen-year-old Antonio reportedly rushed to plead their case with a Spanish officer he had befriended. He persisted until his parents were released.

Whether true in every detail or not, this self-narration as a person who could overcome difficulties with others, even befriend leaders of occupying armies, illuminates Menchaca's self-perception of Tejanos like himself as people of honor, ingenuity, dedication to their families and communities, and resourceful survival through a lifetime of turmoil and social change. These qualities are further evidenced in Menchaca's exposition of his relations with key leaders during the struggle for Texas independence such as James Bowie, Sam Houston, Antonio López de Santa Anna, and a Comanche chief whom Menchaca identifies as "Cassamiro" and claims he convinced not to burn and plunder San Antonio.[26]

It must be recalled that Menchaca dictated his memoirs in the 1870s, by which time Bowie's fame was legendary and still growing. Menchaca relates Bowie's arrival in San Antonio, marriage to Ursula María de Veramendi, and heartfelt loss at her death in a cholera epidemic. The first contact mentioned between Bowie and Menchaca in the memoirs was a confidential and urgent letter Bowie wrote him just before the December 1835 Texan siege and takeover of San Antonio from Mexican forces. After the Texan victory, Bowie and Menchaca reportedly were reunited for the first time since the death of Bowie's wife. Menchaca describes their encounter as a touching reunion in which Bowie,

> as soon as he saw him [Menchaca], put his arms around his neck, and commenced to cry to think that he had not seen his wife die. He said "My father, my brother, my companion and all my protection has come. Are you still my companion in arms?" he asked. Antonio answered, "I shall be your companion, Jim Bowie until I die." "Then come this evening," said Bowie, "to take you to introduce you to Travis, at the Alamo." (22)

Menchaca goes on to narrate his leading role in organizing a ball in honor of Davy Crockett, at which Menchaca states that he was present when Bowie, Crockett, and William Barret Travis first received the news that Mexican forces under General Santa Anna were marching toward San Antonio.

After he fled San Antonio with his family and was conscripted into the Texas army, Menchaca was part of the force under General Sam Houston that retreated eastward. He asserts that he personally confronted Houston when he learned that the Tejano troops under Juan Seguín's command were ordered to guard horses rather than engage the Mexican army in the battle of San Jacinto. According to the memoir, Houston said that Menchaca impressed him because the Tejano "spoke like a man" (26). Consequently Houston allowed that the Tejano soldiers join in the fighting.

Once the battle was won and Santa Anna was taken prisoner in the Texas camp, Menchaca reportedly served as interpreter between him and General Houston. In contrast to his depiction of Santa Anna as an unsavory character when he provided some recollections for the historical research of former Texas president Mirabeau Buonaparte Lamar in 1857, in his memoirs Menchaca recounts no derogatory anecdotes about Santa Anna. Rather, Menchaca states that he secured a hot meal for the ravenously hungry Santa Anna, protested a Texan guard's refusal to let him see the Mexican general with this meal until he was granted admission (allegedly through the intercession of Houston himself), conversed with Santa Anna about the general's previous military service in San Antonio during the Mexican War of Independence, and even offered him financial support to assist with his needs while in captivity. Unlike the many Texas soldiers who wanted to execute Santa Anna in retribution for the killing of their comrades at the Alamo and Goliad, Menchaca states that he treated Santa Anna with the respect of a prisoner of war, a depiction of his actions consistent with the account in José María Rodríguez's memoirs.[27] Menchaca notes that Santa Anna was so moved by this kindness that he "saw tears come to his eyes and he cried like a child" (86).

Menchaca's diverse friendships and alliances reveal the Tejano dilemma of choosing sides as they were caught between opposing forces in the crucible of violence that was San Antonio. Nowhere is this dilemma more clearly expressed in the memoir than in the narration of the September 1842 Mexican occupation of San Antonio under the forces of General Adrián Woll, whose last name the memoir mistakenly renders as "Bull." Menchaca relates that Woll had him arrested along with several Anglo-Americans who had pledged to defend the city and then accused the Tejano of being "the greatest traitor to your flag unhung and you deserve to be shot 25 times through the head but General Santa Anna who thanks you for the kindness you did him asked me if I captured you to spare your life" (115–16). General Woll reportedly did so with the condition that Menchaca promise to never take up arms against Mexico again. Menchaca agreed but then immediately began to plea for his Anglo-American friends, asking Woll that those to be taken away as prisoners to Mexico be allowed to travel via wagon or horseback rather than on foot. He also describes himself as a mediating force between Woll and Jack Hays, the commander of the Texas troops that amassed to retake San Antonio. Menchaca reportedly warned Woll that he had better leave town peaceably because Hays was about to attack, but to no avail. After the two forces fought and Woll prepared to withdraw, Menchaca reiterated his plea that the Mexican general show respect for his Anglo-American prisoners and not force them to walk all the way to Mexico. Then he purportedly delivered a letter from those prisoners to Hays stating that Woll had treated the prisoners well and that no undue harshness should be shown him if he was taken captive, though an account written at the time of this incident states that the prisoners' communiqué asked Hays to treat San Antonio Tejanos respectfully, not Woll, out of gratitude for *their* kindness to the prisoners.[28] As he did with other noteworthy leaders, Menchaca implied that he had a close relationship with Hays, who "was much rejoiced to see me alive and well" (122).

Next, Menchaca states that after Woll's retreat he and some Anglo-American allies successfully resisted a proposal to burn San Antonio. Though Menchaca's recollection of this proposal arising in 1842 is not corroborated in any other primary source, similar propositions had been proffered as early as 1836. After the battle of San Jacinto, General Felix Huston commanded Juan Seguín to destroy the city, an order that Seguín convinced President Sam Houston to rescind.[29] Anglo-Americans who advocated the town's destruction argued that San Antonio's isolation enabled the Mexican army to plant spies there and easily capture it. Through an interpreter, Menchaca reportedly responded to such arguments with a speech "bitterly opposing the sacrifice of San Antonio to the flames," reminding his hearers that his aging mother and other residents "would be left destitute by the burning of the town" (126). Menchaca's recollection of defending his hometown against both Mexican attack and Anglo-American destruction, all within the space of a few short weeks, reflects the Tejano dilemma of being caught between opposing armies. It also epitomizes Menchaca's self-narration of his Tejano capacity to survive by cultivating relations of respect, even friendship, among the leaders of various groups who came into the nexus of San Antonio life.[30]

What emerges from the pages of Menchaca's memoir is the story of a man who prided himself in his heritage, his personal and family honor, and his capacity as a survivor. Like other Tejanos, Menchaca had many opportunities to succumb to bitterness and despair. His friends and neighbors had lost their lives in the insurgencies of the Mexican War of Independence and the Texas Revolution, regardless of which side they chose in the conflicts, or even if they attempted to remain neutral. Living in the city that has had more battles fought in or around it than any other in what is now the United States, he had witnessed many atrocities. In his early years perennial tensions with Indians had also led to attacks and counterattacks. As successive national governments claimed sovereignty over San Antonio, he was among the population caught in between, on one occasion having to defend his hometown from both the Mexican and the Texan armies. His political career and activism, like those of his contemporaries, had relatively limited influence on the new Anglo-American regime that gained ascendancy in his hometown.

Menchaca's life narration—however embellished or errant in detail—reveals a vision of humanity that he undoubtedly held with many other nineteenth-century Tejanos who endured the tumult of that century in Texas. Proudly accentuating his encounters with such diverse figures as James Bowie and Spanish military commanders, Comanche chiefs and Antonio López de Santa Anna, Sam Houston and Davy Crockett, General Adrián Woll and Texas Ranger Jack Hays, his fellow Tejanos and San Antonio's growing Anglo-American population, Menchaca displayed a remarkable capacity to remember both friends and supposed enemies with similar respect. His memoir adds to the collective biography of nineteenth-century Tejanos an insightful portfolio of the characteristics Tejanos valued and sought to deem their own: an unwillingness to forget that their ancestors were the original founders of places like San Antonio, maintenance of internal equilibrium amid the many changes they faced throughout their nineteenth-century lives, and the *aguante* (unyielding endurance) without which they would not have lived to tell their tale.

Notes

1. Quotations from Hewitt's speech in this and the following paragraphs are taken from the copy of his presentation in the *San Antonio*

Herald, 5 March 1859. The speech was also reprinted in the *San Antonio Daily Herald,* 9 March 1859.

2.   James Newcomb, "Introduction," in Antonio Menchaca, *Memoirs* (San Antonio, Tex.: Yanaguana Society, 1937), 11; *San Antonio Express,* 2 November 1879; *Northern Standard* (Clarksville), 6 March 1845, as cited in James Ernest Crisp, "Anglo-Texan Attitudes toward the Mexican, 1821–1845" (Ph.D. diss., Yale University, New Haven, 1976), 402; Edward Tabor Linenthal, *Sacred Ground: Americans and Their Battlefields* (Urbana: University of Illinois Press, 1991), 61–62.

3.   Juan N. Seguín, *Personal Memoirs of John N. Seguín from the Year 1834 to the Retreat of General Woll from the City of San Antonio in 1842* (San Antonio, Tex.: Ledger Book and Job Office, 1858), reprinted in both edited and unedited versions in Jesús F. de la Teja, ed., *A Revolution Remembered: The Memoirs and Selected Correspondence of Juan N. Seguín,* 2d ed. (Austin: Texas State Historical Association, 2002), 71–122; José Antonio Navarro, *Apuntes históricos interesantes de San Antonio de Béxar escritos por el C. Dn. José Antonio Navarro, en noviembre de 1853. Y publicados por varios de sus amigos* (San Antonio: privately printed, 1869), facsimile reprinted in David R. McDonald and Timothy Matovina, eds., *Defending Mexican Valor in Texas: José Antonio Navarro's Historical Writings, 1853–1857* (Austin: State House, 1995); J[osé] M[aría] Rodríguez, *Rodríguez Memoirs of Early Texas* (San Antonio, Tex.: Passing Show Printing, 1913; reprint, San Antonio, Tex.: Standard, 1961); Menchaca, *Memoirs.*

4.   San Fernando Cathedral Baptismal Register, vol. 4, entry no. 450, Catholic Archives at San Antonio, Chancery Office, Archdiocese of San Antonio; Frederick C. Chabot, "Foreword," in Menchaca, *Memoirs,* 9.

5.   Chabot, "Foreword"; *New Handbook of Texas,* s.v. "Glanton, John Joel" (quotation).

6.   Stephen L. Hardin, "Efficient in the Cause," in *Tejano Journey, 1770–1850,* ed. Gerald E. Poyo (Austin: University of Texas Press, 1996), 66 (first quotation), 67; Charles Merritt Barnes, "Alamo's Only Survivor," *San Antonio Express,* 12 May 1907 (second quotation). The Esparza account continued in the 19 May 1907 issue of the *Express;* it is reprinted in its entirety in Timothy Matovina, *The Alamo Remembered: Tejano Accounts and Perspectives* (Austin: University of Texas Press, 1995), 77–89, quotation at 82.

7.   Quotations from Menchaca's memoirs are cited in context with page numbers given in parentheses. The only known copy of the first 40 percent of the document is the transcription in Menchaca, *Memoirs,*

13–28. Thus cited page numbers in this range come from that source. The remainder of the memoir in its original handwritten form, which Charles Merritt Barnes transcribed from Menchaca's dictation, is at the Center for American History, University of Texas, Austin [CAH]. It is marked with pages numbering 68–155; cited quotations from this portion of the memoir are labeled accordingly. Since correcting the spelling and grammatical errors in both these sources would be distracting because they are so numerous, and in order to give the reader a rendition of the original text, I cite all quotations literally and correct only minor errors as needed to make statements intelligible and more accurate in historical detail.

8. Rodríguez, *Rodríguez Memoirs of Early Texas*, 62; Hardin, "Efficient in the Cause," 60; Henry Stuart Foote, *Texas and the Texans* (Philadelphia: Thomas Cowperthwait, 1841), 2:310. See also Hardin, *Texian Iliad: A Military History of the Texas Revolution, 1835–1836* (Austin: University of Texas Press, 1994), 213.

9. De la Teja, ed., *Revolution Remembered*, 113, 163. See also Seguín, *Personal Memoirs of John N. Seguín*, 18.

10. [M. B. Lamar] to Major Jones, 11 March 1839, in Charles Adams Gulick Jr. and Katherine Elliott, eds., *The Papers of Mirabeau Buonaparte Lamar* (Austin: Von Boeckmann-Jones, 1973), 2:489–90; Sam Houston to the Texas Senate, 18 July 1842, in Amelia W. Williams and Eugene C. Barker, eds., *The Writings of Sam Houston, 1813–1863* (Austin: University of Texas Press, 1938–43), 3:105–6; Houston to certain citizens of San Antonio, 18 May 1843, in ibid., 3:390–93; Joseph Milton Nance, *Attack and Counter-Attack: The Texas-Mexican Frontier, 1842* (Austin: University of Texas Press, 1964), 243, 273, 305, 318, 323–25; Frederick C. Chabot, *The Perote Prisoners: Being the Diary of James L. Trueheart, Printed for the First Time Together with an Historical Introduction* (San Antonio, Tex.: Naylor, 1934), 100 (first quotation); Joseph Milton Nance, ed. and trans., "Brigadier General Adrian Woll's Report of His Expedition into Texas in 1842," *Southwestern Historical Quarterly* 58 (April 1955): 533 (second quotation). For other eyewitness accounts of General Woll's 1842 occupation of San Antonio which mention Menchaca, see Rodríguez, *Rodríguez Memoirs of Early Texas*, 17–18; E. W. Winkler, ed., "The Bexar and Dawson Prisoners," *Quarterly of the Texas State Historical Association* 13 (April 1910): 295, 314.

11. Sam Houston, appointment of an Indian escort, 7 February 1844, in Williams and Barker, eds., *Writings of Sam Houston*, 4:251; Fane Downs, "The History of Mexicans in Texas, 1820–1845" (Ph.D. diss.,

Texas Tech University, Lubbock, 1970), 248; Henry W. Barton, *Texas Volunteers in the Mexican War* (Waco, Tex.: Texian Press, 1970), 118.

12. *San Antonio Herald*, 7 April 1876, 3; Gifford White, *1830 Citizens of Texas* (Austin: Eakin, 1983), 101; "A Joint Resolution for the Relief of Antonio Manchaca," 22 December 1838, in *Laws of the Republic of Texas Passed the First Session of Third Congress* (Houston: Intelligencer Office, 1839), 21; Gifford White, ed., *The 1840 Census of the Republic of Texas* (Austin: Pemberton, 1966), 15; V. K. Carpenter, comp., *The State of Texas Federal Population Schedules Seventh Census of the United States, 1850* (Huntsville, AR: Century Enterprises, 1969), entry 179, 1:121; *San Antonio Herald*, 25 September 1857. For a brief overview of the Cart War, see John J. Linn, *Reminiscences of Fifty Years in Texas* (New York: D. and J. Sadlier, 1883; reprint, Austin: State House, 1986), 352–54; J. Fred Rippy, "Border Troubles along the Rio Grande, 1848–1860," *Southwestern Historical Quarterly* 23 (October 1919): 103–4; Larry Knight, "The Cart War: Defining American in San Antonio in the 1850s," *Southwestern Historical Quarterly* 109 (January 2006): 319–36.

13. White, *1840 Census*, 12–18; Carpenter, *State of Texas Federal Population Schedules*, 1:111–89; White, *1830 Citizens of Texas*, 79–112.

14. Antonio Menchaca, Deposition, 1 January 1856, Antonio Fuentes File, Memorials and Petitions, Texas State Archives, Austin [TSA]; Menchaca, Deposition, 28 July 1856, Carlos Espalier File, Memorials and Petitions, TSA; Juan N. Seguín, "Application for Pension," 2 October 1874, in De la Teja, *Revolution Remembered*, 187–88; Tejano citizens to Stephen H. Darden, 12 January 1875, in James M. Day, ed., "Texas Letters and Documents," *Texana* 5 (Spring 1967): 81–84, quotations at 84; Menchaca, Deposition, 24 August 1860, Court of Claims Voucher File 2557 (Francisco Esparza), General Land Office, Austin; Newcomb, "Introduction," 11.

15. Newcomb, "Introduction," 11.

16. "Minutes of the City Council of the City of San Antonio from 1837 to 1849, Journal A" (typescript, CAH); De la Teja, *Revolution Remembered*, 43; Houston to certain citizens of San Antonio; Joseph Milton Nance, *After San Jacinto: The Texas-Mexican Frontier, 1836–1841* (Austin: University of Texas Press, 1963), 206.

17. "Minutes of the City Council of the City of San Antonio from 1837 to 1849, Journal A"; "Journal of City Council B, January 1849 to August 1856, City of San Antonio"; and "Journal of City Council C: April 1, 1856 to February 21, 1870, City of San Antonio," City Clerk's Office, San Antonio; Sam Houston to Howell Cobb, in Williams and Barker,

Writings of Sam Houston, 7:451–52; *Alamo Express* (San Antonio), 1 October 1860, 3; *Mooney & Morrison's General Directory of the City of San Antonio, for 1877–78* (Galveston, Tex.: Galveston News, 1877), 43.

18. Arnoldo De León, *The Tejano Community, 1836–1900* (Albuquerque: University of New Mexico Press, 1982; reprint, Dallas: Southern Methodist University Press, 1997), 30–31; De León, *They Called Them Greasers: Anglo Attitudes toward Mexicans in Texas, 1821–1900* (Austin: University of Texas Press, 1983), 56–57.

19. *San Antonio Express*, 2 November 1879; *New Handbook of Texas*, s.v. "Manchaca, Texas."

20. Rodríguez, *Rodríguez Memoirs of Early Texas*, 34, 38.

21. The buffalo story can be found in various documents in the Bexar Archives, including several references that mention José Antonio Curbelo as the individual charged by Governor Domingo Cabello to take buffalo to the king. See, e.g., "Estado de la fuerza," 31 January 1783. A somewhat inaccurate representation of the story is in Frederick Charles Chabot, *With the Makers of San Antonio* (San Antonio, Tex.: Artes Gráficas, 1937), 155.

22. Charles Merritt Barnes, *Combats and Conquests of Immortal Heroes: Sung in Song and Told in Story* (San Antonio, Tex.: Guessaz and Ferlet, 1910), 76–81; S. J. Wright, *San Antonio de Béxar: Historical, Traditional, Legendary* (Austin: Morgan, 1916), 121–22, 127–28. Another account states that Margil de Jesús miraculously discovered a spring near Nacogdoches, although it cites the earlier works of Barnes and Wright, who gave the site as San Antonio. E. G. Littlejohn, "The Holy Spring of Father Margil at Nacogdoches," in *Legends of Texas*, ed. J. Frank Dobie (Austin: Texas Folk-Lore Society, 1924), 204–5.

23. *Western Texas* (San Antonio), 14 October 1852.

24. For an overview of these eventful years in San Antonio history, see Félix D. Almaráz Jr., *Tragic Cavalier: Governor Manuel Salcedo of Texas, 1808–1813* (Austin: University of Texas Press, 1971); Jesús F. de la Teja, "Rebellion on the Frontier," in Poyo, *Tejano Journey*, 15–30. Menchaca's account of Arredondo's harsh reprisals against San Antonio residents is consistent with his reminiscences that former Texas president Mirabeau Buonaparte Lamar recorded while conducting historical research in 1857. Notes taken from Menchaca and Barrera, [21 January 1857], in Gulick and Elliott, *Papers of Mirabeau Buonaparte Lamar*, 6:339–40.

25. José Antonio Navarro attested that the secretary of this ruling group was Mariano Rodríguez, a leader not mentioned on Menchaca's list of appointed officials; José María Rodríguez states Mariano

Rodríguez was his distant relative. Historian Carlos Castañeda cites primary documents to show Gutiérrez himself led the governing body after the insurgent victory, but he makes no mention of local officials, much less a Canary Islander–dominated ruling elite. Navarro, *Defending Mexican Valor in Texas*, 47; Rodríguez, *Rodríguez Memoirs of Early Texas*, 52–54; Carlos Castañeda, *Our Catholic Heritage in Texas, 1519–1936* (Austin: Von Boeckmann-Jones, 1936–58), 6:102–3. See also Navarro, *Apuntes*, 15.

26.   In some passages of Menchaca's memoir the name is spelled "Cassimiro." The only other reference I have found to this Comanche leader is in the work of Joseph Milton Nance, who spells his name "Casemiro" but does not reference any incidents with him at San Antonio akin to those Menchaca recounts. Nance, *Attack and Counter-Attack*, 111, 189.

27.   Notes taken from Menchaca and Barrera, in Gulick and Elliott, *Papers of Mirabeau Buonaparte Lamar*, 6:338; Rodríguez, *Rodríguez Memoirs of Early Texas*, 14.

28.   Samuel Maverick, one of the prisoners, recorded this version of the communiqué in his journal, noting that "the Mexican population here" had supplied and assisted the Anglo-American prisoners "in the most liberal manner." Rena Maverick Green, ed., *Samuel Maverick, Texan: 1803–1870. A Collection of Letters, Journals, and Memoirs* (San Antonio, Tex.: privately printed, 1952), 174.

29.   Felix Huston to Sam Houston, 14 November 1836, Catholic Archives of Texas, Austin; Houston to Juan Seguín, 16 January 1837, in De la Teja, *Revolution Remembered*, 152–53, 111–12; Linn, *Reminiscences of Fifty Years in Texas*, 294–96. See also Seguín, *Personal Memoirs of John N. Seguín*, 15–16; *Telegraph and Texas Register* (Columbia), 25 October 1836.

30.   For the Tejano dilemma of being caught being opposing loyalties and military forces, see Jesús F. de la Teja, "The Making of a Tejano" in *Revolution Remembered*, 1–70; Timothy Matovina, *Tejano Religion and Ethnicity: San Antonio, 1821–1860* (Austin: University of Texas Press, 1995), esp. 24–48. The interpreter Menchaca mentions in this passage is an attorney named Barnes; this is not the Charles Merritt Barnes to whom he dictated the memoirs, who was not yet born when these events occurred.

Carlos de la Garza's petition for a league of land. Although the family had possessed the land for many years, the lack of a title required Garza to seek a title from the Irish empresarios James Power and James Hewetson, who had established their headquarters at the site of the former Mission Nuestra Señora del Refugio. Note that Garza signed with an X.

Courtesy Spanish Collection 43/9, p. 1, Texas General Land Office, Austin.

CARLOS DE LA GARZA

LOYALIST LEADER

Alonzo Salazar

THE BIOGRAPHY OF CARLOS DE LA GARZA is more than the story of his life. He lived during the critical period that encompassed the end of the Spanish empire in Mexico, the birth of the Republic of Mexico, and the revolution that created the Texas Republic. He was born and died at the southern end of the great cattle triangle between the Guadalupe and San Antonio rivers, where Texas ranching was born. The region between Presidio La Bahía (later Goliad) and the juncture of the Guadalupe and San Antonio rivers witnessed a wide range of events, from the explorations of French and Spanish frontiersmen, to encounters among Spanish padres and soldiers and Indians, to confrontations between the Spanish military and pirates and filibustering Anglo-Americans. It was the site of the last Spanish mission founded in Texas, Nuestra Señora del Refugio. The region's landings and ports of El Sabinito, El Muelle Viejo, El Bergantino, and El Copano were Spain's and Mexico's Gulf gateway to Texas. De la Garza's ranch and village below Goliad on the San Antonio River represented the region's last Spanish frontier.

Carlos de la Garza was born in 1807 at Presidio La Bahía del Espíritu Santo de Zúñiga, better known as Presidio La Bahía. His parents, José Antonio and Rosalia de la Garza, were in possession of the De la Garza ranch at the time of his birth. Presidial soldiers such as José Antonio acquired ranches along the San Antonio River with hopes of receiving titles once the missions were secularized. The ranch has been in the family for hundreds of years according to oral family history; two hundred years is certain. Located on prime terrain, the ranch and roads leading to the ferry sat above the floodplain, with the homestead on a bluff on the left bank of the river and the ferry upstream at the bottom of a ravine. The river's elevation rapidly declines into the coastal marshlands as it winds into the Guadalupe River and San Antonio Bay. Midway between the Gulf and La Bahía, the ranch served as a waystation and sentinel for the presidio. A Spanish presence existed in the area long before the De la Garzas and final location of Presidio La Bahía at Goliad.

In 1829, De la Garza married Saltillo native Tomasita García and built a hand-hewn double log cabin at the family ranch. They had two sons and one daughter: Rafael Carlos, Vicente, and Refugia. The ranch and community that developed around their home came to be known in Texas as Carlos Rancho and Ferry Crossing. The roads from the ferry led to Goliad, Victoria, Refugio, Texana, and the Gulf ports at La Vaca and Copano bays, pathways of immigration and commercial activity long since forgotten. It was a thriving community by 1830 and served as a place of refuge for the citizens of Goliad, Victoria, and Refugio during dangerous times before, during, and after the Texas Revolution. The ranch comprised the Santa Gertrudis chapel, a school, blacksmith shop, commissary, barrel house, and ferry crossing.[1]

This Tejano enclave was home to Badeños—La Bahía settlers and their families descended from Spanish presidio soldiers. Born to the saddle, they raised, broke, and trained horses. On these horses they patrolled beyond Goliad's territorial jurisdiction, comprising the vast territory between the Nueces and La Vaca rivers up to a vaguely defined boundary at Cíbolo Creek between Goliad and San Antonio. Like their ancestors, the Badeños also worked vast herds of cattle on the rich pasturelands between the San Antonio and Guadalupe rivers, considered the cradle of Texas ranching.[2] In the 1780s area ranchers had helped supply Spanish general Bernardo de Gálvez with more than 10,000 head of cattle and horses in support of his campaign against the English during the American Revolution. Badeño soldiers and cowboys drove the beeves east to Louisiana, where General Gálvez supplied American patriots and his own army from these herds. Texas cattle, particularly from La Bahía's jurisdiction, proved a deciding factor in his victorious campaign over British strongholds along the entire Gulf coast and the Bahamas Islands.[3]

Continual political turmoil in Spain and Mexico resulted in misadministration and neglect of Texas at the end of the eighteenth century and years leading to independence in 1836. Events in early nineteenth-century Europe adversely affected the families of La Bahía during De la Garza's childhood. Napoleon Bonaparte's invasion of Spain in 1808 and the abdication of the Spanish throne to Napoleon's brother Joseph by King Ferdinand VII set in motion a series of events leading to New Spain's independence. Already dissatisfied with Spanish rule, the American colonies rejected French rule, and the struggle for independence began. Father Miguel Hidalgo Costilla declared against bad government on 16 September 1810 at Dolores, Guanajuato, and the independence movement spread to Texas.

José Bernardo Gutiérrez declared independence for the Republic of Texas on 6 April 1813 at San Antonio. This independence would come to an abrupt end four months later at the hands of General Joaquín de Arredondo at the battle of Medina outside San Antonio. Arredondo left Texas in ruins, and the population declined thereafter. The 1813 revolt was Texas' deadliest and most devastating attempt at independence, which would have to wait another generation.

The families of Presidio La Bahía would endure four separate attempts to establish independence from Spain and Mexico between 1812 and 1836, each involving attacks on the presidio. The Gutiérrez-Magee expedition captured the presidio in November 1812, proceeded to San Antonio, and secured a surrender of Spanish forces. The Henry Perry expedition failed to capture the presidio in June 1817, and the James Long expedition succeeded in 1821 only to surrender to Spanish royalist troops from San Antonio three days later. The final effort in October 1835 resulted in the presidio's capture by a company of Texians led by George Collinsworth of Brazoria and local Tejanos under Plácido Benavides of Victoria. La Bahía's population was overwhelmed and suffered at the hands of the rebels in each attack, with the campaign of 1835–36 being the most destructive. First came the abuse and destruction of La Bahía at the hands of Colonel Fannin's men, then the execution of his command by the Mexican army, followed by the depredations committed by the Texian Army at Victoria under General Thomas Rusk's command after Santa Anna's defeat in the battle of San Jacinto.

In 1829 La Bahía's status was raised to *villa*, the political status of a capital of a territorial jurisdiction, and the town was renamed Goliad. Its municipal territorial jurisdiction included Victoria, Refugio, and San Partricio, diluting the Badeño vote and political influence to the benefit of the newly arrived Irish of San Patricio and the De León colonists at Victoria. Goliad's Badeños and Victoria's colonists were of different stock with divided interests. The Badeños were local military families whereas the majority of Victoria's colonists were newly arrived Mexicans. The contested election of De León's son-in-law Rafael Manchola to alcalde of La Bahía in 1829 illustrates the influence De León exerted over La Bahía. The Badeños protested Manchola's election to jefe político Ramón Múzquiz in San Antonio only to have Múzquiz rule in Manchola's favor.[4] This political schism would appear during the Texas Revolution, with the majority of La Bahía's Tejanos actively opposing independence while the De León family and Victoria supported the revolution.

The Spanish secularization decree of 10 April 1794 declared that the padres in Texas had accomplished their work. This was not the case, though, at the three missions at La Bahía and Refugio; missions Espíritu Santo, Rosario, and Refugio received extensions. The three missions were secularized by Mexico in 1830, allowing their lands to be granted.

In 1834 Irish-Mexican empresarios James Power and James Hewetson received coastal bend land grants from the Mexican government, and the old Spanish mission of Refugio became the center of the predominately Irish settlement. The Mexican government provided grants for existing Tejano ranchers within the settlement, including Carlos de la Garza. He obtained a grant of one and one quarter leagues of land. By all accounts, he welcomed and accommodated his new neighbors. This was not the case with all native Tejanos, as Andrés Tijerina's chapter on Rafael Manchola makes clear. There were cultural, political, and religious differences among the newly arrived colonists and the Tejanos.

Many assume that all of the Power and Hewetson colonists were Roman Catholics, but such was not the case. The colony was intended as a Roman Catholic settlement, but the cholera epidemic of 1833–34 decimated the newly arrived colonists. The empresarios petitioned the Mexican government to allow others to take their place, and permission was granted. Among the replacement colonists were Germans, Englishmen, Scots, Canadians, and North Americans, some Protestants. Many of them learned from De la Garza and the residents of his community the skills required to survive on the Texas frontier. Among his closest friends and neighbors were the families of Nicholas Fagan and Tom O'Connor. Texas' war of independence would put these friendships to the test, since De la Garza opposed the revolt from its inception.

By 1835 Goliad was the Gulf port of entry and a communications line for San Antonio. It consisted of about two hundred homes and businesses of all types, a population of about six hundred, and buildings ranging from dirt floor *jacales* to two-story limestone mansions. The *aduana* (customhouse) of the port of Goliad was a two-story limestone building located across from the presidio. General Martín Perfecto de Cos landed a punitive expedition at the nearby port of Copano in September 1835 and proceeded to Goliad. General Cos had orders from General Santa Anna to expel troublemakers and disarm the colonists. By the time he left Goliad for San Antonio, General Cos had managed to infuriate peaceful Texians and loyal Tejanos against General Santa Anna's centralist government. Texians' worst fear, a centralist dictatorship, had become reality, and the Tejanos were forced to choose between the federalist Constitution of 1824 and Santa Anna. After General Cos departed for San Antonio, George Collinsworth and Plácido Benavides captured the presidio with the help of local Badeños early in the morning of 10 October 1835. Communication and supply lines to San Antonio were cut and the revolution began for Goliad.

The capture of Goliad and occupation by Colonel James Fannin forced De la Garza into the Texas Revolution, which began over constitutional issues between centralist and federalist factions in Mexico. In 1834 centralist president Antonio López de Santa Anna moved against the federalist congress and began undoing the Constitution of 1824. Federalists, which included most of the Tejano leadership, favored the strong states' rights government under the constitution. For Texans, Santa Anna's centralist actions raised fears of dictatorship and threatened to postpone separation from Coahuila, a partnership that many in Texas felt was detrimental to the region's interests.

Badeños fared poorly during the American occupation of Goliad. Carlos Rancho came under suspicion as a haven for Mexican spies, and Colonel Fannin sent his forces against it at least twice. His men arrested several residents of the community, including their priest, Father José Antonio Valdez.[5] During these raids De la Garza reluctantly furnished Texian forces with supplies including horses, cattle, and carts.[6] In Goliad, Colonel Fannin's men broke into and plundered Mexican homes. These acts earned Fannin's men the nickname *mesteños* (mustangs) and prompted De la Garza to lead the families to his ranch to guarantee their safety.[7] The behavior of the Texians contributed to his decision to oppose Texas revolutionary forces. Thus, De la Garza actively supported the Mexican cause and provided General José Urrea's advancing army intelligence on Colonel Fannin's troop count and activities. Colonel Fannin eventually paid a dear price for alienating and underestimating the importance of the Tejano military families, including De la Garza, who were quite familiar with the region and in many cases had earlier supported the revolt.

De la Garza's principal contribution to the Mexican effort to preserve Texas was his leadership of a two-hundred-man militia unit known as the Guardia Victorianos. Composed of Tejanos, Mexican soldiers, and Karankawa Indians, they were a well-disciplined frontier guard in the tradition of the *compañías volantes* ("flying companies"), a product of Spanish frontier military experience with mounted Indians.[8]

In early March 1836 the Guardia Victorianos went on the offensive, raiding south of Goliad and initiating a series of engagements known as the battle of Refugio. After the initial engagement, De la Garza proceeded to San Patricio and established contact with the advancing Mexican army of General Urrea. The timing of the Refugio raid coincided with General Urrea's defeat of Texian forces at the battles of Agua Dulce and San Patricio. Colonel Fannin's reaction was to delay his retreat from Goliad to Victoria. He responded by sending Kentuckian Amon King and twenty-eight men to Refugio.[9]

After gathering the Refugio families, King delayed his return to Goliad. He attempted to engage a band of Mexicans camped out at the Estevan López ranch on the Mission River below Refugio. Finding the ranch abandoned, King burned it and subsequently led his men into an ambush set by De la Garza on the outskirts of Refugio.[10] King withdrew into Mission Nuestra Señora del Refugio and sent for help. In what proved to be a disastrous move, Colonel Fannin again divided his command by dispatching his second in command, Lieutenant Colonel William Ward, and his Georgia battalion to relieve King's command, which the Guardia Victorianos held under siege at the Refugio mission. Colonel Ward and some 120 men successfully reinforced King on the evening of 13 March. Ward and King quarreled over who held command, however. King claimed that he was first on the ground, Ward that he held superior rank. Each refused to serve under the other, resulting in a divided rebel command at Refugio. Meanwhile, Mexican cavalry under Captain Rafael Pretalia and infantry commanded by Colonel Francisco Garay had reinforced the Guardia Victorianos. The forces of King and Ward managed to escape temporarily under cover of night.[11]

After ambushing and killing eight Mexicans, King became disoriented and found himself back at the Refugio mission by daybreak, where he was discovered and engaged by the combined forces of De la Garza's Guardia Victorianos and Colonel Garay's infantry. King defended himself in a motte on the south bank of the Mission River. The fight lasted from late morning until dark, when under cover of night King and his men escaped. De la Garza and the Guardia Victorianos pursued them, finally overtaking and defeating them at the John Malone ranch the following morning.[12]

Among those captured by the Guardia Victorianos was Nicholas Fagan, De la Garza's neighbor. Unwilling to bear responsibility for his friend's death, De la Garza released Fagan with instructions to return to his home. The remaining prisoners were tied with a single rope and marched back to Refugio,[13] where De la Garza remanded King and his men to General Urrea. The next day King and his men, except two Germans and six Refugio colonists, were executed by German-born Lieutenant Colonel Johann Holzinger.

Colonel Ward and the Georgia battalion also managed to escape during the night of the thirteenth. However, De la Garza and Colonel Garay learned from a captured courier that Ward planned to retreat to Victoria from Refugio.[14] With this intelligence, the Guardia Victorianos and Mexican cavalry pursued the Georgia battalion to Victoria, which the Texians discovered occupied by General Urrea's forces. Colonel Ward and his men attempted to escape by reaching Dimmitt's Landing on the lower La Vaca River. Exhausted, famished, without ammunition, and surrounded by General Urrea's forces, the Georgia battalion voted to surrender on the road to Dimmitt's.[15]

The battle of Refugio is one of the lesser-known engagements of the Texas Revolution, but its consequences were significant. Colonel Fannin unwisely split his forces and delayed his retreat to Victoria for a week largely as a result of De la Garza's activities. King's refusal to return to Goliad before engaging De la Garza at Refugio contributed to a series of events leading to the ultimate defeat of Colonel Fannin's Texian forces by General Urrea's at the battle at Coleto Creek. Years later General Vicente Filisola, in his critical analysis of Urrea's published military diary, confirmed De la Garza's importance to the outcome of the engagement: "Sr. Urréa omits that on the 12th he was met on his departure from San Patricio by 30 well-armed and mounted citizens from the villa of Goliad, and among them several soldiers from the company of La Bahía del Espíritu Santo, all under the orders of Don Carlos de la Garza, who served in a commendable way in the operations of the 14th against the Refugio Mission, according to the report of Sr. Garay and subsequent ones that were contributed, due to their detailed familiarity with the terrain."[16]

The Texian Goliad campaign of 1836 concluded with the execution of Colonel Fannin's men as rebels in accordance of Mexico's Tornel Decree of 1835. It is at this juncture that the dilemma faced by many Tejanos since the inception of the revolt squarely confronted De la Garza, who, unwilling to treat all Texians as mere enemies, intervened to save from execution several of his friends and neighbors captured with Colonel Fannin. General Santa Anna had ordered the execution of the "perfidious foreigners," overruling General Urrea's order "to treat the prisoners with consideration." Through De la Garza's efforts several colonists were spared, among them John and

Nicholas Fagan, James Byrne, Edward Perry, and John and Anthony Sydick. Nicholas Fagan had escaped execution a second time.[17]

After the battle of Coleto, De la Garza and the Guardias Victorianos were attached to the victorious Mexican army of General Urrea, which continued to work its way up coastal Texas. Their advance came to a halt a month later, on 21 April, when the Mexican army found its fortunes reversed after General Sam Houston's victory over General Santa Anna at San Jacinto. The Mexican armies of generals Urrea and Filisola, following the orders of General Santa Anna, now a prisoner of war, began their withdrawal from Texas to the Rio Grande in the following weeks.

De la Garza was not alone in leading resistance against Texian forces at Goliad during the revolution. In fall 1835, General Cos and his Mexican army arrived at the strategically important port of Copano. Guadalupe de los Santos, Manuel Sabriego, Juan Moya, Agustine Moya, Father José Antonio Valdez, and De la Garza greeted him and pledged their loyalty to the Mexican cause.[18] This loyalty bore tragic consequences for all after the revolution. Guadalupe de los Santos died in Mexico City while attempting to receive compensation for his services. Manuel Sabriego left Texas with the retreating Mexican army and continued his military career in Mexico. Father Valdez went to Mexico and died in Saltillo. The Moyas were murdered while in the custody of Goliad County Sheriff Phil Fulcrod. De la Garza alone returned home to live a respected citizen of the Republic of Texas.

De la Garza returned to his ranch and braced himself for the arrival the Texian army. When General Thomas Rusk, now in command, arrived in Victoria, he ordered Tejano families on both sides of the Texas Revolution removed from their homes and ranches in June 1836.[19] Some were exiled to Mexico and Louisiana; others had left with the retreating Mexican army. General Rusk sent a company of men to Carlos Rancho with orders directing De la Garza off his land and out of Texas. Informed of General Rusk's order, De la Garza and his Texian friends were waiting. Rusk's soldiers read him the orders directing him to leave his home. De la Garza listened but ignored the order. His friends stepped in and told the soldiers, "You can read it to him, but you don't touch him," and "None durst molest him."[20] De la Garza and his family would successfully defend their land against various threats over the course of the next decade.

Conditions for Tejanos quickly deteriorated after the battle of San Jacinto. Anglo-American veterans and newcomers were quick to settle and claim the most desirable tracts of land in Victoria, Goliad, and Refugio counties. In his memoirs, John J. "Juan" Linn, alcalde of Victoria wrote: "After the burial of the remains of Col. Fannin's men General Rusk returned to Victoria. A great number of his men were new-comers and required the utmost exertion of their general to control them. Their creed was the total extermination of the Mexican race and the appropriation of their property to the individual use of the exterminators."[21]

Widespread banditry affected Carlos Rancho the same way it did the rest of the Tejano population. Texian army lieutenant John Browne wrote of the all too numerous outlaws who characterized postwar Texas: "A group of twenty of these men met in a Goliad public house and planned to burn down Carlos Rancho and take all the cattle." In an 1839 official army report to the secretary of war, Browne wrote:

> When I arrived in Victoria I found it filled with a set of men who had given themselves the title of *a band of brothers*. I soon found that what they said was law. They are all in the cow stealing business, and are scattered all over this frontier. Mr. Cornelius Van Ness of Victoria says he thinks Judge James Allen at Carlos Rancho is silently connected with them. I have been told that they drove off from Carlos Rancho a caballarda [*sic*] belonging to José Aldrete and Colonel Juan Seguin; that the owners know well where the property is but dare not recover it. Also the cow stealers when on the Nueces the other day took from a party of Mexican traders all their property and killed eight of them.[22]

Despite the circumstances, De la Garza worked to restore the family's fortunes; he was respected, but resented for his role during the revolution. He oversaw his farming and livestock operations, defended against Indians, ran his commissary, and operated the ferry. Early in the time of the republic, the ranch was a post for Texas Rangers, and it served as the Refugio County seat several times.[23] Nevertheless, Carlos Rancho was not yet entirely safe. What may have been the last attempt to remove De la Garza from his ranch occurred late in the life of the Republic of Texas. In August 1845, General Thomas T. Williamson of Shreveport, Louisiana, acquired a series of land scrip granted to Thomas Green of Richmond, Virginia. Williamson sold the scrip to New Orleans land speculator Thomas B. Lee. Lee arrived in Victoria to claim his land, which was along the left bank of the San Antonio River and included the De la Garza grant. Unlike what occurred to the De León clan in nearby Victoria, De la Garza's friends in the community would not permit a miscarriage of justice. Again, De la Garza successfully defended his property.[24]

Overcoming all obstacles, De la Garza soon headed a thriving community. Roman Catholic priest Jean Marie Odin, the first bishop of Texas and an acquaintance of De la Garza's friend Juan Linn, noted in his early travels to the region that the population of Carlos Rancho exceeded the residents living in the towns of Victoria, Refugio, and Goliad combined.[25] De la Garza himself assisted the Catholic Church in Texas in those early days by allowing his ranch to serve as the headquarters for the Vicentian priests and as refuge for parishioners after the great Comanche raid on Victoria in 1840.[26] He also sheltered families during the Mexican invasion of 1842, when Lieutenant Colonel Ramón Valera established his headquarters at Rancho de las Mujeres near San Patricio.[27] And, having accepted Texas independence, De la Garza provisioned the republic's punitive expedition in response to the 1842 Mexican raid.[28]

South Texas remained an Indian frontier in the mid-nineteenth century, and De la Garza was as much involved in defending against Indian attack as he was in defending against Anglo bandits and Mexican armies. In 1842, Comanches murdered his neighbor Johnson Gilleland and his wife Mary and took their children Rebecca and William captives. De la Garza, Nicholas Fagan, and Tom O'Connor rescued the Gilleland children from the San Antonio River bottom, where they had been left for dead, and brought the orphaned children to the ranch.[29] Texas army general Albert Sydney Johnson was himself headquartered at Carlos Rancho during the Gilleland murders and pursued the Indians. As late as 1852, De la Garza participated in the battle of Hynes Bay, the region's last engagement between Texans and the Karankawa Indians, after which the surviving Karankawa agreed to leave the country.[30]

De la Garza's ranch came to be widely celebrated as a place of shelter. Among those to find refuge at Carlos Rancho was Jimbo, "the wild man of Navidad," a former African slave owned by Zebrian Lewis of Victoria. From the end of the Civil War until his death in 1884, the ranch was home to Jimbo, or "Kunta," as the African American was known to the De la Garzas. De la Garza and his wife Tomasita also offered spiritual shelter to numerous children by serving as godparents at their baptisms. One significant request came early on, when Miguel Zaragoza and María Seguín asked De la Garza and Tomasita to sponsor the baptism of their son. Zaragoza was a captain in the

Mexican army garrisoned at Goliad, and María Seguín a relative of San Jacinto hero Colonel Juan Seguín. Their son Ignacio would lead the Mexican army against the French at Puebla on 5 May 1862.[31]

By the time of De la Garza's death, Carlos Rancho had ceased to serve as a refuge from Indians, bandits, and Mexican expeditions. However, Carlos Rancho remained a waystation and haven for Mexican immigrants and Tejanos well into the twentieth century. Numerous Victoria County families lived at the ranch over the years. Stones in the De la Garza family cemetery bear the names of Y'barbo, Flores, De los Santos, Hernández, Olivares, Moya, Vasques, and Tijerina. Records indicate that a post office named Carlos, Texas, existed at the site until 1886.[32]

De la Garza passed into history on 30 December 1882. Tomasita, his wife of fifty-three years, joined him in 1897. Both died and were buried on the old Carlos Rancho. The sad fact is that he did not write memoirs and no one who knew him wrote his biography. He took with him to the grave much of the early nineteenth-century history of the region encompassing Goliad, Refugio, and Victoria counties. His saber now rests where he was born, at Presidio La Bahía. Texas.

De la Garza was a product of the Spanish military and colonization in Texas. He was a soldier, pioneer, cattleman, farmer, and Texas stalwart. He was born Spaniard and died American. His lifetime spanned five of six flags that flew over Texas, those of Spain, the Republic Mexico, the Republic of Texas, the Confederate States, and the United States. He lived during Mexico's attempts for independence, from Father Miguel Hidalgo's failed campaign of 1810 to the success of Agustín de Iturbide and Vicente Guerrero's Plan de Iguala of 1821. In between he lived through the filibustering campaigns and captures of Goliad by the Gutiérrez-Magee expedition of 1812, the first Texas revolution of 1813, the failed attempt by Henry Perry in 1817, and the James Long expedition of 1821. In 1824 he saw the colonization of San Felipe de Austin by Stephen F. Austin and Martín De León's colonization of Guadalupe Victoria. He survived the cholera epidemic of 1833–34, the Texas Revolution in 1836, the Great Comanche Raid of 1840, the Mexican invasions of Rafael Vásquez and Adrián Woll of 1842, the Cart War of 1857, the American Civil War, and the yellow fever epidemic of 1867.

De la Garza was born at Texas' most fought-over and captured presidio during an era of brutal invasions, revolutions, and Indian depredations. Yet he was able to survive and prosper in this environment. A natural-born leader and humanitarian, he acted in the best interest of the region's population in difficult circumstances. They trusted and supported him, especially during the American occupation of Goliad. When confronted by Colonel Fannin's men at Carlos Rancho, the Badeños, wrote Dr. Joseph H. Barnard in his journal,

> received us kindly, and treated us with hospitality, professed the warmest hospitality to our cause, and denied having any communication with the Mexican Army. They gave as a reason for leaving town and coming here, that many of the volunteers were unruly and turbulent, and disposed to impose on them and their families, and that to avoid any quarrels with them they had removed. They succeeded in blinding us to their real disposition.[33]

Prudent militarily when circumstances rendered him powerless, he acted decisively when victory was attainable. He picked, won, and survived his battles. After the defeat of Texian forces, he put his life on the line defying General Santa Anna by facilitating the escape of his Texian revolutionary friends from execution in Goliad. After the revolution, he remained in good standing and was respected by his former military rivals. He facilitated the transition of his Tejano community from a defeated Mexico to the United States of America. Regarding the large-scale Tejano depopulation after the revolution, Paul D. Lack writes in *The Texas Revolutionary Experience*, "Exceptional ones like Carlos de la Garza remained to keep the Tejano heritage alive."[34]

That heritage of service extended to De la Garza's descendants. The family's military service spans the American Civil War, two world wars, the Korean and Vietnam wars, numerous invasions, and two Iraq wars. Rafael Carlos, first born of Carlos and Tomasita, died in service to the Confederacy. Seven generations later, Army Corporal Lee Pedraza III became Victoria's first casualty of the 2003 Iraq invasion. A direct descendent of Carlos de la Garza and Tomasita, Corporal Pedraza sustained debilitating injury in combat.[35]

As to the land that De la Garza worked so hard to acquire, make productive, and defend, the story runs the same course as for most Tejano families. Julia Y'barbo de la Garza was the last major landowner of the old Carlos Rancho. She was a seventh-generation Tejana and direct descendant of Antonio Gil Y'barbo, and the widow of first cousins Rafael II and Jesús de la Garza, both grandsons of Carlos de la Garza. Julia and her family came into control of Carlos Rancho after the death of her second husband Jesús in 1910. The families of Jesús

II, Carlos, and Ynocente de la Garza, great-grandchildren of Carlos, remained on the ranch more than two hundred years after the first Garza settled on the banks of the San Antonio River. Yet in the course of the twentieth century, sales, divided legacies, and diverging interests steadily chipped away at Carlos Rancho.

A State Historical Marker honoring Carlos de la Garza was dedicated in 1999. Nearly five hundred visitors participated. The marker is located on the De la Garza family Catholic cemetery. Participating in the program was Nicholas Fagan descendent James Matthews, who served as keynote speaker. The cemetery is the oldest private cemetery in Victoria County. It is located on the remnants of the old rancho on the San Antonio River Road.

If Carlos de la Garza were to return two hundred years after his birth, what would he think of the region and society? He would be pleased to see the coastal bend still in the United States, a somewhat civilized, less violent society. A beef-eating society with affinities rooted in the Great Cattle Triangle. He might be amused to see his Spanish legacy continued by multicultural Texan cowboys sporting hats, boots, chaps, and lariats, driving mustangs and longhorns to the rodeo. What would he think of his descendents who sold the very land he so valiantly fought to keep? A trailblazer in his own right, he would understand the decision to move on. He made no provision to keep the ranch intact; he stipulated in his last will and testament that it be "divided equally to his children and thereafter." He knew this guaranteed the fragmentation and eventual sale of the land.

To see his descendents and those of his Celtic and Anglo friends bearing the names of Fagan, O'Connor, Matthews, and Johnston continue a friendship established 180 years earlier would make him proud. He would find it sad and ironic that the nation's deadliest immigration tragedy occurred at the edge of his ranch, the refuge and waystation that saved the lives of many immigrants. He would be pleased to see his homestead now a Catholic spiritual renewal center and retreat available to all regardless of faith—this made possible by De la Garza family friend Gus Schmidt, who purchased the land from the family and bequeathed it to the Roman Catholic Diocese of Victoria.

When at the family cemetery, I find myself contemplating the family, people, and events that occurred on this ranch and in the region over the past two hundred years. What happened to the forty families Bishop Odin celebrated mass with in the rancho's Santa Gertrudis chapel during the early days of both the republic and the

Texas Catholic Church? What are the stories of the immigrants who passed through here after disembarking at the ports of El Copano or Indianola? Was a photograph ever taken of Carlos, Tomasita, or the home he built for her in 1829, the double log cabin "La Casa Grande," as it was called? So much historical and genealogical research remains to be done.

Notes

1. Hobart Huson, *Refugio: A Comprehensive History of Refugio County, from Aboriginal Times to 1955* (Woodsboro, Tex.: Rooke Foundation, 1953–55), 1:160–61; Kathryn Stoner O'Connor, *The Presidio La Bahia del Espiritu Santo de Zuñiga, 1721 to 1846* (Victoria, Tex.: Armstrong Printers, 1984), 250; *Handbook of Texas Online*, s.v. "Carlos Rancho."

2. Jack Jackson, *Los Mesteños: Spanish Ranching in Texas, 1721–1821* (College Station: Texas A&M Press, 1986), 52.

3. Robert H. Thonhoff, *The Texas Connection with the American Revolution* (Burnet, Tex.: Eakin Press, 1981), 46.

4. Franklin Madis, *The Taking of Texas, a Documentary History* (Eakin Press, Austin, 2002), 53–59.

5. John Critten Duval, *Early Times in Texas* (Austin: Steck, 1935), 3 1.

6. Carlos de la Garza folder, Republic of Texas Audited Military Claims, Archives Division, Texas State Library, Austin.

7. Duval, *Early Times in Texas*, 30; Roy Grimes, ed., *300 Years in Victoria County* (Victoria, Tex.: Victoria Advocate, 1968), 85.

8. Andrés Tijerina, *Tejanos and Texas under the Mexican Flag, 1821–1836* (College Station: Texas A&M University Press, 1994), 86.

9. Huson, *Refugio*, 1:288, 293, 294.

10. Ibid., 294; Roy Grimes, *Goliad: 130 Years After: Refugio and Guadalupe Victoria, March 1836–1966. Day-by-Day in the Words of Men Who Were There* (Victoria, Tex.: Victoria Advocate, 1966), 55–56.

11. Huson, *Refugio*, 1:321; Grimes, *Goliad*, 73; *Handbook of Texas Online*, s.v. "Refugio, Battle of."

12. Vicente Filisola, *Memoirs for the History of the War in Texas*, trans. by Wallace Woolsey (Austin: Eakin Press, 1985–87), 2:195.

13. Grimes, *Goliad*, 71.

14. Huson, *Refugio*, 1:301; Grimes, *Goliad*, 73; Filisola, *Memoirs*, 2:195.

15. Huson, *Refugio*, 1:367; Filisola, *Memoirs*, 2:213; Grimes, *Goliad*, 108.

16. Gregg J. Dimmick, ed., John R. Wheat, trans., *General Vicente Filisola's Analysis of José Urréa's Military Diary: A Forgotten 1838 Publication by*

an Eyewitness to the Texas Revolution (Austin: Texas State Historical Association, 2007), 28.

17. O'Connor, *Presidio La Bahia*, 251.

18. Huson, *Refugio*, 1:214.

19. Ibid., 1:398.

20. O'Connor, *Presidio La Bahia*, 253; Huson, *Refugio*, 1:398. James and Hillary Matthews, brothers and Fagan descendants, related to me family oral history describing the confrontation between General Rusk's soldiers and De la Garza and his Texian friends.

21. John J. Linn, *Reminisces of Fifty Years in Texas* (Austin: State House Press, 1986), 200.

22. Huson, *Refugio*, 1:428–29.

23. O'Connor, *Presidio La Bahia*, 250; *New Handbook of Texas*, s.v. "Carlos Rancho."

24. Thomas Lee, 7 August 1845, Deed Record, Victoria County Clerks Office, Victoria, Tex.; Ana Carolina Castillo Crimm, *De León: A Tejano Family History* (Austin: University of Texas Press, 2003), 96.

25. Sister Marie Sheridan, "Bishop Odin and the New Era of the Catholic Church in Texas, 1840–1860" (Ph.D. diss., St. Louis University, 1938), 98; Huson, *Refugio*, 1:459–85.

26. James Talmadge Moore, *Through Fire and Flood: The Catholic Church in Frontier Texas, 1836–1900* (College Station: Texas A&M University Press, 1992), 63.

27. Huson, *Refugio*, 1:463; Grimes, *300 Years*, 168.

28. Carlos de la Garza folder, Republic of Texas Audited Military Claims, Archives Division, Texas State Library, Austin.

29. Tom O'Connor Sr., "Nicholas Fagan, Texas Patriot," *Victoria County Genealogical Society* 23 (Spring 2002): 4.

30. *Handbook of Texas Online*, s.v. "Hynes Bay, Battle of"; Huson, *Refugio*, 1:552.

31. Communication from Emilio Vargas II, Ignacio Zaragosa Society, Goliad, Tex., including letter and article on General Zaragosa from Professor José Gutiérrez Almguex, Galeana, N. L.

32. *Handbook of Texas Online*, s.v. "Carlos Rancho."

33. Joseph Barnard, *Dr. J. H. Barnard's Journal: from December, 1835 to March 27th, 1836, Giving an Account of Fannin Massacre*, reprint (Goliad, Tex.: Goliad Advance, 1988), 19.

34. Paul D. Lack, *The Texas Revolutionary Experience: A Political and Social History, 1835–1836* (College Station: Texas A&M University Press, 1992), 207.

35. "Changed in an Instant: A Land Mine Took a Victoria Soldier's Arm, but not His Spirit," *Victoria Advocate*, 7 March 2004; "A Hero's Welcome Home: Wounded Victoria Soldier Returns to Throng of Family, Friends," ibid., 21 March 2004; "Hurt in Iraq, Victoria Soldier Remains Upbeat in Rehabilitation," ibid., 15 April 2004.

IN THE NAME OF THE

REPUBLIC OF TEXAS,

FREE, SOVEREIGN AND INDEPENDENT.

To all to whom these Presents shall come: I *David G. Burnet* PRESIDENT OF SAID REPUBLIC, *send* GREETING:

BE IT KNOWN, *That reposing special trust and confidence in the courage, patriotism and ability of* Juan N. Seguin *I have nominated, and by and with the advice and consent of my Cabinet, and in virtue of authority vested in me, do constitute and appoint the said* Juan N Seguin *to the* RANK AND OFFICE OF Lieut Colonel in the Regular *Army of Texas: Making it hereby the duty of the said* Juan N Seguin *carefully, diligently and faithfully to discharge all his duties as such* Lieut. Colonel o *to conform himself strictly to the Rules and Regulations that have been, or may hereafter be adopted, for the government of the Army of this Republic, and to be obedient to all the lawful orders of his superior Officers.*

And it is hereby further enjoined, *That the said* Juan N Seguin *do compel all Officers and others under his command to render a prompt and complete obedience to all his lawful orders appertaining to the Public Service, and to see that they fail not in the discharge of their respective duties.*

For all which, *this present Commission shall be his sufficient warrant, which is to take effect from the* 30th of May last *Given under my hand at* Velasco *this* Seventeenth *day of* September *A. D. 1836 and of the Independence of the Republic of Texas the* First

By order of the President,
John A Wharton
See of War

David G Burnet

TELEGRAPH (COLUMBIA) PRINT.

In the aftermath of San Jacinto, Juan N. Seguín was probably the most popular Tejano in the Republic of Texas. Having executed several military details successfully, he received a lieutenant colonel's commission from the interim government. A little over two years later the town of Walnut Springs changed its name to Seguin in his honor. Controversy soon hounded Seguín out of Texas for a six-year exile, and his reputation never completely recovered.

Courtesy Texas Adjutant General Service Records, [401-10], Texas State Library and Archives Commission.

JUAN N. SEGUÍN

FEDERALIST, REBEL, EXILE

Jesús F. de la Teja

To whom did Texas belong? It is a question for which
Juan Seguín would have had a clear and ready answer in January
1834, when at age twenty-seven he took the reigns of power as jefe
político of the department of Béxar. Texas belonged to men like his
father Erasmo and his relatives the Flores and even the rival Navarros
and Veramendis. As the other essays in this anthology suggest, these
men had navigated the treacherous waters of the Mexican War of
Independence, had advocated the development of the province their
grandparents and great grandparents had settled for a century, and
had welcomed and formed alliances with the recently arrived Anglo-
American settlers. But Texas also belonged to these new Texans—the
cotton farmers from the United States who had quickly carved farms
and plantations out of raw land with the promise of prosperity just
around the corner. And, because Mexico had at least in principle accepted the French revolutionary ideals of liberty, equality, and broth-
erhood, Texas might also belong to free people of African descent and
to Indian peoples who had peaceably settled in Texas, opened their
own farms, and seemed intent on becoming productive members of
society.

Texas certainly did not belong to others who laid claim to it. Texas
did not belong to the Coahuila politicians who had belatedly passed
some of the reforms that Texans had long demanded while conspir-
ing to sell off the province's lands through various schemes that prof-
ited few but themselves. The struggle between politicians in the rival
would-be capitals of Saltillo and Monclova for control of the state
government threatened the progress and stability that Texas enjoyed.
Texas also did not belong to the national government in Mexico City,
which seemed to teeter between states' rights federalism and strong
government centralism. From far off Mexico City, what could such
men understand of frontier needs? Texas certainly did not belong
to the United States, although it had claimed it as recently as 1819.
Although the treaty of 1828 had finally been ratified by both nations
in 1832 and Texas' boundary with the United States set, the Americans' track record with regard to former Spanish possessions did not
inspire confidence. Texas also did not belong to Indian peoples such

as the despised Karankawas and Comanches, who refused to accept Euroamerican civilized ways. After a century of chronic warfare with the indigenous peoples, Tejanos saw the unacculturated tribes as impediments to progress.

If the answer to the broad question of who had a stake in Texas' future was clear to Juan, many other questions, small and large, required investigation, consideration, and resolution. Just how should Texas respond to the national government's arrest for treason of Stephen F. Austin, the principal architect of Anglo-American settlement in the province? How should Texas respond to the mounting political crisis in Coahuila occasioned by the rivalry between Saltillo and Monclova politicians? Now that the state legislature had divided the province into three departments, how might Texas retain its cohesion? Most important, in the face of the centrifugal effects exerted by Anglo-American economic and political forces on one side and Mexican cultural and political forces on the other, just what course of action should he take?

For Juan Seguín, born in 1806 on the eve of Mexico's long struggle for independence, raised in partial exile as his father fought charges of treason to the Spanish crown, and now maturing in the shadow of the political instability into which early national Mexico had descended, the choices were not simple. Juan had not been raised to avoid difficult choices, however. Through his father he could trace his family's presence in Texas to the earliest days of the province, where a great-great-grandfather had served as a presidio soldier. His great-grandfather, the first Seguín in San Antonio, had established the tradition of public service, holding municipal office various times. Santiago Seguín, his grandfather, had established another family tradition—political activism—as he challenged successive governors before being removed to Saltillo. Juan's father Erasmo was no stranger to controversy and political activism, and he walked a fine line between loyalties.[1]

Juan's family, therefore, was part of San Antonio's social, economic, and political elite. As members of the Spanish, or criollo, sector of the population, Juan's family enjoyed a status equivalent to that of "white" in a society that, although it had officially given up race as a legal principle, nevertheless put much stock on the perceived racial-ethnic background of its members. Between the ranching interests handed down from the time of his great-great-grandfather and his Seguín ancestors' successful business ventures, the family was among the more affluent of the community. Municipal, state, and national government positions added to the Seguíns' prominence in the city that they and their ancestors had helped develop, and Juan was fully expected to rise to a place of prominence in the community.

Juan's own story must therefore be set against a twofold backdrop of strong family traditions of civic leadership and momentous political changes that required both careful judgments and decisiveness. Born in October 1806, Juan was not quite four years old when Father Miguel Hidalgo raised the cry of rebellion against bad government. His father's exile to Coahuila during the Mexican War of Independence and the confiscation of the family's property must have served as a dual lesson for Juan. On the one hand, he learned that being on the losing side brought on severe consequences that could wipe out a family's fortunes overnight. On the other hand, he also learned that with patience, perseverance, and flexibility a family could survive any errant choice.

The family's recovery of its property by the early 1820s afforded Juan a chance to enter the world of adulthood with opportunities to rise to the top of San Antonio society. Despite the turmoil, he learned to read and write, to work cattle and farm, and to conduct business and public affairs. By the time his father was away in Mexico City in 1823–1825 representing Texas in the constitutional congress, seventeen-year-old Juan was helping his mother run San Antonio's post office and representing the family in local affairs. As the "man of the house," he worked to obtain credit from local merchants when the family ran out of money, and he protested against efforts to impose what he felt was the unfair tax burden of supplying thirty cartloads of stone for local public works.

In the political crisis of 1824, Juan, not yet able to participate openly in politics, nevertheless must have played a part in representing his father's position on the vital issue of Texas' fate as part of Mexico. Although Erasmo had left for Mexico as an advocate of territorial status for Texas, he had come around to the belief that the unsettled state of the national government made union with Coahuila a better option. Juan must have been influential in convincing city leaders that his father's change of position was the only logical response to the situation in the capital, and that the inclusion of a provision allowing Texas to form a separate state at a later date was evidence that his father had not sold out the province.

Juan was also acting as surrogate for his father with Stephen F. Austin and his colonists. One of Juan's earliest surviving letters was addressed to Austin in April 1825. In it the eighteen-year-old Seguín informs Austin that his father will soon arrive from Mexico with good news regarding his mission on behalf of the colonists. He addresses the Anglo-American in a confident and familiar tone. In a postscript Juan even admonishes Austin not to forget "to tell me if you have received the correspondence I sent you, as well as that which I send you now." Juan's relationship with Austin was further strengthened by his family's hosting of Stephen's younger brother Brown for an extended stay so he could learn the Spanish language and Mexican culture. In August 1826, on his way to Saltillo, Brown had opportunity to return the favor. He wrote his brother from San Antonio asking him to pay *"very particular* . . . attention *to Juan for my sake,* for I am certainly *indebted* to his family for inumerable favors. [Should] he want a new supply of provisions, furnish him with the best, let it cost what it may. Also he will want letters of recommendation to persons in New Orleans which I wish you to furnish him with. He goes on to purchase goods, probably to the amt of $1000 or $1,200. Also tell Mrs. Picket to have some good *butter* for him to take along on the road."[2]

From an early date, then, Juan was comfortable among Anglos who showed evidence of respecting and appreciating Tejanos and Mexican ways. These early experiences surely helped shape Juan's opinion that Tejanos and Texians (as the Anglo-American settlers were increasingly referring to themselves) were in partnership to develop Texas for the benefit of both groups.

By his twentieth birthday Juan had established himself as a family man and struck out on a business career. In January 1826 he married Gertrudis Flores de Abrego, scion of another old San Antonio family whose male members were among the town's most important ranchers. That same year he set out on his first business trip to New Orleans, which he undertook in partnership with, among others, Juan Martín Veramendi. Subsequent business trips led Juan into the Anglo-American business world and one of the more controversial aspects of Texas-Mexico relations—land speculation. By 1833, Juan had acquired a one-league (4,428 acres) grant from the state government, which he promptly sold to Indian trader and entrepreneur Michael Menard, who in turn located the land at the eastern end of Galveston Island. The practice of grants being bought and sold on speculation turned out to be one of the stated grievances by Texians against Mexico, although it continued into the republic period. Although a minor player, Juan remained involved in land speculation until his forced exile in 1842. At that time some of his other business deals that had soured also became "evidence" of his treason against Texas. Whatever the case, like his father and the other leading Bex-areños, Juan continued to combine business activities and public service throughout his life.[3]

By the time he entered politics at age twenty-two, Juan had amassed considerable experience in public affairs. His education in civics was very different from that of his Anglo-American friends and partners, but no less important. He had been born into a monarchical system, grown up during a period of revolutionary warfare, and matured during the birth of Mexico as a nation-state, a process in which competing forms—monarchy, centralized republic, and decentralized democracy—were still being experimented with and fought over. Nevertheless, a comment by jefe político Ramón Múzquiz, the man Juan would replace five years later, makes clear that Juan would still need more seasoning when he served his tour of duty as alcalde of San Antonio: "Don Juan Nepomuceno Segin is very talented for his age, but he needs practice in order to be a good administrator of Justice."[4] A successful one-year tenure as alcalde led to other political offices in succeeding years, and Juan remained in public service to Texas in one form or another until 1842.

Political life in Texas after 1829 increasingly revolved around three great themes.[5] First, ideological issues were separating politically active Mexicans into two camps—those who supported strong states' rights and those who supported a strong national government in which the states were mere administrative units. The first group became known as federalists because they advocated a federated form of national government in which the states exercised most authority. The second group became known as centralists, because they would place all real power in a national government. In this matter Juan's opinion fell in line with his father's and that of most other prominent Bexareños, who saw the country's future in a union of states enjoying significant authority over local resources and development issues, much as in the United States. Consequently, Juan was a federalist by training and conviction.

The second theme was the status of Texas within the Mexican republic. As the state legislature made it increasingly difficult for Texas slaveholders to feel secure in their property, and as land speculation became increasingly perceived as a paramount corrupting influence, Texians became increasingly militant about their desires for separate statehood. Juan was not foolish, however. In 1832 and 1833 he had joined his father and Veramendi, Navarro, and the rest of

San Antonio's leadership in advising the restive Texians to be patient and follow the law in presenting their grievances against Coahuila and federal officials. Mexico City's unwillingness to address separate statehood for Texas led Austin, who was in the national capital attempting to gain the government's ear on the matter, to write a letter to the ayuntamiento of San Antonio advocating separation even without the consent of the Coahuilans. When the letter reached the government's hands, it led to Austin's arrest in January 1834.

The third great theme was the future status of the Texians. As early as 1826 the first warning signs of the perils of Anglo-American colonization had been raised when followers of East Texas land agent Haden Edwards launched a revolt and declared independence at Nacogdoches. Although Austin's and the other Texian settlements had united against the rebels, Mexican officials took note. Two years later, when General Manuel de Mier y Terán conducted an inspection tour of Texas, he became alarmed by the absence of Mexican influence in the eastern part of the province. His recommendations for bringing the situation under control were incorporated into the Law of 6 April 1830, which almost completely forbid further Anglo-American colonization in Texas, called for strengthening of the military's presence in the province, and eliminated the further importation of slaves, among other features. This restrictive law, along with efforts to start collecting tariffs, contributed to Texian restiveness that expressed itself in the conventions of 1832 and 1833. Austin's departure for Mexico City to present the Texians' grievances to national authorities seemed to calm matters, but it proved simply to be the calm before the storm.

Elected to serve as the city's alcalde in 1834, on January 1 Juan found himself not taking up the magistrate's staff of office but accepting the post of interim jefe político for the department of Bexar. At age twenty-seven Juan was the chief administrative officer for the Tejano-dominated southern portion of Texas. Unfortunately for him, 1834 proved a year of momentous shifts in Mexican politics, the collapse of Texas-Coahuila relations, and to top it all off the peak of a cholera epidemic that had been sweeping through the region for a year.

It was during his time of service that the federalist-centralist struggle heated up, in both Coahuila y Texas and the rest of the nation. Just a few days into office, Juan received the news of Austin's arrest. The news must have saddened him, especially since the arrest was made by order of Mexico's federalist interim president Valentín Gómez Farías. Austin had managed to get a hearing before Santa

Anna and Gómez Farías, who seemed sympathetic although unwilling to move too quickly. The national government did request the state legislature to pass reforms along the lines sought by the Texians, and in November 1833 the federal congress repealed the part of the Law of 6 April 1830 that prohibited further settlement by immigrants in the border states. In light of these actions, Austin's letter seemed all the more the act of an ingrate. From the Texas side, the arrest confused matters greatly, as anti-Austin elements in the Texian population attempted to undermine his standing.[6]

As the year progressed the federalist-centralist struggle turned into open rebellion, putting Juan in a difficult position. In May, Antonio López de Santa Anna switched political affiliations and, now acting as a centralist, removed from office his radical vice-president Gómez Farías, who had been acting president during Santa Anna's protracted absence from the capital. Federalists around the country, including the state legislature of Coahuila y Texas sitting in Monclova, declared themselves opposed to Santa Anna's new government. Saltillo's politicians, eager to regain control over the state government, responded to Monclova's declaration with one of their own, branding the state government there illegal. By fall 1834, limited fighting had broken out between militia units supporting Monclova and Saltillo, and Santa Anna had appointed his confidant, General Martín Perfecto de Cos, to restore order.

Not that the state legislature had not attempted to carry out the reforms suggested by the federal government to redress some of the problems brought up by Austin the previous year. March 1834 witnessed passage of laws dividing Texas into three departments, thus giving Texians additional political clout in the legislature. The legislature also authorized new municipalities at Matagorda and San Augustine. English became an official language for conducting public business, and freedom of conscience was granted, provided its expression did not cause public disturbance. The same legislation attempted to reform the public lands administration, calling for special commissioners to issue titles and regulating land sales and grants. Another law passed in April provided for an American-style judicial system, going so far as to allow for jury trials in the language of the accused. Unfortunately, the legislature also opened up more Texas lands for sale, made large grants to individuals, and generally gave the impression of being in the hands of speculators.[7]

Ramón Múzquiz, the incumbent jefe político, was not up to the task of dealing with the growing turmoil. He resumed office in

March, releasing Juan to return to the post of alcalde, but not before having to carry out an assignment to meet with the Comanches on how to jointly counter recent Tonkawa hostilities. However, by the beginning of July Múzquiz, who had previously been ill, was forced to resign his post, and Juan resumed the function of jefe político in the midst of a cholera outbreak that threatened chaos as families fled the city. Cholera had decimated Coahuila the previous summer, taking the life of Texas' most important friend in state government, interim governor Juan Martín Veramendi.[8]

If cholera panic and increasing tensions in Coahuila were not enough, in August Juan was confronted with the arrival of Juan Almonte, an inspector sent by the national government to report on conditions in Texas. Almonte had secret instructions, however, which required him to find out the political mood in Texas, particularly with regard to dissident sentiment among the Texians. Although we have no documentation, he certainly must have met with Juan to discuss the political climate. What opinion Juan expressed in August to a representative of the national government, we can only speculate. There is no reason to believe that he was not as circumspect in his comments to Almonte as he was a month later in his reply to Commandant General Pedro Lemus, when the general informed him that he had taken steps to calm the growing tensions between Monclova and Saltillo: "Carrying out the charge given to me by Your Lordship, I have used my influence so that, with a unity of opinion, the authorities of the department should show the proper deference to the newly named governor, and cooperate in this manner toward restoring the state to that peace that it so much requires for its prosperity."[9]

Circumspection was no longer possible once Juan discovered how badly the situation had deteriorated in Coahuila. On 1 September the Texas delegates to the state legislature wrote to their "Fellow Citizens of Texas," urging the convocation of a convention in November. Soon after, word arrived that Martín Perfecto de Cos, a close associate of President Santa Anna, was to relieve Pedro Lemus of his command and enforce the national government's will on the factions fighting for control of the state government. For Juan this sequence of events proved decisive. Although a federalist, he had been willing to let Monclova handle its own fight against Saltillo. When the national government became involved, however, he could no longer hold back. The danger of centralist intervention in local affairs required action. Juan began hosting private gatherings, or *tertulias*, at which a Tejano course of action began to emerge.[10]

On 7 October, heeding the wishes of the province's representatives in Monclova, Juan called a public meeting in San Antonio that declared a need for all of Texas' municipalities to decide on a course of action. A manifesto issued by Juan Seguín and other inhabitants of Texas called for a consultation on 15 November 1834. The manifesto signed by Seguín and most other prominent Bexareños made the following arguments: Saltillo's arbitrary action to disavow the Monclova government was wrong, but so was Monclova's removal of Governor Vidaurri and installation of Juan José Elguézabal, a military man, "since it is not derived from the constitutional principle, or in its absence, from the sovereignty of the people as it should be." Furthermore, since the deadline for holding elections has passed and the competing governors disputed each other's authority, "such events have completely dissolved the constituted authorities of the state, and involved her in anarchy; and it is to be feared that Texas (where order and union prevails) will be involved in the general confusion, if timely measures are not taken before she feels the want of [good] government."[11]

In communicating the community's decision to his counterparts at San Felipe de Austin and Nacogdoches, Seguín painted the situation as dire: "I have the honor to forward to Your Lordship the enclosed resolution enacted by this citizenry on the 7th instant, by which Your Lordship and the worthy citizens subordinate to you will be informed of the chaotic circumstances in which the State of Coahuila y Texas finds itself, and of the complete anarchy that reins in almost all its towns."[12] He went on to ask that representatives be appointed from every municipality to meet at San Antonio on 15 November "to legally and without restraint treat all matters that may relate to our security and the interests of the inhabitants. And, all of this having met with my complete approval, I have the satisfaction of communicating it to Your Lordship."

News of Seguín's move did not take long in reaching the national government. On 22 October General Cos, who had not yet left the coast for Saltillo, sent Juan a not very subtle warning:

> I am informed that Your Lordship, capriciously considering the state leaderless, is moving to disavow the authority of His Excellency the Governor, which officer exercises his office legally. . . . I deeply hope that Your Lordship, turning your attention to your fatherland, will desist from those projects whose evils are impossible to calculate if they are carried out. . . . I

invite you in the name of the Nation not to trespass the limits of your authority nor to make bad use of the influence that you have, and to preserve it in order to use it in favor of your fatherland.[13]

As matters turned out, Juan did not need to heed Cos's warning, and he must have been sorely disappointed and confused by the response his call for a convention got from the Anglo-American parts of Texas—silence. From Almonte's late 1834 correspondence with various Texians it is clear that Juan had miscalculated the interests of the Anglo-American population in the federalist-centralist struggle. Peter Ellis Bean wrote to Almonte from Nacogdoches at the beginning of November that Juan's call for a convention had just arrived in the town, "but I believe none will go from here, nor from San Felipe de Austin, because here no one wishes now to take part in such things. But in order that a change of that nature not come to pass, it is necessary to apply some timely remedy. Otherwise, there will be a disastrous war that will take many sacrifices to end, unless beforehand troops—well prepared ones—are sent to prevent a disturbance."[14] Samuel M. Williams, Austin's partner and one of the leading land speculators in Texas, also wrote to Almonte in early November and claimed that although Henry Smith, the jefe político for the department of the Brazos, which include all of the Austin colonies, had quickly called for an election, he had been unsuccessful:

> In this place and the upper part of this colony the inhabitants did not wish to participate in the election, and this to a certain extent cooled the ardor of our Chief. But he did not cease his activities, because his vanity caused him to attribute that gesture to the efforts of Austin's personal friends. . . . Thus, the interests of the farmers has put that issue to sleep, and doubtless it will be forever for the way it was proposed.
>
> I personally opposed the latest convention, because in it they wished to assume powers not recognized in our laws and constitutions. I am also opposed to the current plan, and I have played a big role in its defeat.[15]

How does one interpret the behavior of the Anglo-American parts of Texas, especially in light of their having held two conventions, in 1832 and 1833, which were as extralegal as the one Juan hoped to convene? Rather than merely asserting that the Texians were reticent to take any action that might jeopardize the safety of Stephen Austin, who was still being jailed in Mexico City, the answer may well rest on differences in perceived interests. Texians at this point did not much care who was in charge, so long as there was still the possibility that they could continue to live autonomously and gain title to their land grants. They did not care much for the federalists who had controlled state government and were perceived as being in league with the land speculators. Land speculators like Samuel M. Williams still hoped to salvage the situation to their benefit by appearing to be supportive of law and order. Neither group was by now much concerned with the political principles underlying Juan's call for a convention. The year came to an end in the midst of the proverbial calm before the storm, and Juan turned over the office of jefe político to his successor, Angel Navarro, on 1 January 1835.[16]

Tejanos and Texians began to see eye to eye again in the course of 1835. Austin's release and the passage of various reforms did not meet Texian demands for separation from Coahuila. Continued instability in Coahuila at one point led to the interim governor's call for aid from the Texas municipalities. "Citizens of Texas," wrote Governor Agustín Viesca, "rise up in arms or sleep forever! Your dearest interests, your liberty, your properties, and even more, your very lives, depend on the whims of your most enraged enemies. Your destruction is already decided, and only your resolve and characteristic energy can save you."[17]

Federalist jefe político Angel Navarro responded to General Cos's strong-arm measures by refusing to disband the local militias and calling for militiamen from Goliad and Béxar to attempt a rescue of the state government. In May, Juan led a force that included both Tejanos and Texians to Monclova to rescue the state government, but they returned empty-handed when Viesca ordered the local militias that had been assembling to defend the government to disband.[18] His recognition of the national government's determination to stamp out local autonomy, combined with his "disgust with the weakness of the governor who had given up the struggle," brought Juan home resolved "to use all our influence to rouse Texas against the tyrannical government of Santa Anna."[19]

Later in the year, when Cos arrived in Texas and demanded the arrest of William Travis, Samuel Williams, Lorenzo de Zavala, and José María Carvajal, all associated with the federalist cause, Juan must have been confirmed in his belief that Tejanos and Texians again had the same fight. Throughout summer 1835, while Austin reconciled with the Texian members of the War Party, Juan was conducting his own survey of the temperament among the population of Texas. In early October, while the battle of Gonzales was setting the revolution in motion, Juan met with the Tejano families of the San Antonio River ranches to enlist their support for the cause. It was at this point that he gave up his status as militia commander and joined the ranks of Austin's Federal Army of Texas as a captain. All of his actions to this point, and those of the Texians and Tejanos with whom he had collaborated directly, pointed to a spirited defense of federalism against the centralists' usurpation of power behind Santa Anna.

Just when Juan came to the realization that few of the Texians had ever thought of the fight as a struggle for constitutional government is a mystery. According to Leandro Chávez's 1874 pension application for service during the war, "About on the middle of the month of November 1835, he was on his way from the rancho to the City with his ox-cart, when he found himself surrounded by a party of armed men under the command of John N. Seguin, said party was mainly of friends and playmates of affiant; they told him that they were gathering in order to declare Texas independent from Mexico, that the most part of the young men were in favor of that move."[20]

Of course, after thirty years and in hopes of gaining a pension for his service, Chavéz may have embellished the motives of Seguín and his men, but it is possible that independence talk was in the air. There was certainly no compromise on Juan's part as his company participated in driving General Cos and his forces out of San Antonio during what has come to be known as the siege of Béxar in December. Nevertheless, on 22 February 1836, when the defenders of San Antonio withdrew into the Alamo, Juan and his comrades in arms were still defending the Constitution of 1824 against centralist arbitrary rule. When he left the Alamo on the night of 28 February with another plea for assistance, he was still in the service of the Mexican state of Texas. If he was shocked by the actions of the convention on 2 March 1836, that shock must have been tempered by the knowledge that two fellow Bexareños, José Antonio Navarro and Francisco Ruiz, had signed their names to the document. Unlike the Victoriano Plácido Benavides, by the time he and his men lobbied with Sam Houston to be allowed an active part in the battle of San Jacinto on 21 April 1836, Juan clearly had thrown his fortunes in with the Texians.

Juan not only accepted but embraced Texas independence. As military commander of San Antonio in early 1837, it fell to him to lead the burial services for the Alamo defenders, and his words on that occasion attest to his identification with the new republic: "Companions in Arms! These remains which we have the honor of carrying on our shoulders are those of the valiant heroes who died in the Alamo. Yes, my friends, they preferred to die a thousand times rather than submit themselves to the tyrant's yoke. . . . The venerable remains of our worthy companions as witnesses, I invite you to declare to the entire world, 'Texas shall be free and independent, or we shall perish in glorious combat.'"[21]

In the second, third, and fourth congresses he served as a senator from Bexar County and continued his struggle for the rights of all Texans, but now more specifically his fellow Tejanos. Understanding that democracy stands on the shoulders of just laws and an informed populace, he strove to make those laws understandable to the people he represented. In February 1840 he addressed the Texas Senate:

> Mr. President, the dearest rights of my constituents as Mexico-Texians are guaranteed by the Constitutions and Laws of the Republic of Texas; and at the formation of the social compact between the Mexicans and the Texians, they had rights guaranteed to them; they also contracted certain legal obligations of all of which they are ignorant, and in consequence of their ignorance of the language in which the Laws and the Constitution of the land are written. The Mexico-Texians were among the first who sacrificed their all in our glorious Revolution, and the disasters of war weighed heavily upon them, to achieve those blessings which, it appears, are destined to be the last to enjoy.[22]

Juan's sensitivity to the precarious situation of all non-Anglo-Texans probably moved him to side with Wily Martin's efforts to gain approval from the Texas Congress to allow his emancipated slave Peter to remain in the republic. The 1836 constitution denied citizenship to people of African ancestry and to Indians. Only through direct legislative approval could free people of color even remain within the republic. Peter's case was the first to test the provision, and opponents feared that allowing the rather wealthy freedman to remain, even if he had aided the cause of Texas independence, would set a bad precedent. Sitting on the committee treating the matter, Juan sided with the majority in favor of granting the petition, and Peter went on to become the first emancipated slave permitted to remain within the republic.[23]

Despite his political and military service, Juan, like other Tejanos, remained suspect of disloyalty from an early date. In December 1840

Adolphus Sterne felt compelled to comment in his diary that news had arrived from San Antonio that Juan had "not joined the Enemy." It could not help that Juan had become involved in Mexican political affairs, taking sides with General Antonio Canales in the abortive effort to establish a Republic of the Rio Grande among the northeastern Mexican states. When Canales defected to the national government, Seguín was left exposed, having raised a company of men in which he had invested over $3,000 to equip. Soon he was engaged in a smuggling operation designed to extract him from debt, but it only brought him into contact with Mexican military men who ostensibly were determined to recover Texas for Mexico.

By spring 1842, when General Rafael Vázquez invaded Texas and briefly captured San Antonio, Juan had been fully compromised. In 1841–42 he had served as mayor of San Antonio under increasing threat from Anglo-American newcomers who branded him a traitor but whose true intent was to drive out the most powerful individual who stood in the way of their land speculation schemes. People knew that Juan had been in communication with the Mexicans, and some even suspected that he had betrayed the Santa Fe expedition. Returning to San Antonio from the expedition that pursued Vázquez back across the border, Juan found himself threatened by a determined group of Texians and unable to get a commitment of support from President Houston. Juan resigned as mayor in mid-April 1842 and fled with his family to Mexico.

On arriving in Tamaulipas, he claims in his memoirs, the authorities gave him the choice of enlisting in the army or going to jail as a traitor to Mexico. Unable to offer his family any protection from jail, he chose to organize a company of mounted volunteers from among those Tejanos who had chosen Mexico over Texas after the revolution. In Texas the condemnations came fast and furious from throughout the republic. When the news reached distant Nacogdoches, an indignant Adolphus Sterne commented in his diary that "Col. Seguín has joined them, and as is usually case, when our warm Friends turn against us, they become the most inveterate foes, I am satisfied, that it will be so in this case." But not all Texans believed what on the surface appeared to be a case of treason. Sam Houston, then president for the second time, wrote to Juan's father Erasmo: "I pray, Sir, that you will not suppose for one moment, that I will denounce Colonel John N. Seguín, without a most perfect understanding of the circumstances of his absence. I rely upon his honor, his worth, and his chivalry." Anson Jones, last president of the republic, on the eve of Texas' annexation in summer 1845 commented: "Col. Seguín fought as well at San Jacinto as any man there; but has been forced by bad usage to quit the country, and, as is said, has turned traitor; but I am unwilling to believe it."[24]

For six years Seguín patrolled the Texas-Mexico border as a member of the Mexican military, however. When war came between the United States and Mexico, he fought at the battle of Buena Vista and other engagements in the north, all the time under pursuit from Ben McCulloch and his company of Texas Rangers. They never did catch him.

By the end of the war Juan was homesick and weary. In April 1848 he wrote to his staunch defender Sam Houston about wanting to take his family "to my native place [Béxar] and to remain for the rest of my days peacefully occupied as a laborious citizen." And so, risking his and his family's safety at the hands of those who remained unconvinced of his devotion to Texas, Juan returned to San Antonio and began to rehabilitate his political fortunes. By 1852, despite a continued lack of English proficiency, he won the post of Bexar County justice of the peace, and he was reelected two years later. He also began serving as president of his election precinct and went on to serve as a member of the platform-writing committee for the Democratic Party in Bexar County and member of the Mexican Texan Citizens of Bexar County.

Still the attacks came. McCulloch, who had not managed to destroy Seguín a decade earlier in northern Mexico, tried to do it now from the floor of the Texas Legislature, where he continued to accuse Seguín of treason and was indignant that such a man should be allowed to participate in the state's public affairs. It was these accusations of "barbarous and unworthy deeds" that drove Seguín to write his memoirs in 1858, thus joining his fellow Tejano José Antonio Navarro in publishing accounts of the Mexican and Texas wars of independence intended to educate Anglo-Texans, many of whom had arrived after the fact, that Tejanos too had served the cause of Texas.

Juan had remained involved in Mexican affairs during the 1850s. He continued to conduct business there and had relatives throughout the north, including up and coming Ignacio Zaragoza, a cousin on his mother's side of the family. During Mexico's War of the Reform (1858–61) he led militia troops in the Nuevo León-Tamaulipas-Coahuila region, and during the War of the French Intervention (1862–67) he led troops at the battle of Puebla (Cinco de Mayo) and elsewhere. Nevertheless, he maintained his Texas ties and must have felt himself a citizen of both nations. The War between the States was not his war, however, and Reconstruction politics had little to do with his views of Texas. Although he served briefly as Wilson County judge in 1869, he had for years been preparing for a final move to Nuevo Laredo. His son Santiago was a rising star in local politics, and the aging Tejano felt the need for the protection of strong young sons. We know that he returned at least twice to Texas, in 1874 to file for a war of independence pension, which he received, and in 1882. In 1887 he petitioned for a pension from the Mexican government, but because all of his service had been as a volunteer, he was denied.[25]

Juan N. Seguín died in 1890 in Nuevo Laredo, largely but not entirely forgotten. The year that he applied for his Texas pension, he communicated with Reuben Potter and Edward Miles of the Texas Veterans Association about his activities. The latter served as his attorney on the pension issue. In his late years he gave an interview to a reporter from the Laredo *Times* and corresponded with Texans regarding the revolution. Missing from these communications are the events of 1834 and 1835 that brought about the Texas Revolution and such radical change to Juan's life. People wanted to know about Travis, and Bowie, and the heroism of the Alamo: Juan Seguín was only too happy to oblige.

Notes

1. This essay draws generally from my biographical essay "The Making of a Tejano," in Jesús F. de la Teja, ed., *A Revolution Remembered: The Memoirs and Selected Correspondence of Juan N. Seguín* (Austin: State House Press, 1991; 2d ed., Austin: Texas State Historical Association, 2002).

2. Eugene C. Barker, "Native Latin American Contribution to the Colonization and Independence of Texas," *Southwestern Historical Quarterly Online* 46 (4), www.tshaonline.org/publications/journals/shq/online/v046/n4/contrib_DIVL4342.html, accessed 17 January 2007.

3. William C. Davis, *Lone Star Rising: The Revolutionary Birth of the Texas Republic* (New York: Free Press, 2004), 116. More work needs to be done on land speculation throughout the history of nineteenth-century Texas, but for a summary of some of the principal grievances at the time of the revolution, see Eugene C. Barker, "Land Speculation as a Cause of the Texas Revolution," *Southwestern Historical Quarterly Online* 10 (1), www.tshaonline

.org/publications/journals/shq/online/vo10/n1/article_6.html, accessed 20 January 2007.

4. De la Teja, *Revolution Remembered*, 18.

5. For a general overview of Tejano perspectives on these issues, see Jesús F. de la Teja, "The Colonization and Independence of Texas: A Tejano Perspective," in *Myths, Misdeeds, and Misunderstandings: The Roots of Conflict in U.S.-Mexican Relations*, ed. Jaime E. Rodríguez O. and Kathryn Vincent (Wilmington, Del.: Scholarly Resources, 1997), 79–95. See also Andrés Tijerina, "The Emergence of Tejano Politics," in *Tejanos and Texas under the Mexican Flag, 1821–1836* (College Station: Texas A&M University Press, 1994).

6. Josefina Zoraida Vásquez, "The Colonization and Loss of Texas: A Mexican Perspective," in Rodríguez and Vincent, *Myths, Misdeeds, and Misunderstandings*, 68; Gregg Cantrell, *Stephen F. Austin: Empresario of Texas* (New Haven, Conn.: Yale University Press, 1999), 269–75.

7. Vito Alessio Robles, *Coahuila y Texas desde la comsumación de la Independencia hasta el Tratado de Paz de Guadalupe Hidalgo*, 2d ed. (Mexico City: Porrúa, 1979), 1:489–95; Cantrell, *Stephen F. Austin*, 291; Tijerina, *Tejanos and Texas*, 134–35.

8. J. Villasana Haggard, "Epidemic Cholera in Texas, 1833–1834," *Southwestern Historical Quarterly Online* 40 (3), www.tshaonline.org/publications/journals/shq/online/vo40/n3/contrib_DIVL3015.html, accessed 15 March 2007.

9. Quote from De la Teja, *Revolution Remembered*, 130. Jack Jackson, ed., *Almonte's Texas: Juan N. Almonte's 1834 Inspection, Secret Report and Role in the 1836 Campaign* (Austin: Texas State Historical Association, 2003), 174.

10. Andrés Reséndez, *Changing National Identities at the Frontier: Texas and New Mexico, 1800–1850* (Cambridge: Cambridge University Press, 2005), 158.

11. Jackson, *Almonte's Texas*, 295–96.

12. De la Teja, *Revolution Remembered*, 132.

13. Ibid., 133.

14. Jackson, *Almonte's Texas*, 298.

15. Ibid., 299.

16. On Texian attitudes toward the government in Coahuila as a result of land speculation, see Barker, "Land Speculation as a Cause of the Texas Revolution."

17. Alessio Robles, *Coahuila y Texas*, 2:22.

18. Ibid., 2:23–25; Reséndez, *Changing National Identities*, 159–60; Lack, *Texas Revolutionary Experience*, 20–22.

19. De la Teja, *Revolution Remembered*, 76.
20. Pension claim of Leandro Chávez, Republic Claims, Texas State Archives, Austin (microfilm PE reel 208, frames 483–96).
21. De la Teja, *Revolution Remembered*, 156.
22. Ibid., 174.
23. Harold Schoen, "Free Negro in the Republic of Texas III," *Southwestern Historical Quarterly Online* 40 (2), www.tshaonline.org/publications/journals/shq/online/vo40/n2/contrib_DIVL1280 .html, accessed 17 March 2007.
24. All quotes in De la Teja, *Revolution Remembered*, 44, 49.
25. Seguín, Juan N., XI/III/4–5980, Secretaría de la Defensa Nacional, Mexico City; Pension claim of Juan N. Seguin, Republic Claims, Texas State Archives, Austin (microfilm PE reel 237, frames 687–96). In *Revolution Remembered*, I wrote that it was most likely Juan Jr. who served with Zaragoza at Puebla. An examination of Juan's file in the Mexican military archives has proved that statement in error. Although all that remains in the file are copies of the original documents, Juan's petition and other corroborating documents make clear that he remained active in Mexican military affairs until 1871, that is, until he was about sixty-five years old.

CONTRIBUTORS

CAROLINA CASTILLO CRIMM obtained the PhD from the University of Texas at Austin and is professor of history at Sam Houston State University. She is a Minnie Stevens Piper Professor and winner of the Mary Jon and J. P. Bryan Texas History Teacher award. Dr. Crimm is a fellow of the Texas State Historical Association and a member of its board of directors. Her numerous publications include *De León: A Tejano Family History* (University of Texas Press, 2004), which has won the Presidio La Bahía Award from the Sons of the Republic of Texas, a San Antonio Conservation Society Book Citation, and the Texas Old Missions and Forts Restoration Association Book Award.

JAMES E. CRISP holds the PhD from Yale University and is associate professor and assistant department head of history at North Carolina State University. He has been a Rockefeller Humanist-in-Residence fellow at the University of North Carolina at Chapel Hill and has won the H. Bailey Carroll Award from the Texas State Historical Association for best article in the *Southwestern Historical Quarterly.* He is the author of *Sleuthing the Alamo: Davy Crockett's Last Stand and Other Mysteries of the Texas Revolution* (Oxford University Press, 2005), which was a History Book Club featured selection and winner of the T. R. Fehrenbach Book Award.

JESÚS F. DE LA TEJA earned the PhD from the University of Texas at Austin and is professor and chair of the Department of History at Texas State University–San Marcos. Appointed by Governor Rick Perry as the inaugural Texas State Historian, he is a fellow and former president of the Texas State Historical Association, an honorary member of the Sons of the Republic of Texas, and winner of the Americanism Medal from the Daughters of the American Revolution. Among his numerous publications is *A Revolution Remembered: The Memoirs and Selected Correspondence of Juan N. Seguín* (2d ed., Texas State Historical Association, 2002), winner of the Summerfield G. Roberts Award of Sons of the Republic of Texas.

STEPHEN L. HARDIN obtained the PhD from Texas Christian University and is a professor of history at McMurry University. He is a fellow of the Texas State Historical Association, a fellow and board member of the Grady McWhiney Research Foundation, a member of the Texas Institute of Letters, and the winner of the Texas Historical Foundation's Award of Merit for contributions as historical advisor for the motion picture *The Alamo* (2004) . His numerous award-winning publications include *Texian Iliad: A Military History of the Texas Revolution* (University of Texas Press, 1994), which won awards from the Westerners International, the American Association for State and Local History, the Sons of the Republic of Texas, and the Texas Historical Commission.

TIMOTHY MATOVINA holds the PhD in religion and culture from Catholic University of America and is professor of theology and director of the Cushwa Center for the Study of American Catholicism at the University of Notre Dame. He has won major grants from the Henry Luce Foundation, Lilly Endowment, and Pew Charitable Trust. He is a multiple award-winning author and editor of books and articles in both history and religion whose publications include *Tejano Religion and Ethnicity: San Antonio, 1821–1860* (University of Texas Press, 1995), which won the Summerfield G. Roberts Award from the Sons of the Republic of Texas and the Paul J. Foik Award from Texas Catholic Historical Society.

DAVID R. MCDONALD obtained a BS degree in sociology from West Texas State University in Canyon before earning a BA in Spanish literature from the University of Texas at Austin. Before becoming a freelance historian in 2002, Mr. McDonald served as manager and park historian for the Casa Navarro State Historical Park in San Antonio, Texas, for twenty-three years. He has translated and written historical accounts on various aspects of Spanish and Mexican Texas, including *Defending Mexican Valor in Texas: The Historical Writings of José Antonio Navarro* (State House Press, 1995) with Timothy Matovina. He is currently at work on a major biography of Navarro.

RAÚL A. RAMOS has the PhD in history from Yale University and currently is an assistant professor at the University of Houston. He is a recipient of both the Summerfield Roberts Fellowship in Texas History, from the Clements Center for Southwest Studies, Southern Methodist University, and a Mellon Foundation Dissertation Fellowship. His book *Beyond the Alamo: Forging Mexican Ethnicity in San Antonio, 1821–1861* (University of North Carolina Press, 2008) builds on his interest in identity formation in the Southwest, and he is at work on a study that brings the subject forward in time: *American Centenario: Mexican Identity in the American Southwest, 1910*.

ANDRÉS RESÉNDEZ did his doctoral work at the University of Chicago and is an associate professor of history at the University of California,

Davis. He has been awarded a Fulbright Bicentennial Chair in American Studies for Finland and has published extensively on various aspects of Texas and Mexican history. His book *Changing National Identities at the Frontier: Texas and New Mexico, 1800–1850* (Cambridge University Press, 2005) won both the Coral H. Tullis Memorial Award for the best book on Texas history from the Texas State Historical Association and the Award for the Book Making the Most Significant Contribution to Knowledge presented by the Texas Institute of Letters.

ALONZO SALAZAR is a tenth-generation Texan and descendant of Carlos de la Garza. He attended Victoria College and Pan American University and works as a contract control systems designer in the oil, gas, and chemical industry in Houston, Texas. He is also a genealogist and amateur historian with a particular interest in the Garza family, a lifelong interest that developed while running around the walls of Presidio La Bahía as a child. He has made numerous presentations on Carlos de la Garza's role in nineteenth-century Texas history and is at work on a full biography of the Tejano leader.

ANDRÉS TIJERINA obtained a PhD from the University of Texas at Austin and is a professor of history at Austin Community College. He is a fellow of the Texas State Historical Association and a member of the Texas Institute of Letters. He is a founder and board member of Tejano Monument, Inc., which seeks to place a major monument commemorating the contribution of Tejano pioneers to the development of Texas. He is the author of numerous works on Tejano history. His book *Tejanos and Texas under the Mexican Flag, 1821–1836* (Texas A&M University Press, 1994) won numerous prizes, including the T. R. Fehrenbach Award from the Texas Historical Commission and an Outstanding Academic Books Award from the American Library Association.

ROBERT E. WRIGHT, O.M.I., holds the PhD in theology and culture from the Graduate Theological Union, Berkeley, and is associate professor of theology and culture at the Oblate School of Theology in San Antonio. Father Wright serves in various capacities in several organizations, including as vice president of the Texas Catholic Historical Society and on the executive board of the Comisión para el Estudio de la Historia de la Iglesia en Latinoamérica. He has won the Carlos Eduardo Castañeda service award from the Texas Catholic Historical Society. Father Wright is the author of numerous essays and articles, many of them related to the Catholic history of Texas and the Southwest, and has lectured extensively on the subject.

INDEX

ISBN-13: 978-1-60344-152-0
ISBN-10: 1-60344-152-2